How To Do Prison Time Successfully

by

Emanuel Bell

D1731204

FIRST PUBLISHED EDITION, JULY 2022

All rights reserved. No part of this book may be reproduced, scanned, or distributed inany printed or electronic form without explicit written permission. Please do not participate in or encourage piracy of copyrighted materials in violation of the author's rights.

Copyright © 2022 by Emanuel Bell

Cover Design by Kevin Watson Designs

ISBN 978-1-7353845-3-5

Printed in the United States of America

Acknowledgments

To my daughter...thanks for all the support and encouragement
during this project.

To Randy, my editor, for giving me guidance with this book.

To Jeannie my publisher, and Pastor Jason, for believing in me
and helping with getting my book in the hands of people.

To Rich, the creative writing instructor at Solano State prison,
for enrolling me in your class. This is where I learned how to
successfully write a book and get the necessary feedback that I
needed from all the inmates in the class to make it better.

Table of Contents

Introduction

I got locked up on October 19th, 2003. It was a Sunday morning, and I was 24 years old. I began my prison sentence for attempting to murder the mother of my child. I knew nothing about prison life and had no idea what awaited me.

Fourteen years into my prison sentence, I was laying on my bunk, looking back at my journey through prison. I could see how a lot of conflict and trouble that I got into in prison could have been less had I had the proper knowledge on how to do time, and had I known the deception and traps that awaited me in prison. I wished I had found the necessary tools for managing my anger and stress. Thankfully I eventually got the knowledge. That same day I decided to write this book to help people, giving them all the necessary tools and knowledge that's needed to minimize their conflict and trouble in prison.

You can learn from other people's mistakes; so learn from mine and the other inmates' real life stories that I'm about to tell you. In this book, I will give tools to help you do your time successfully. Some of the things in this book came from my lifer homeboys who laced me up with their experiences regarding parole board hearing. For their input, I made sure to go only to my lifer homeboys that had 20 years or more under their belt, and at least 14 years straight without getting into any trouble in prison. In other words, no write-ups or disciplinary actions. So shout out to my lifer-homeboys in prison for giving me some game and knowledge; it really helped me and changed my life for the better. The majority of what is in this book is from my own 17 and a half years of personal experience in prison.

So let's get started.

Footprints in the Sand

One night I dreamed a dream.

As I was walking along the beach with my Lord.
Across the dark sky flashed scenes from my life.

For each scene, I noticed two sets of footprints in the sand,
One belonging to me and one to my Lord.

After the last scene of my life flashed before me,
I looked back at the footprints in the sand.

I noticed that at many times along the path of my life,
especially at the very lowest and saddest times,
there was only one set of footprints.

This really troubled me, so I asked the Lord about it.

"Lord, you said once I decided to follow you,
You'd walk with me all the way.
But I noticed that during the saddest and most troublesome
times of my life,
there was only one set of footprints.
I don't understand why, when I needed You the most, You
would leave me."

He whispered, "My precious child, I love you and will never
leave you
never, ever, during your trials and testings.

When you saw only one set of footprints,
It was then that I carried you.

~ Author Unknown

1

Intake Process

Once you arrive at the county jail and get out of the cop car, you walk inside the doors where the Correctional Officer or CO is going to make you strip out. He's trying to find whatever it is you may have hidden up your butt cavity, under your feet, between your ears, and your hair, between your butt cheeks, under your testicles, or inside your mouth. The CO is going to tell you to squat and cough, lift up the bottom of your feet, flip your ears with your hands, rub your fingers through your hair, grab your testicles and lift them up. After you finish with the search, he is going to tell you to put your clothes back on.

All the money you had in your pockets when you got arrested will now be logged into the County Jail Trust Account. And if you're unable to make bail, you will be able to spend that money on commissary day. All your personal property that the policeman confiscated from you will also be logged into the computer and stored away for you until you leave the county jail. But, if you're unable to make bail and you do get found guilty and are now on your way to prison, all your personal property that the county jail is holding for you will not follow you to prison, only your money will follow you. You will only have 30 days to find a family member or friend that's willing to come to the county jail to pick up all your personal belongings for you. If you can't find anybody to come pick your personal property up from the county jail then it will get disposed of.

While sitting in the county jail holding tank, you will eventually get fingerprinted, get your picture taken, and see the nurse. While you're sitting in the holding cell, you will be able to make a collect call to try to make bail. But if you were arrested on a serious charge like murder, kidnapping, etc, then you will not be able to make bail that night. You will have to wait until you go to court and see the judge so he can set a bail amount for you. You're going to be sitting in that holding cell with about 10 other inmates.

It's very uncomfortable in that holding cell, because it will be very crowded with a bad stench in the air. You're going to have people sleeping on the floor. You might even be sitting next to someone that's trying to stay awake but his attempt is failing, so his head will constantly be bumping your shoulder as he tries to stay awake. You know how it is when someone is sitting down and their head keeps falling sideways as they try to stay up.

I remember when I got arrested and was charged with attempted murder in 2003. As I sat in the holding tank, I was in there with 3 winos that had the holding cell smelling like hard liquor and forest trees. It was like their clothes were made out of leaves and branches, the way their clothes gave off that tree smell. And to make matters worse, one of the winos was sleeping right under the bench where I was sitting. He was tucked way back under the bench and would hit my feet every time he tossed and turned in his sleep. I couldn't stretch my feet out cuz there was other people laying out on the ground in front of me. So I was stuck right there, and just had to deal with the wino constantly bumping my legs as he tossed and turned in his sleep. I wanted to say something but I felt sorry for this homeless man. So I just left it alone.

If you are unable to make bail you will get a plastic wristband which will have your picture, your name, and your booking number. You're going to need your booking number whenever you decide to write a letter or go to the store. When you write a letter, you must always put your booking number next to your name like this; Emanuel Bell #545786. And when you go to the store, you will also have to write your booking number on your store list.

If you were unable to make bail, you will be escorted to the dress-out room, where you will be given some county jail clothes and told to put all your personal clothes inside a bag that the CO will hand you. Your personal clothes will then be stored away for you. You will also get a bedroll consisting of 2 sheets, 1 blanket, 3 boxers, 3 socks, and 3 t-shirts. You will also get a "fish-kit," consisting of 1 golf pencil, 2 stamped envelopes, 1 razor, 1 bar of soap, 1 toothbrush, 1 toothpaste, and a 5-inch comb. There will also be an orientation booklet inside your bedroll, which explains the county jail rules and regulations. There will be things inside your regulation booklet such as what day and time laundry exchange day is, the commissary day, visitation day and hours, etc.

After you're dressed in your county jail clothes, you will then be escorted to your housing unit, which will be either cell living or dorm living. The difference between the two is that cell living will be just you and one other inmate inside a little bathroom-size cell. For dorm living, you'll be in a gym size building with about 120 other inmates with bunk beds lined up about 3 feet apart from one another. The average dorm living houses 120 inmates, but some county jails have 50-men dorms, 16 or even just 8 men dorms.

Watch your thoughts, *they become your words;*

Watch your words, *they become your actions;*

Watch your actions, *they become your habits;*

Watch your habits, *they become your character;*

Watch your character, *it becomes your destiny.*

~ Lao Tzu

2
Cell Living

If you're going to be housed in a cell, there's a lot you must know about cell living. When I first started out with my cell living, I knew nothing about it. And because I knew nothing about cell living, I ended up getting into a lot of arguments and fights with my cellies for a while until I finally learned the proper way to cell-live.

Each time I had an argument or fight with my celly, I would go tell a few of my partners that I was cool about the argument or fight that I had with my celly. And then I would ask them, "Was I in the wrong, or was my celly in the wrong?" And each time I would ask my partners, they would always say I was in the wrong. See, when I first started out cell living, I had the attitude like, "Nobody can't tell me nothing and better not try to tell me nothing. I'm going to do what I want when I want. And whoever got a problem with it, we're gonna handle it."

Looking back now, I can see that every time I had an argument or fight with my celly, all he was trying to do was show me the proper way to cell-live. They wasn't really trying to punk me like I thought they were. I could see that I took it the wrong way when they were trying to tell me I needed to stop doing something, or I needed to start doing something a certain way. After my 4th cell fight, and after my homeboy's told me I was in the wrong for a fight, I decided to start listening to my cellies when they was trying to correct me on something. Listening to them when they would say I needed to be considerate inside the cell.

And I am glad I made that change because now I know the right way to cell-live and be a cool celly no matter who I was celled up with. I want you to know everything there is to know about cell living so you will be a cool celly no matter who you cell up with.

Celly Introduction

When you enter the building that you're going to be housed in, you will walk over to your assigned cell. Don't walk inside the cell without first getting to know your celly a little bit. You start off by first saying your name and where you're from. It's different depending on your nationality. If you're Black, for example, you'd say "I'm Fred from Stockton 44 Crip Gang." If you're Hispanic or Asian, you'd identify your gang affiliation, too. And if you're a nonaffiliate, then tell him that you're an nonaffiliate and that you don't gang bang. But if you're white, your introduction will be a little different. A wood, or white inmate, will be easily accepted by other white inmates, since there's no gang bangin' with them.

Normally, once you say your name and where you're from, your celly will do the same in return. But if he don't say his name, then say, "Hey! What they call you?" And after he says his name, then ask, "Where you up out of?" Then he will tell you where he's from. This introduction is very important before you walk inside a cell.

Even if you told the CO you only want to cell-up with your own gang, you still might get put in the cell with one of your rivals. The CO only knows that you're a Crip or Blood, but not what street you're from. So, it could happen that the CO is going to house you with another Crip or Blood gang-banger, unaware that you're at odds with that particular gang.

So it's your job to check and make sure that the Crip/Blood cell, or whatever gang you in, that the CO got you moving into is not one of your Crip/Blood rivals. Even if you don't gang bang, you would still want to check and find out where your celly is from before moving in. That way you'll know what city or gang he's clicked up with.

Another important thing you would want to do while you're introducing yourself to your potential celly is to get a good look inside his cell to see if the cell is dirty or clean. Because if the cell is dirty, that shows you that he don't like cleaning. At a time like this, you don't need to be dealing with a messy celly. Having a messy celly will only put unnecessary stress on you. Extra stress that you really don't need right now. Being in the county jail is already stressful, and you having to constantly cleanup behind a grown-ass man will only add to the stress. So be sure to get a good look inside the cell before you move in. Look at the cell floor to see if he has trash, dirt, or stains. Get a good look at his sink and toilet, to see if there are stains all on it. Look at his bed to see if it is made up neat or is it all sloppy. If his bed is all sloppy looking, that will let you know that he's lazy and pretty much don't do a good job of cleaning up the cell.

After you both introduce yourselves and you get a good look inside his cell, it's now up to you whether or not you're going to move in there. Because you don't have to move in that cell if you believe the cell was too filthy or if he's connected to one of your rivals. You can simply walk right back over to the CO and tell him/her that you and the guy they want you to cell-up with are not compatible. Once you tell the CO that, he cannot make you go inside that cell because now it's a safety concern. When two inmates are not compatible as cellies, that's like saying he's oil and you're water, and y'all do not mix. Y'all won't get along with one another inside the cell. If the CO asks, "Why aren't y'all compatible?" Just tell him that you and him are two different kinds of people, and the way he programs and does things inside the cell is totally different from your ways. After telling this to the CO, he will definitely find you another cell to move to. And once you get to that cell, go through the same process of introductions and looking inside the cell.

You never want to just walk straight inside a cell. Once you're in the cell and the cell door is shut, you won't be able to get a bed-move until the weekend. If you were to ask the CO if you can get a bed move right now, he will tell you that convenient moves are only done on the weekends and that you will have to wait until then. Even if you try to explain to the CO that you and your celly ain't compatible right now, the CO will still tell you that you need to wait till the weekend for a convenience move. So you will be stuck inside the cell until then and might even get literally "stuck" inside the cell by your celly, and lose your life.

I remember when I was at Soledad Prison in 2008, there was an inmate that just arrived and was housed in my building, called Rainier. Five seconds after moving into his cell on the bottom tier, you could hear hollering coming from that cell. By the time the CO got there, it was too late. The guy that just had moved into that cell got stabbed to death by his celly. And anyone that was at Soledad prison in 2008 in the Rainier building knows exactly what I'm talking about. So learn from his mistake, and avoid putting yourself in a situation like that. Be smart and introduce yourself to your celly like I showed you; make sure he's cool and not one of your enemies before you move in.

Wipe Down and Questions

When you finally do find a celly that you feel compatible with, make sure that you get some disinfectant and wipe down everything before you put your sheets on the mattress and your property in your locker. Another man has been sleeping on that mattress, and there's no telling how many wet dreams he had on that mattress. Your celly should already have disinfectant inside the cell, but if he doesn't have any disinfectant and the CO says they don't have none either, just lather up some soap on a towel and use that.

While you're wiping down your bunk, mattress, and your locker, your celly is going to be asking you all kinds of questions to try to get to know you a little better. When your celly finally asks you what you got locked up for, just tell him what you got charged for and don't go into details about your case. So many inmates make the mistake of telling their cellies all kinds of details about their case, including where he buried the body and gun, only to find out later that his celly was a jailhouse informant. They'll tell the district attorney everything that you told him about your case so that he can get a lesser sentence or maybe even have his case thrown out. Many inmates got convicted that way, so don't go out like them; be smart and keep your case details to yourself and your lawyer. I'm not saying that your celly is a jailhouse informant; all I'm saying is you just never really know who will switch over and become one to try and get his charges dropped or lessened by telling the DA what you told him. Even if you happen to already know your new celly from the streets, still don't go into details about your case.

There are inmates in your county jail that are truly frightened, scared to death, of going to prison. Even if they're only looking at

1 year or 2 years in prison. That hardcore dude that you know from the streets that's now in the same building with you - even he can't be trusted with details about your case, specially if he's facing more than 10 years or a life sentence. He'll put his reputation, loyalty, pride, ego, and dignity to the side if doing so will get him a get out of jail free card. So remember: talk to no one about your case except your lawyer.

Also watch what you say on the county jail phone, because COs listen in on phone conversations. If you slip up exposing important details about your case, the CO will send the recorded conversation to the DA. Those details will then be used as evidence against you at your trial. Same thing with your letters that you're mailing out; watch what you say in those, too, because the CO will read every letter that's coming in for you, and read every letter that's going out by you. If there is evidence they can use against you, they will give those letters to the DA.

I remember when I was in the county jail, I met a guy that was initially in jail for assaulting his pregnant ex-girlfriend. He was looking at 4 years in prison. But one day, he got on the county jail phone and called-up his cousin, asking him to go find his pregnant ex-girlfriend and punch her repeatedly in the stomach so she'll lose the baby. I will never forget the look on his face when he came by my cell one day and told me he had a new charge of solicitation to murder. He went on to say that the CO was listening in on his phone conversation. When he told his cousin to go kill his ex-girlfriend's unborn child, the CO sent the recorded phone conversation to the DA and new charges were filed against him. He was later convicted and received his third strike for solicitation to murder and got a life sentence in prison.

See, the court system knows that some inmates make calls or send out mail to try to get their witness or victims killed. That way at trial, he'll have a better chance at getting found not guilty, because the case is weak without the victim or the witness. The court system also knows that inmates try to make calls or send letters to intimidate their witnesses or victims so that they don't show up to court. Always remember that loose lips sink ships. So be extremely careful with the words that come out of your mouth while in the county jail.

Now that you know why it's not cool to go into details with your celly or anybody else besides your lawyer about your case, here's everything you need to know about cell living...

When you're in the cell and you feel like you need to piss, take your piss; but know that there are different ways of pissing and one of these styles of pissing might be one of your cellys prison-cell rules. I'll explain the different styles of pissing in a prison cell toilet later. But first, it would be wise to ask him about his pissing cell-rules. If he says "just the regular way," just standing up and pissing, you must wipe-down the rim of the toilet with toilet paper as soon as you finish taking your piss. That's just proper piss etiquette. And you best believe that your celly is low-key watching you to make sure you do wipe down the toilet rim after you finish pissing.

He is also low-key watching to see if you wash your hands afterwards. If you fail to wipe or wash, he'll quickly remind you in a checking type of way. "Damn man! You ain't going to wipe the toilet rim down?!" or "Hey man! Wipe the toilet down! What's wrong with you?!" or "What type of dude is you ain't going to wash your hands after you use the bathroom?!" or "Hey man! You forgot to wash your hands!" So be on point and don't let your celly have to remind you and check you like this.

But if it's a crap that you got to take instead of a piss, then there should already be soap hooks up on the wall. This is a way for you to hang your sheet, creating a partition so you can have your privacy while you take a crap. But if there's no hooks already on the wall, don't trip. After you take your crap and get settled inside the cell you can make the hooks. I'll show you how later; but in the meantime, ask your celly can he turn his head to give you a little privacy while you take your crap. Once he turns his head giving you some privacy, make sure to tell him good looking out "thank you."

Before you sit down on the toilet, grab your shower shoes so you can sit on them while you're on the toilet. You could use toilet paper to lay around the toilet bowl rim so you can have a seat cover; but being you only get two toilet paper rolls a week, you will quickly run out of toilet paper. So. a lot of inmates just use shower shoes as a seat cover to preserve toilet paper. There is a rule you must follow while you're taking your crap, and it's called a "courtesy flush." A courtesy flush is when you flush the toilet like every 45 seconds to suck down the fart smell while you're taking your crap. And every time your crap drops, you should flush it. You should also flush every time you fart while you're taking your crap. Being the cells are very small, failing to do this courtesy flush will gas your celly out. If you do forget to do some courtesy flushes, your celly is going to quickly remind you to do some. If he has to keep reminding you about courtesy flushes, your celly will eventually get fed up and lash out at you in an aggressive manner.

I remember when I took my first crap while I was incarcerated, I didn't know nothing about courtesy flushes. As I'm taking my crap, my celly said to me, "Hey man! Are you trying to do a mating call over there?" I asked what he meant, and he went on to say, "You over there trying to make me smell your butt! I'm not interested, and you better start doing some courtesy flushes. Are we going to have a problem up in here?" I remember this other time I forgot to do some courtesy flushes, and another celly I had said, "Damn man! I got sentenced to 7 years in prison, not the gas chamber! Come on man, can you please do some courtesy flushes? You're gassing me the fuck out over here."

But there are some jail/prison toilets that have timers on their toilets, allowing you only two toilet flushes every 5 minutes. If you try to do 3 flushes within 5 minutes, the toilet will lock up on you for 30 minutes so you can't flush at all. If your toilet has a timer on it, you won't be able to do any courtesy flushes. Then you and your celly will have to just deal with the smell of fart unless you cover your nose up when one of y'all is taking a crap. The proper way to take a crap on a timer toilet is by using your first flush to flush your first load of crap down. Then try to time it in your head when 3 minutes go by, then flush again. Even if no crap comes out, because that will be your courtesy flush, Then just wait 2 more minutes for the toilet to reset, giving you another 2 flushes within the 5 minutes. And you repeat this flush process until you're finished taking your crap.

Courtesy flushes are also used to flush farts. When you got to fart, go over to the toilet and sit down on it with your clothes still on, then fart and flush the toilet at the same time. This is how farts gets sucked down from the toilet suction as you're sitting on it. Some cellys don't trip on flushing farts. All that getting up and down off the bunk can mess up your mood when you're trying to relax and watch a movie. So instead of flushing the farts, some cellies will just have a nasal spray with smell-good oil in it and just spray the bottle every time one of y'all fart. Some cellies will just say, "If you got to fart just fart." But make sure to say "excuse me" whenever you do fart, and he won't even be worrying about spraying any smell good oil or worrying about flushing the fart. So come to an understanding with your celly regarding the way y'all are going to be handling the farts inside the cell, because every celly is different. And know that whoever was in the cell first has more say on how to deal with farts inside the cell.

Rules about farting while one of y'all are eating is another thing. Do y'all hold the farts while someone is eating or do y'all flush them? Normally, farts are to be flushed when your celly is eating, but you do have those cellys that would rather you hold your farts while he's eating. So make sure you get this understanding with your celly.

I remember when I first got sent to prison in 2005 at Ironwood State Prison Level 3. My first prison cell fight was about a fart. At this time I had an attitude like "Nobody can't tell me nothing and they better not try to. I do what I want!" I had just moved in the cell with a dude, and he gave me the rundown on how things are going to be done inside his cell. He told me we didn't have to flush our farts, we should always say "excuse me" whenever one of us farted. But when one of us is eating food, we would have to go flush the fart. I had agreed to his fart rules.

I was assigned to the bottom bunk and my celly was assigned to the top bunk. One day while watching TV on my bunk, I farted and said "excuse me." My celly quickly jumped down off his bunk and said to me, "Man, I was up there eating, dog. You just farted while I was eating." He said he thought that we had an understanding that when one of us is eating that we would flush our farts. I told my celly, "My bad. I didn't know you were up there eating." He said, "All right, man, but don't let it happen again. Next time, look up there to see if I'm eating when you about to fart. I said, "alright," and I went back to watching my TV show.

Me and my celly only lasted three weeks, because 2 days later I had to fart again while watching TV. I was too comfortable and didn't feel like getting up to flush my fart, even though I knew my celly was up there eating food. I had just watched him make something to eat and jump on his bed. So I thought to myself, "I'll just make my fart silent. That way my celly won't hear it." With my clothes on, I grabbed my butt cheek and pulled it to the side: a little trick I learned to do to make my fart silent. When I farted, it came out silent...but it just so happened to be one of those silent and deadly farts. When I got a whiff of my fart, I thought "Damn, he's going to smell this." And sure enough, he did.

My celly hopped down off his bunk and said to me in an angry tone, "Did you just fart?!" I looked at him and said, "What are you talking about?" He said, "Don't play dumb with me, man. You just farted again while I was eating. What do you think? That I'm a punk or something? Is that what it is? You think I'm a punk!" But before I could even answer, my celly stole on me in the face, and kept his punches coming, knocking my headphones off my head. I was trying to get off my bunk, but the way I was sitting on my bunk and the way he was standing throwing punches made it hard for me to get up.

I was finally able to get up off my bunk when he stepped back and asked me again, "Do you think I'm a punk?!" I got up off my bunk just in time 'cause he charged me and swung, catching me on the eye. But I caught him, too; on the right side of his face. We both started exchanging blows. His head went down some, and that's when I was able to get him in a guillotine choke hold. He was leaning forward and I was standing in front of him with my arm wrapped around his neck. As I pulled upward with my forearm pressed hard against his Adam's apple, I pulled upward and began squeezing his neck with all my might. He started wiggling like a fish that just got pulled out of the water. I could feel his Adam's apple on my forearm as I'm squeezing and pulling upward with everything I was made of. He started to make this loud wheezing sound. His breathing soon turned into a crackling-wheezing sound. But I still was not letting go.

I will admit this dude was kicking my butt before I was able to get him in a guillotine choke hold, and I know he would continue kicking my butt if I was to let him out of it. So I wasn't letting go. I just kept squeezing with all my might. His crackling wheezing breathing sound started getting slower and slower. He began frantically tapping me on my leg, tapping and tapping until I finally released my grip. I released my grip on his neck and quickly stepped back into a fighting stance. But he dropped to the floor like a sack of potatoes and started taking in long deep breaths at a very fast pace.

I began to panic. I went from fight mode to panic mode. I knelt down beside him and started saying, "Breathe man! Breathe! Breathe..." it took him about 10 minutes for him to finally get his breathing back to normal. He got up and jumped on his bunk. After he got on his bunk, we talked for a while and came to an understanding that we will remain cellys, but when one of us is eating we must respect the person that's eating and flush the fart. So we shook hands on it and agreed to remain cellys.

The next day he checked to see if his TV still worked, as it had fallen down off his top locker during our fight. The day before, when we were exchanging blows, I had backed up into his TV cord that was along the wall and accidentally knocked his TV down. But it was him swinging at me that caused me to back up into his TV in the first place. So when my celly was trying to say I owe him for breaking his TV, I told him that he caused me to bump into his TV cord, so it wasn't my fault but his. But he was not trying to hear that.

So we started arguing; with him saying I owe him for his TV, and me telling him I don't owe him anything because he's the one that caused me to bump into the cord. As we were arguing, the cell door opened up and the CO announced over the loud speaker for my celly to report to the program office. As my celly started walking out the cell he told me that he ain't playing with me and that I better get him his money for his TV. As soon as he said those words, I rushed him and started socking him. There was a CO nearby so our fight ended very quickly. But I got written up for the fight.

RULES VIOLATION REPORT — STATE OF CALIFORNIA, DEPARTMENT OF CORRECTIONS

CDC NUMBER: V-69940 INMATE'S NAME: BELL HOUSING NO.: AFB4-128L LOG NO.: A06-03-0001

VIOLATED RULE NO(S): 3005 (c) SPECIFIC ACTS: MUTUAL COMBAT LOCATION: AFB4-DAYROOM DATE: 04/03/06 TIME: 1410HRS

CIRCUMSTANCES: On MONDAY, APRIL 03, 2006, at approximately 1410 hours, while performing my duties as "A" Facility Building Four(4), Control Booth Officer, I saw Inmate BELL, CDC# V-69940, AFB4-128L, attack his cellie _____, while _____ was walking out the cell in front of BELL. _____ had been called to the Program Office. BELL started punching _____ on the back of his head and upper torso. I yelled out to the inmates to get down and hit the alarm while monitoring the situation. Both Floor Officers, JENKINS and ROQUE, responded towards the inmates at which time both inmates got down on the floor and were cuffed up by the floor staff. Both inmates were escorted out of the building by responding staff. BELL IS NOT an inmate participant in the Mental Health Services Delivery System at CCCMS/EOP/MHCB level of care. Inmate BELL is aware of this report.

REPORTING EMPLOYEE: J. MENDEZ CORRECTIONAL OFFICER DATE: 4-14-06 ASSIGNMENT: AFB4-CONTROL OFFICER RDO S: S/SU

REVIEWING SUPERVISOR'S SIGNATURE: S. WIGGINS CORRECTIONAL SERGEANT DATE: 4-14-06

So learn from my mistake and don't fart while your celly is eating. And try your best not to break none of the cell rules that you and your celly established for the cell.

As you're establishing the fart cell rules with your celly, this would also be a good time to learn all his cell rules about how he goes about cleaning the cell and how y'all going to go about taking turns cleaning up the cell. Every celly got his own cell rules on cleaning the cell and how they take piss inside their cell. Being as your celly was in the cell first, you must respect and follow his cell rules because that's the way things are done in prison/jail. Whoever was in the cell first has more say so on how things are to be done inside the cell. Now I know you're probably thinking that isn't fair and that he doesn't pay any bills for the cell, so why do he get to have more say so on how things are going to be done inside the cell? This has been a prison rule that was established decades ago by inmate prisoners.

There's three different ways inmates take a piss in the cell. In the first way, as you're standing up pissing, you will be repeatedly flushing the toilet. The main reason why some inmates choose this style of pissing is to keep the piss from splashing everywhere as the piss hits the toilet water. Another way is standing up pissing without having to repeatedly flush the toilet. You just take a piss the regular way you did before you came to prison. The third way is you pull your pants down, but keep your boxers pulled up, sit down on the toilet, snake your thing out from the side of your boxers, and piss. This style of pissing is also used to keep the piss from splashing everywhere. Most inmates normally choose this style of pissing.

And when it comes to cleaning up the cell, inmates have different ways on how that's done, too. This was always weird to me. When I would move into somebody's cell and they'd give me the rundown on how they clean up their cell, some inmates will say only use the toilet water to clean the cell and don't use the sink water. You dip the floor towel into the toilet water, wring the towel out, and wipe the floor. But then you have other inmates that would say don't use the toilet water; use only the sink water to clean the floor.

Whichever style of cleaning my cellies chose, I never complained. I just went right along with it. Because I learned that inmates will get offended if you try to switch their style of cleaning up the cell. Trying to change his way of cleaning will only result in him giving you the silent treatment. That's something you don't need right now, just starting out with a new celly. So once again, just go along with however he chooses to clean the cell. Even if I felt he was going too many days without cleaning the inside of the toilet bowl or the cell walls, I will still just follow the cleaning rules that he established for the cell. I figure, who am I to just move in somebody's cell and start trying to change up the way he goes about doing things.

You're celly also got the right to include in his cell rules. Like there is not going to be any pruno making inside the cell. Or no smoking, or cell phones, or knives. Or no traffic coming to the cell - meaning all your homeboys need to not keep coming by the cell to talk to you through the cell door. Most inmates don't like traffic coming to the cell, because this will cause the cell to become "hot." If a CO thinks that much traffic is going on at a cell, he'll assume there's got to be some type of illegal business going on there. So eventually the CO will come by and search the cell.

Being as your celly was in the cell first, he also has the right to be the one that stays in the cell if ever y'all were to ever fall out and become incompatible as cellies. You're the one who has to move out. This is another prison rule that was established by inmates decades ago, and it's to be respected

The number one reason cellies fight each other is because the inmate that just moved inside the cell isn't respecting the cell rules that was established by the inmate that was in the cell first. This normally happens because the inmate that just moved in the cell will have control issues. He wants things to be done his way and his way only, and will start trying to change up the cell rules that have already been established by the inmate that was in the cell first. Once this type of power struggle begins, it will be like two lions in the jungle fighting each other to see who will be the king of the jungle. But in this case it would be too cellies fighting each other to see who will be the king of the cell.

Here's an example of what it will be like when you first move into someone's cell. He will get at you like, "Hey man, when we use the bathroom in here, we sit down to piss. And when you clean the cell floor, don't use the sink water. Use the toilet water. Just dip the towel in the toilet, wring it out, and hit the floor." He might tell you, "There ain't going to be no traffic at the door. And I don't want no smoking in this cell. All right?" Or he might be the type that don't use toilet water and got totally different cell rules and will get at you like, "Hey man, when we pissing here you make sure you flush the toilet repeatedly as you're pissing to keep the piss from splashing everywhere. And whenever you gotta fart, we flush them. And there ain't going to be no knives in here, or no type of contraband, etc."

Whenever I first moved into someone's cell, after he gave me the rundown on how he does things inside his cell, I always told my cellies to just tell me if there's anything that I'm doing that annoyed or bothered them. Don't hold it in, but let me know what it is and I'll start trying to work on myself to fix the problem. That way I'm not annoying or frustrating them, and we can continue being compatible as cellies. Cellies like it when you first move in and tell him something like that, because it shows that you're a respectable person and is willing to fix a problem That way y'all can remain being compatible as cellies, as opposed to just having the attitude like "I do what I want."

Cleaning the Cell

Here's the normal way that inmates clean the cell. If you clean the cell this way, you'll be doing a good job and your cellie will be proud of you. First, roll your mattress back, pick everything up that's on the floor, and put it on your bunk. Next, take one of your shower shoes or a dry floor towel and sweep the floor. After you finish sweeping the floor and pick up all the dust, it's time to mop. Take your floor towel, wet it, and wipe the floor down with it. Then take your disinfectant and sprinkle some on the floor and once again wipe down the floor. You're now finished with the floor. Now you can take everything that you put on your bunk before you started cleaning the floor and put it all back where it belongs. Be sure to wipe your bunk down, just in case dust was left behind from all the stuff you just took off your bunk. Now put the floor towel where it needs to go so it can dry out. Next, grab the sink towel, pour some disinfectant on it, and wipe the sink down. After you finish wiping the sink, put the sink towel where it needs to go so it could dry out. Finally, grab the toilet scrubber, pour some disinfectant inside the toilet and get to scrubbing. Be sure to not only clean the inside of the toilet, but also disinfect around the toilet bowl area too.

Getting an Understanding

If your celly is the type that got contraband in the cell, you gotta get an understanding. Say the CO happens to pull a sneak attack and searches the cell and finds his contraband such as pruno, knife, drugs, cell phone, tattoo gun, etc - you will get a write up, too, if your celly don't own up to his contraband. And the messed up thing about this is, him not owning up to his contraband just might have you end up catching another write up when you lose your cool and punch your celly in the face. All because he didn't want to own up to his contraband. So get an understanding that you want nothing to do with it and he needs to own up to his contraband if the CO happens to ever find it in the cell.

I remember during my 17 and a half years in prison, I had 6 different cellies that all kept their word with me like they said they would if ever the CO were to come in the cell and found their contraband. Two of my cellies got caught trying to make pruno in the cell, but they manned up to it and said I had nothing to do with it and that the contraband was theirs. The 4 other cellies that I had that also got caught with contraband, all got caught with a cell phone. And each time they told the CO that I had nothing to do with the cell phone and that the cell phone was theirs. Luckily, all my cellies kept their word when they told me they'd take the rap if ever the CO comes in. Had they all not taken ownership of their contraband, I would have gotten a total of 540 days extra added to my sentence, which is 1 and a half years total. So get this understanding with your celly, cuz you don't need extra time added to your sentence because of someone else's wrong doing.

Homie Care Package and a Bad Celly

When you arrive at a new building, an inmate will probably come by your cell to ask you where you're from. Once you tell him where you're from, he will then go tell someone from the hood or city that you said you're from. A little bit later, your homeboy will come to your cell door and ask if you are straight and if you need anything like food, deodorant, toothpaste, etc. This is your chance to get yourself a care package from your homies to hold you over until you make it to the store. But if you have no homies in the building, and you have no money on your books to go to the store, then you'll have to do a little sacrificing to get you some deodorant or toothpaste or whatever.

The kind of sacrifice I'm talking about is selling your breakfast, lunch, or dinner tray to one of the prison ballers in your building. Every building has a prison baller, so it will be very easy for you to find someone to buy your county jail/prison meals in exchange for some stuff you need. Hopefully your county jail cell living is the kind that allows you to walk in and out of the cell as you please, opposed to the 23 hour a day lockdown, which hinders you from leaving the cell. Because when you're able to walk in and out of the cell whenever you want to, it makes it easier for you to find somebody to buy your meals such as, your chicken, hot dogs, cheeseburgers, etc. A dinner like this goes for a dollar each.

Yeah, your stomach might growl for a while during the day when you sell your meal, but the sacrifice is well worth it. Now you won't be walking around all musty smelling or with bad breath. You would now have your deodorant and Colgate toothpaste. Same thing if you're in prison and you have no homies to give you some hygiene, you can sell your meals there, too, to get yourself some supplies. But in the meantime, until you get yourself a deodorant, do periodic sniff checks under your arms to see if you're funky and wash away the funk. Nobody wants a musty celly, and you better believe your celly won't put up with your foul odor for too long. That also goes for your socks, feet, sheets, clothes, and butt. You need to keep the smell down in every area you could get funky.

That's why it's important that you don't fall into that habit of sleeping all day to try to escape the reality of being in jail/prison, which a lot of inmates do when they first arrive at the county jail.

Once you fall into that sleep-all-day program, you will become very lazy and start to slack up on the things you should be doing; things like washing your clothes, cleaning the cell, washing your body daily, and keeping your hygiene up. If you don't do these things, you'll likely get into an argument with your celly due to your foul odors. And once you become a bad celly, word will get out fast about you throughout the whole county jail/ prison, making it even harder for you to find a new celly when the time comes.

I know you're probably wondering, "How does the word about you being a bad celly get spread throughout the county jail?" Well, when your celly goes to the yard or dayroom, he's venting. He's letting out some of the steam you caused him, telling inmates about how you're getting down inside the cell. And when your celly goes out to court and is waiting in the holding tank, he will see inmates that he knows that are in different buildings that will be returning to their different buildings after court. He will tell them about how smelly, filthy, or whatever your doing in the cell. This is how the word about your bad ways spreads like wildfire, making it hard for you to find a new celly when the time comes.

Nobody wants a celly who got a bad reputation of being a bad celly. Nobody wants to deal with all the unnecessary stress that comes with having a bad celly. Even inmates from your hood or city will be reluctant to accept you as a celly if you have a reputation of being a bad celly. So program like a normal inmate to keep from getting a bad celly reputation. Just follow the ways that I'm teaching you throughout this book and you'll be okay.

But what if it's not you but your celly who's got the bad reputation?

You need to sit him down and address the issue that's bothering you in a calm and respectful manner. You don't want to sound like you're checking him, cuz that will only cause him to not want to hear what it is you got to say. He will get defensive with you. If he doesn't try to fix the problems you brought up, y'all are now incompatible as cellys and one of y'all must now move out of the cell. But being you were in the cell first, he will now have to move out the cell. That's the prison rules.

Some cellies don't respect this prison rule, and get smart saying, "I'm not moving nowhere, you move!" If he gets at you like that, be smart about the situation and don't act on impulse. Don't rush your celly and start punching him in the face as soon as those words leave his mouth. If y'all are from different cities/cars* [Car - numerous inmates that are from the same city or gang that got each other's back. *When you're in the same car as an inmate he has your back and you're supposed to have his back.*] and you beat him up hella bad, as soon as the cell doors open up, he's going to go run and tell all his homies about the fight that y'all just had. And once his homies see how busted up he got, they gonna want some get-back. And if you don't got any homies from your car inside the building with you, then things could get real ugly for you.

But still be smart about the situation, even if you do got homies in the same building with you. Don't take off on your celly for getting at you foul like that. You want to try to avoid getting your homies into an unnecessary wreck with another car. If you can, always take the smart way to handle a situation like this. The proper way to handle this problem is to go get the shot caller to your cellie's car and let him know everything that's going on with you and his homie (your celly). Also let him know how you were in the cell first and now his homie is saying he ain't moving nowhere. Also let your celly's shot caller know the reason how y'all became incompatible as cellies. Once you tell him all that, he will see that his homeboy is in the wrong. He will see that his homie now gots to move out of the cell. So the shot caller will not only help you out by finding his homeboy a new cell to move to, but he'll also go check his homeboy for getting disrespectful like that, knowing you were in the cell first and he was in the wrong.

See, most shot callers have common sense and try to avoid unnecessary crashes with another car/crew. So when you bring an issue to a shot caller regarding an inmate in his car, it's his duty to look at everything you tell him about his homie and then make the right logical decision. He will see who was in the wrong and who was in the right in the situation. It's also the shot caller's duty to keep everyone in his car in check, making sure all his homies are not making the car look bad and to make sure all his homies are following the politics for the car. Also make sure you tell the shot caller that you're trying to go about this whole situation with your celly peacefully. That way the shot caller can see that you're not looking for trouble; all you're trying to do is get this issue with his homie taken care of in a peaceful manner.

But before you go and holler at your celly's shot caller, make sure you let the homies in your car know what's going on first. Let them know your intention to holler at your celly's shot caller. Also try to have one or two homies from your car go with you when you holler at your celly's shot caller. This shows that you do have people to back you up if things don't turn out peacefully like you plan.

But even if you don't have any homies on the yard with you, you can still go holler at your celly's shot caller by yourself. Once you explain everything to him, he will see that his homie is in the wrong and will help you fix the problem with his homeboy. It just looks better when you do have homies with you when you go to holler, showing that you got people to back you up.

Your celly's shot caller will be bringing everything up that you told him about your celly. So know that once your celly enters the cell, he will know that you got at his car about him. But if his shot caller talked to him and got at him the way a shot caller is supposed to get at one of his people, then you shouldn't have to worry about your celly coming in the cell tripping on you and getting at you aggressively. Instead, your celly should be respectful once he enters the cell and just be waiting patiently and peacefully until his homies find him a new cell to move to. But every inmate is different. He might be the type that don't care about nothing and don't care about going home. So I can't really say exactly what your celly will or won't do when he enters the cell after you got at the shot caller. You got some inmates that's trying to go home, and then you got some inmates that don't care about going home. So what type of celly you will have, I don't know...

But be alert and have your shoelaces tight while you're waiting for your celly to return to the cell. If your celly comes into the cell and starts tripping on you for getting at his shot caller, be set to defend yourself. But it's best to be the bigger man and put your pride and ego to the side, trying to quickly diffuse the situation with your celly. If he comes into the cell trying to fight you, just tell him, "Hey man, you can have the cell I'll move out." Some inmates will look at you like you a sucka for moving out of the cell when you were in the cell first and you moved out because you and your celly were having problems. But the majority of the inmates see that you're just staying focused on getting out of prison and home to your family, and that you're not going to let something that belongs to the state keep you from that. When you weigh the consequences about fighting over a cell, you'll see that it's really not worth it. If things end in a cell fight, it's a high possibility that you just might end up accidentally killing your celly and catch a whole new charge of murder. Or worse you may end up losing your own life during the cell fight.

Many inmates have caught a murder charge or lost their life during a cell fight. I'll never forget this one that happened at Solano Prison where a dude ended up killing his celly during a cell fight. Then he cut out his insides and flushed it all down the toilet. He put the remains of the body in a trash bag and dumped it in the trash can. Right after dumping the body in the trash can, went to dinner chow and started a riot by taking off on another race. The inmate that killed his celly eventually got caught that same day; it was all on the news.

There's plenty of stories I can tell about an inmate killing their celly during a cell fight, but I'll just tell you one last story. If you saw that classic movie Boyz in the Hood, remember that actor that was riding in the back seat of that red car holding the 12-gauge shotgun and was wearing all red? That guy that shot and killed Ice Cube's brother Ricky at the end of the movie? Well, he also got killed in real life by his celly at Pelican Bay Prison. It's true. After acting in Boyz in the Hood, years later in 2005, he got locked up for murder and was sentenced to life in prison. He was sent to Pelican Bay

Prison and ended up getting into a cell fight with his celly, and his celly killed him during the cell fight.

So know that these cell fights can be dangerous. There is no one there to break the fight up when one of y'all is getting the life squeezed out of you from a chokehold. So with that in mind, it does not make you a punk for moving out of the cell when you and your celly become incompatible, even though you were in the cell first.

In 2010, I was in an out-of-state prison at Tutwiler Mississippi. I was way out there because the California prison system was overcrowded at the time, so they sent a lot of us California inmates to either Arizona, Mississippi or Oklahoma. While I was at the Mississippi prison, there was this one guy...I don't want to say his real name, so I'll just call him Steve. Steve had a reputation of being a bad celly; he just couldn't get along with none of his cellies. I watched as Steve moved from one cell to another cell to another.

At the time, I had been in a cell by myself for almost a month. I was loving the peace of mind that being in the cell by yourself brings. I didn't have to worry about a celly complaining about something or just being in the way when I needed to do something like piss or whatever. One day I heard a bunch of arguing while I was watching TV. I went to my cell door to see what was going on and noticed that the arguing was coming from a cell to the left of me. I listened some more to see if all that arguing was coming from one of my partners that was housed four cells down, but it wasn't. I noticed that the voice was Steve. Steve was arguing with his celly. About five minutes later all the cell doors opened up for the dayroom and I watched as Steve left the building.

Minutes later, he came back with the counselor. They approached me as I sat in the dayroom, and Steve asked me if he could move in the cell with me. I shook my head "no" and told Steve that I didn't think it was a good idea since I didn't think we'd be compatible as cellys. The counselor was standing right there when I told him that, and she said, "Mr Bell, your cell is the only cell that's open right now and we need a place to house Steve because he and his celly are not getting along inside the cell." I told the counselor that me and Steve won't be compatible as cellies either. The counselor said, "Are you refusing a celly, Mr Bell?" I said "no" because two things could happen when you refuse a celly in prison. The first thing is they will tell you to put your hands behind your back and you will be handcuffed and escorted to the hole. Then the CO will pack all your property up and then tell the inmate that you had just refused as a celly to go ahead and move into your cell. The second thing that could happen to you if you refuse a celly is you'll get a write-up, which will now give them an opportunity to take away your packages, yard time, dayroom time, or phone time. I didn't need either of them so I just simply told the counselor, "No, I'm not refusing a celly." The counselor said "Good," then turned to Steve and told him to pack his stuff up from his old cell and go ahead and move into my cell.

That night, me and Steve got into our first argument. Something he was wearing had the cell smelling hella foul. I politely and respectfully asked him if he could do something about that foul odor, he responded by saying, "Man, stop tripping!" I said, "Come on, man. Don't do me like this. If I had on something that was smelling, and you brought it to my attention, I would not only wash my clothes in the sink but I would also take a birdbath to keep everything cool between us as cellys." I asked Steve again if he could do something about that funk and he ignored me, so I asked him again and he still gave me the silent treatment. I gave up on it and went to sleep shortly after. That night I tossed and turned in bed. I never could sleep good when adrenaline was flowing through me and I'm pissed off.

The next night, I still had the same problem with my celly. Again he had the cell smelling foul. I stood up off my bunk and tapped him lightly on the shoulder to get his attention while he sat on his top bunk watching TV. When I finally got his attention, he looked at me and said, "What's up?" I said, "Man, you killing me with that smell! Can you please do something about that smell?" He responded by saying, "Man, can you leave me the hell alone?! I'm trying to watch TV!" I answered, "Oh no! I can't live like this! You need to do something right now about that smell..." Steve didn't say nothing. In fact, he went right back to watching his TV. I then said, "Look man I don't know who the hell you think I am, but you got me messed up. You ain't gonna be up in here disrespecting me like this." Steve still didn't respond to me.

That's when I lost my cool and fired on him, catching him on the left side of his face. I kept the punches coming as he tried to get off his bunk. Steve fell off his top bunk trying to get off the bunk and landed hard on the floor. And that's when I got over him. He was curled up in a ball, and I began punching him and stomping him in the face. Steve said, "All right, all right, all right!" while I landed blows. Eventually, I stopped assaulting him and backed up some by the door. He got up, looked at me and I told him, "All you needed was to do something about that smell and all of this could have been avoided." Steve said, "All right man. From now on I'll start keeping the smell down... Are we still cool?" I said, "Yeah man, but you gotta keep the smell down in this cell. I can't live like that." He agreed, so we shook hands and remained cellys.

But as the days went on, Steve continued giving me problems. He left stains in the sink, food droppings on the floor. When I brought it to his attention, he would always say, "My bad, man. I'll be more careful." One day, as I was cleaning up the cell, I moved everything from underneath the bottom bunk so I could clean under it. When I got to my cellies' side of things underneath the bunk, I pulled a pair of pants. When I went to lay them on his top bunk, a rolled up towel fell out of the pants. I picked up the rolled up towel, and noticed it had a few socks wrapped around it to hold it in a rolled up position. I also noticed the rolled up towel had a glove in the center of it. I looked closer at the glove and noticed that the glove was all greasy inside and a weird, sour smell filled the cell from the towel. I took the rolled up towel and tied it up in a plastic bag and decided I'll ask my cellie about it when he came back. I finished cleaning the cell, and sat back waiting for my celly to walk in.

When Steve finally came into the cell, I held up the bag with the rolled up towel and asked him "What the hell is this thing that's giving off this weird sour smell?" He came over to me and grabbed the bag out of my hand. "Why are you going through my stuff?!" he asked. I told him, "I wasn't going through your stuff. I was cleaning the cell up and I had to remove all your things from underneath the bunk. When I pulled your pants from underneath the bunk, this rolled up towel fell out of it." Then I asked him again. "What in the hell is this and why is there a glove inside the towel?" Steve said, "Don't worry about it, man. And mind your business!" I said,

"Come on, man. Don't be acting funny like that with me, tell me what this is." Steve then said, "All right, man. I'ma tell you what it is but don't be telling people about it." I said okay. He told me, "It's a fe-fe." I asked what a fe-fe was. Steve explained that a fe-fe is something you have sex with. He told me the greasy glove part in the center of the rolled up towel is what you penetrate. I quickly stopped him and said to him, "Say no more. I done heard enough." Steve grabbed his pants from under the bed and wrapped his fe-fe back in it.

Have you ever asked somebody a question and you regret asking as soon as you get the answer? Well, that's how I felt. I now knew the weirdo stuff my celly was doing inside the cell when I ain't there. I realized that those days when I was complaining to my celly about the foul odor that was coming off of him it was that same exact sour smell I was smelling from the rolled up towel. I got angry from the thought of this dude humping on this fe-fe while I was out of my cell. It made me even angrier, knowing those days when I walked in the cell it had that weird sour smell in the air from him reusing that same gunk inside the glove over and over again without changing it. That was the funk I complained about.

I constantly found myself arguing with Steve. Even after our talk, there were days I would walk inside the cell and that weird sour smell would be in the air. Over and over and over, I kept telling him to stop funking up the cell, but it kept happening. Eventually, I had had enough. I told Steve that this ain't working out and that he had to find another cell to move to. Steve said he didn't have another place to move to. I knew he was telling the truth, being I had seen Steve bounce from one cell to the next cell and the next cell because he couldn't get along with his cellies. So I just went along and told Steve that he can have the cell. I told him that I'd move out, which I did that following weekend.

See, prison is already stressful. And to be in the cell with someone that's putting unnecessary stress on you is not cool. It would have been silly for me to keep having those arguments with Steve. Yeah, I hated losing my cell. But I would have lost my joy, peace of mind, and my cool if I had stayed in that cell. That could have easily resulted in me catching a murder charge, cuz Steve was hella frail. I done kicked his butt already and I knew I was gonna do it again. Some inmates might look at the way I moved out the cell as being scared, since I was in the cell first and Steve should have been the one to move out the cell. But I don't look at it like I'm scared; I look at it like I had just jumped over an obstacle - an obstacle that was likely going to keep me in prison longer, with a possible murder charge from a cell fight. You got to remember the goal: when you go to jail or prison the goal is to get out of there and get back to your family. Anything that's making it hard for you to reach that goal...you need to try your best to either stay away from it or get away from it! Getting your freedom back should be way more important than a cell.

I want to tell you about these dudes I knew when I was in Arizona Prison...

Remember, the California prison system was sending a lot of California inmates out of state due to overcrowding. Now, I don't want to say these two inmates' real names, so I'll just call one of them Gene and I'll call the other one Mike. Mike and Gene were both cellies from different crip gangs. Gene had four of his crip homies in the same building with him. Mike had homies from his crip gang at the prison, but none of his homies were in the same building with him; all his homies were all in different buildings. Everything was cool between these two cellies until one day. Gene lost his $20 bag of meth and claimed that he lost it inside the cell. Gene searched everywhere in the cell but couldn't find his meth bag. Being as Mike was in the cell at the time Gene lost his meth, Gene accused Mike of stealing it. I don't know every word that was said inside the cell right before the fight happened, but I do know it was all behind Gene losing his bag of meth and accusing Mike of stealing it. And I know this because Gene told all of us the reason behind the fight in the cell.

Gene also told us that it was his celly, Mike, that threw the first punch inside the cell. Not only did Gene lose his bag of meth, but he also lost the fight and a front tooth along with a deep cut above his left eye and a busted lip. Mike suffered no injury during the fight.

When the cell doors opened up for dayroom time, Gene quickly went and told all his homies what just went down inside the cell. While he was talking, Mike just went over and sat down in the dayroom. While Mike was sitting in the dayroom, one of Gene's homies approached him. With Gene and his homies standing close by, Gene's homie said to Mike, "Let me holler at you for a minute." Mike stood up and started walking with Gene's homie to the back of the building while Gene and his other two homies followed close behind them. Once Mike and Gene's homie got to the back of the building, Gene homie quickly stole on Mike. Then Gene and his other 2 homies all jumped in as well.

Mike was jumped by 4 inmates while the whole dayroom just watched. Mike ended up on the ground, and that's when things got real bad for him. Gene and all his homies punched and stomped on Mike while he laid on the ground. The CO eventually saw all the commotion that was going on in the back of the dayroom and ran over to stop the beat down that Mike was getting. Gene and his homie heard the inmates in the dayroom making police siren calls. Inmates do that alarm call to warn other inmates that the CO is coming. So Gene and all his homies scattered while Mike laid motionless on the ground. This Arizona prison had security cameras set up all over the place, so the CO rewinded the camera to see who caused this beat down on Mike. Gene and all his homies eventually ended up getting caught when medical assistance had to come and scoop Mike up off the ground. His injuries were so severe that the prison medical team was unable to treat him. Mike was sent to an outside hospital suffering two broken ribs and a broken jaw. Gene and all his homies were all charged with the assault on Mike. The charge was assault with great bodily injury, or GBI, which is a strikeable offense. They all had to go to court and ended up getting extra time added to their sentence.

So if you're thinking about just taking off on your celly when you have no homeboys in the building, and your celly has got homies in the building with him, you might want to think about what happened to Mike. Cuz this exact same beatdown can happen to you.

Bitter Celly

It's not good to be in the cell with someone that is bitter and negative. Their negative energy can easily rub off on you, causing you to become bitter and negative just like them. You could be sitting on your bunk feeling good with your positive energy on full. Then all of a sudden your bitter, negative celly gets to complaining or nit-picking, talking bad about people, being Debbie-downer, constantly talking about hurting people or complaining about how the CO or somebody else did him wrong. All of a sudden, you begin to feel your positive high energy begin to lessen.

You got to be careful with these type of cellies. They love to nit-pick and complain about little things that you're doing inside the cell, things that are not really anything; but he will try to make it seem like it's something just to have something to complain about. Maybe you left a little drop of water on the floor; a little drop of water that would dry up in about 5 minutes. But here he is, making a big deal out of it. Or maybe you turn on the light because you need it for a little bit, but he wants to complain about the light.

Not only do these bitter cellies sap your positive energy away, but they are also extremely detrimental to your health. They wind up making you feel depressed, sad, angry, frustrated, annoyed, and agitated with all his bitterness and complaining. Don't allow bitter cellies to emotionally drag you down with them. Don't keep letting your celly steal your joy. Know that there are negative, bitter cellies that don't want to see you happy, laughing, and smiling. They would rather see you miserable and unhappy like them. Remember, misery loves company. So if you end up with a bitter celly like that, do your mental health a favor and get a cell move quick.

Playing the Hard and Tough Role

A lot of inmates will play the hard role with you at first when you move in the cell with them. They will barely speak to you or say nothing at all to you for a while. But as the days go on he'll open up to you when he sees that you're following all his cell rules, you're not a dirty person, and he sees that you're cool. He'll lower his guard some, and become friendlier and more talkative to you.

The reason why a lot of cellies act this way at first is because he's feeling you out. He's checking to see if you're a cool person and will follow all his cell rules. Another reason why some inmates will play the hard role with you at first is because there's a nervousness that goes through inmates when we first get a celly that they don't even know. The nervousness comes from thinking that the new celly might be a j-cat or weirdo, and they might just have to put hands on him if he starts acting up in the cell by being hella disrespectful or crazy. But that nervousness will diminish when they see that the new celly is gonna be alright.

When I was in prison, pretty much all my cellies that I didn't know played the hard role and quiet role with me at first. I remember this one dude that played the hard, quiet role with me after I just moved in the cell with him. He was 6'8" tall and weighed at least 280 pounds. I tried to talk to him the first day I moved in, but he would only give me short responses. He didn't laugh at all. He was always serious. But after a week went by, he seen that I was cool and was following all his cell rules. Then he turned into a gentle giant. He started offering me some of his food, cracking jokes with me, and even laughing out loud. He became so talkative, he started talking me to death!

After so many of my cellies started by playing the hard role with me, I stopped taking it personally whenever they would act like that. I knew what was going on. I was being tested and watched to see if I'm even a cool dude that is following all his cell rules. You should just expect this. But know that as time goes by and you are following all his cell rules and are not dirty, he will start letting his guard down, becoming more talkative and friendly with you. Being played the hard role and seeing the reason my cellied played it, I also started acting that way too with all the new cellies that I got. If my cellie didn't have nothing when they first moved in with me, I wouldn't just open up and tell him he could use my TV, hot pot, hair trimmers, etc. I waited to see if he's cool and if he was following my cell rules. If he did, I would begin to offer him stuff, even offering him deodorant or toothpaste if he didn't have any. So I would advise you that if you're in the cell first and you get a celly that you don't know, before you open up to him and be hella friendly and talkative, see if he's even cool and respecting your cell rules. You don't want to open up to a celly from the start because he might just be one of them inmates that's very disrespectful towards you, rude, dirty, and not following none of your cell rules.

Cell Time

Most county jails are on a 23-hour a day lockdown, but some are not. So if your county jail cell living allows you to come and go out the cell as you please, it's impossible that you give your celly some cell time. In prison there's always an hourly unlock, and with every unlock you can leave the cell and give your celly some cell time. So if your county jail allows you to walk in and out of the cell as you please, be courteous and give your celly at least an hour of cell time.

Inmates will use their cell time to meditate or talk to their higher power, or just enjoy the peace of mind that being in the cell by themselves brings. A majority of the inmates will use their cell time to relieve themselves: in other words to jack-off. By not giving your celly any cell time so he can relieve himself, will cause him to become frustrated with you. And chances are once he starts getting frustrated with you, he will start trying to run you out of the cell permanently. Here's a look at some of the things cellies will do to try to run their celly out of the cell.

When a celly is eating, he'll fart; or all of a sudden say that he gots to take a crap, or will start blowing his nose while his celly is eating. He will purposely leave stains and crumbs all in the sink and on the floor. He'll even start giving you the silent treatment inside the cell. Or he'll start rapping or singing out loud while you're trying to read a book or watch TV. Some will purposely turn the volume up high on his TV while you're trying to sleep. He'll even purposely give off foul odors from his body or clothes inside the cell knowing that this foul odor will really bother you.

He'll be doing all types of stuff to try to irritate his celly in hopes that his celly will finally throw in the towel and say "I can't take this anymore! I'm moving out." If an inmate was in the cell first he's more likely to do those things to run his celly out of the cell. And sometimes inmates that wasn't in the cell first will still try those things to run there celly that was in the cell first.

So if you're not giving your celly any cell time, then your celly will have no choice but to jack-off at night time while you're sleeping. And what straight man wants to be doing something like that with another man nearby, sleeping above, or underneath him on a bunk? And let's just say you had to get up to use the bathroom in the middle of the night. That means your celly will have to stop trying to bust-a-nut when he hears you getting up off your bunk at night to use the bathroom. He would then have to roll over and play-sleep. And just like any man that's had to suddenly stop in the middle of trying to ejaculate, that man will grow irritable, agitated, and frustrated with that person and might even hold a grudge. So avoid putting your celly through that. Believe me when I tell you that it will cause y'all to eventually fall out and become incompatible as cellys if you don't give him any cell time.

What's Said In the Cell Stays In the Cell

Cellies are always talking inside the cell. There's going to be times when your celly is going to open up to you and talk to you about his personal business and personal problems. He might talk about things that's going on in his life right now, that's either stressing him out or bothering him. It's really important to know that when you're celly vents to you about his personal stuff, you don't go outside the cell and start telling inmates what he told you. Because if it gets back to him that you told someone his business or personal stuff, it will cause him to feel like you betrayed his trust and that he can't trust you anymore.

Here's the problem with when a celly feels like he can't trust you any more. Without trust you don't have communication. And without communication inside the cell, tension will eventually rise. And if nothing is done about the rising tension inside the cell then it's inevitable that y'all will become incompatible as cellies. Then your celly will start doing the things inmates do to try to run their celly out of the cell. Or he might just avoid doing the little things and just flat out tell you that this ain't working out as cellies and that you got to move.

I remember when I was at Calipatria State Prison level 4 in California, from the end of 2006 to the beginning of 2007. I had just moved in with my celly. He wasn't too cool at first, but once he started seeing that I was following all his cell rules and that I was a cool dude, he let his guard down some, opening up to me, and becoming more talkative and friendly. He told me that before he came to prison on this murder charge, he was living good with lots of money, a boat, a house, and nice foreign cars. One day me and my cellie signed up to use the phone. I used the phone first and then my celly went. I was watching TV in my cell waiting for him to get off the phone. When he was off, my cellie walked in the cell and angrily told me that his wife is filing for divorce. My celly then went on to say that without his wife by his side, he'll start doing bad, he'll be unable to get any more money for packages or the store. As time went on, the divorce papers finally came in the mail. And from that day on, my celly was not the same person. He no longer laughed the way he used to and I noticed his energy level got low.

One day my celly stayed in for yard but I went. I was chilling over by the benches talking to one of my partners. A friend of my celly walked up to me and asked me where my celly at, so I told him that my celly stayed in the cell. His friend asked me how my celly was doing, and I told him that my celly is stressing big time right now because his wife filed for divorce. "Damn, man. I'm sorry to hear that," his friend said. "Tell him I said wah's up," and then he walked away.

The next time we had yard, I decided to stay in the cell but my celly ended up going. When my celly got back from yard, he stormed into the cell all heated, asking why I was out on the yard the other day telling people his personal business. I said, "What are you talking about?" My celly told me that the dude who was asking about him told him what I said about him. My celly told me, "What's said in the cell is supposed to stay in the cell, man! I don't know where you been doing your time at, but you was out of pocket for telling someone my business. I don't even feel comfortable talking to you anymore." My celly then went on to say that our communication inside the cell is over, and that he will no longer be talking to me.

A week and a half went by without him saying a word to me. Being it was his cell since he was in the cell first, and I didn't like the tension that was now inside the cell, I went ahead and moved out. So learn from my mistakes. Don't let this be the reason why you and your celly fall out like me and my celly did.

Sharing With Your Celly

Even though your celly is not from where you're from, still treat him as though he were. Once you see that he's cool with you and is follwoing all your cell rules, offer him some cookies or whatever when you open them. Even when you grab an already open bag of cookies, chips, or whatever you're eating, still offer your celly some. By doing that, you will show your celly that everything is cool between y'all inside the cell and that you ain't just thinking about yourself. Sharing like that not only keeps y'all both on sharing terms inside the cell, but will also cause him to take a likeness towards you. Then, if he sees you getting into an argument with an inmate, he will come to your aid. He'll have your back or will try to diffuse the situation for you. Also, once you're celly takes that type of likeness towards you, he will also be your ears and eyes in prison/ jail. So now when your celly hears some inmate talking crap about you, or someone plotting to do you some kind of harm, your celly will quickly let you know.

You don't want to be stingy with your food, constantly eating in your cellys face. By doing that, you're pretty much saying to your celly "I don't give a crap about you," and in return your celly is going to start feeling the exact same way towards you. Your celly won't be your eyes and ears for you in prison/jail and he won't have your back. Even though you might not be in the same car as him, sharing opens up a person's heart. Not sharing? Well that hardens a heart.

Let's say you happen to fall off your top bunk and hit your head on the toilet or floor and get knocked unconscious or have a seizure inside the cell. Your celly may not even try to get you medical assistance by yelling "Man down! Man down!" underneath the cell door. Instead, your celly is likely to just stare at you while you're on the cell floor. Your celly is likely to think back to all the days when you made that food sound good as you smacked it in his face. And he'll just stare at you while you suffer on the floor.

If you get in a fight and have to go to the hole, the CO tells your celly to pack up all your personal property and hand it over to him. If you have been stingy with your celly, there's a high possibility you may come up short on some of your property. Your celly might just strip you for your CDs, food, hygiene, clothes etc. To minimize the chances of your celly pulling a stunt like that, simply be generous with your food. Also remember sharing is caring, and when you share you warm a person's heart up to where they'll start to take a liking towards you. Any animal that you feed and continue to feed will take a liking towards you. Remember that human beings are animals, too.

Don't Be a Burden on Your Celly and Know How to Say No

There are times when you won't have any money and are unable to get any packages or get to the store, but your celly is getting packages and store. Even when you want something he has, you have to learn to say no sometimes when he offers you some of his food. You don't want to become a burden on him. See, your celly will offer you some of the food that he's eating and he will continue to offer you food. But if you always take it, eventually your celly will start to feel like you're getting heavy on him, causing him to run out of his food way faster than he normally would have, had he not been feeding you. But this feeling only occurs when you're not sharing back with your celly.

So what you do is, the first time he offers you some food, accept it. That way you don't make him feel weird for rejecting his offer. But the second time he offers you some food, don't accept it. Just tell him that you're cool right now even though you really do want some. See, you want to accept and decline, accept and decline. But decline more than you accept.

By doing this, you keep your burden load from getting too heavy on your celly. If you regularly do this, your celly will eventually see what you're actually doing. He will see that you're not trying to be a heavy burden on him, and that will help your celly respect you more and like you more for lightening up the burden load on him. Don't worry about whether or not you're offending your celly by declining his food offers to you. Trust me, it will be way better for you to make him feel offended than it would for you to make him feel like you're being a heavy burden on him.

See, cellies offer food to their celly at first to try to be nice and cool. But if you're broke or not doing any sharing back, you will become a burden on your celly. And after a while, you will notice the little switch up on his attitude towards you.

I remember a few times when I was in prison, my support system wasn't able to help me with some stuff I needed. When I was doing bad at the time, my celly would ask me if I wanted some of the food he was eating. I would ask him what kind of chips they are or what kind of cookies they are. When he would tell me, I would lie and say I don't like those kinds of chips or cookies. This was my way of cutting down his food offerings and lessening the burden. By saying I didn't like those kinds of chips, cookies, or whatever, he stopped asking me if I wanted some.

But he will offer me some other kinds of cookies, chips or whatever, and I would accept it. Sometimes my celly would offer me some cookies, sliding the cookie bag back some, exposing like 6 or 7 cookies and telling me to go ahead and grab some. But I will always only take 1 or 2 cookies. Or if my celly was offering me some chips and told me to hold out both my hands so he can pour some chips in my hand, I would always only hold out one hand and tell him to just pour me a little bit. See, I would accept and decline, except and decline. But I would always decline way more than I would accept, and I only accepted a little bit.

I know from experience how people switch up once you become a burden on them, so I equipped myself with acting this way when I'm doing bad and am being offered stuff.

It's kinda similar to how a family member invites a relative to come stay with them "just until they gets back on their feet." But as the months go by, the relative is in the house eating up the food without helping out with buying any groceries; they don't help at all with the bills and rent. The day will eventually come when that family member is going to start feeling the heavy burden load that the relative is putting on him. Once this occurs, the family member is going to start switching up in such a way that the relative is going to want to ask the family member, "Are you trying to run me out the house?"

So don't be a burden on your celly. Learn how to accept and decline. And if you're broke and unable to share back, take very little when you do accept.

Nip It In the Bud

When your celly is doing something that annoys you or bothers you, you need to nip it in the bud or he will continue doing it. I believe a person should not nip things in the bud the first time someone does something that's annoying or bothering them, but for sure the second time they do it. A lot of times people will do something that's annoying or bothering only one time and will never do it again. So let it go the first time; but the second time your celly does it, nip it in the bud. Y'all both got to live in that cell and he shouldn't be robbing you of your peace of mind, the same way you shouldn't be robbing him of his peace of mind.

Your cell should be a place of relaxation and peace of mind. If your celly is annoying you or bothering you, talk to your celly about the problem, but don't get at him aggressively. If you do, he might feel like you're trying to check him or punk him and that will make him not want to listen to what it is you're trying to say. Getting at him aggressively will only cause him to match your aggressiveness. And you know how things can turn out when two people are arguing back and forth aggressively. So instead, get at him in a calm, relaxed, respectable type of way. When you talk to people that way, they're more willing to listen to what it is you got to say and are willing to compromise to fix the problem that he's causing you.

If I had a dollar every time I had to nip something in the bud with one of my cellies...I wouldn't be rich, but I will for sure have at least $32. I remember this one celly that had just moved in with me. I was assigned to the bottom bunk and he was assigned to the top bunk. The prison was cell-feeding all us inmates cuz we were on lockdown due to the COVID-19 pandemic. The morning after he moved in, we were served breakfast. I handed him his breakfast tray as he sat on his bunk and I took my breakfast tray and went and sat down on my bottom bunk and started eating.

As my celly was eating his breakfast, he decided to hang his bare feet down from his bunk, where I sat about a foot away from him eating my breakfast. Then he started cracking his toes. I was chewing on my food and looked up at him and gave him a look like "are you serious right now?" He looked down at me and said, "Good morning, bunky." I said "good morning" back trying my best not to show my frustration at the moment. I got up, grabbed my bowl that was in my locker, and scraped my breakfast in it, figuring that I'll just eat it later. I have always been the type of celly that wouldn't nip something in the bud the first time somebody does something that annoys me or bothers, but will nip it in the bud the second time they do it. I'm hoping that maybe they'll just do it this one time and won't do it again.

That night at dinner, my celly didn't hang his bare feet down as I ate my food.

The next morning, I handed him his breakfast tray as he sat on his top bunk, took my breakfast tray and sat on my bottom bunk and started eating my food. Right when I started chewing my food, my celly hung his bare feet down and started cracking his toes. I looked up at him and said in a calm relaxed voice, "Can I ask you a question?" My celly said, "Yeah, go right ahead." I said, "If you were sitting at a restaurant table with your girlfriend, eating a steak, and then out of nowhere some dude comes and sits at the table right next to you and your girlfriend and he takes off his shoes and socks, and then kicks his bare feet up on his table and starts cracking his toes - how would that make you feel?" My celly saw where I was going with this story and quickly lifted his feet back up on his bunk. "Oh, my bad man. My bad," he apologized. I said to my celly, "I appreciate that, man, cuz it's hard to eat my food with them dogs hanging down on me like that." My celly then said , "My bad, man. Again.That it won't happen again." And it never did.

See, it's not just what you say but how you say it. As a man in prison, none of us wants to feel like we're being checked, punked, or bullied. Always remember you could catch more bees with honey then you can vinegar.

Different Outside the Cell Than Inside the Cell

People are different people in different settings. For example a man hanging with his homies will act totally different when he's hanging with his wife; or a person hanging with his friends will act totally different when hanging with his pastor.

If you don't have a celly and you're out trying to find you a new one, know that a lot of inmates are totally different outside the cell then they do inside the cell. You may see a guy outside the cell and think he'll be a cool celly; but find that he's dirty or a nit-picker, a complainer, or into all sorts of weird stuff once he moves in. He could be one person outside the cell, and someone you never thought he'd be once inside the cell.

I remember this one dude I met at a prison in Oklahoma. I always played chess and worked out with this one dude. He was hella cool; in fact, he was my number one partner at that prison. The celly I had was getting ready to transfer to another prison. When he finally got transferred to the other prison, my chess and workout homeboy asked if he could move in the cell with me. I told him he could and he moved in that following weekend. I was proud that he was in the cell with me. But it wasn't long until I realized I made a big mistake.

The first night with him in the cell there was a big problem. He snored. And I mean he snored loud. I was able to drain out some of his snoring by putting my earplugs in and turning my fan on high. This was something that I learned to drain out a celly's snoring. Then a few days later, I learned that he didn't like cleaning! I tried to get him to clean the cell floor, and he said it was my duty since I was on the bottom bunk. He constantly made messes and would not clean them up, and we kept having arguments about it. Eventually, I had enough of him and told him that it ain't going to work out with us being cellies.

A few days later he found himself a new cell to move to. But when I'd see him in the dayroom he wouldn't even say what's up or ask me to play chess or work out with him anymore. He was a totally different person outside the cell then he was inside the cell.

So know that you can have a homie that's hella cool with you outside the cell, there's a possibility he ain't that cool once y'all become cellies.

Perfectly Placed

The cell lockers inside the cell have no doors, so you can see everything that your celly has in his locker. Some cellies have everything perfectly placed inside their locker, to where if anything was moved or out of place from how he had it, he'll notice. So if you're out of lotion, grease, coffee, or whatever, and you figure you could just sneak inside your celly's locker without him knowing - I would advise you not to. Unless, of course, you and your celly are cool like that and he gave you permission to go inside his locker. That goes for your celly's appliances, too. If he told you not to mess with none of his appliances, don't do it.

You do have inmates that will tell you not to touch his stuff, and then perfectly place a CD inside his CD player a certain way so he'll know if it was tampered with. Or he'll set his volume knob at a certain place and know if you messed with it. There are a lot of things he could use to set a trap for you, so when he comes into the cell and sees it out of place, he'll know you've been tampering with his stuff.

I remember when I was in an out-of-state prison in Arizona. My celly told me not to touch none of his stuff, because we weren't cool like that. One day at yard time, I decided I was just going to kick back and chill inside the cell while my celly went to the yard. My CD player was broken and I had ordered one from a prison vendor called Wlakenhorsts. My celly had a boombox, and had also just got his quarterly package. He had ordered a CD called Sharp On All Four Corners - Corner1 by the rap artist E-40. My celly loved playing that E-40 CD, and I started to like that CD a lot, too. My favorite track was number six. So I decided to sneak and play his boombox while he left for yard, wanting to listen to track six a few times. I walked over to his boombox and checked to see if the E-40 CD was already in there. It wasn't, so I checked the CD case that was on his locker. I flipped through the plastic sleeves until I finally found the E-40 CD. I pulled out the CD and went back to the boombox, took out the CD that was already in the boombox and put the E-40 in and quickly went to track six. When the song kicked in, I bounced my head up and down and started doing my little dance. After listening to the song a few times I decided that was enough. I figured I better get the CD back in its sleeve before my celly gets back from the yard. I opened up the boombox, took the E-40 CD out and put the E-40 CD back in the plastic sleeve case that it was in. Then put the CD that was in the boombox before back.

When my celly got back from the yard, he was all sweaty and asked me if I needed to take a piss before he took a birdbath. I told him I was good, hung up the sheets along the wall to give him privacy as he birdbathed. Then he went to put some music on his boombox like he always did before he birdbathed. I was watching TV, but kept looking over to my celly to see why the hell he was staring at his boombox the way he was. He walked over to his locker and began staring at his locker the same way he stared at his boombox. Then he turned to me and said, "You been touching my stuff?" I asked what he was talking about. He said, "I know you been touching my stuff, because I purposely left my boombox volume on three, and right now it's on five. And I purposefully left a staple on the right corner of my CD case and now the staple ain't there." I was lost for words so I just looked at him with a puzzled look on my face like "Huh?" A few seconds went by, and my celly said, "I ain't playing with you, man. You touch my shit again, we gon' tear this mother f***ing cell up." Being as I was in the wrong, I didn't bark back. Instead, I just nodded my head up and down in agreement and went back to watching my TV. After that day, I did in fact start leaving all his stuff alone. I now knew he was planting traps, perfectly placing things inside in his locker and appliances.

In 18 years in prison, I had 3 different cellies who told me not to touch their stuff. At first, I didn't understand why they were acting funny like that about their stuff. Later, I understood why they acted that way. They had hella years to do in prison, and were just trying to make sure their appliances and stuff lasted a long time. With a hella time to do they can't afford for their stuff to be breaking or running out of stuff too fast. There may be inmates that you cell up with, too, that don't want you to touch any of their stuff. Respect their rules. If he told you not to touch his stuff, you could expect that he has numerous traps set inside the cell that will alert him whenever you've been tampering with his stuff.

Since some inmates will lay traps for you inside their cells after they have told you not to touch their stuff, here's a look at some of the traps that your celly may lay out for you. He'll open up a Folgers jar of coffee and neatly lay something like a tiny piece of paper on top of the coffee grounds; he will have two objects in his locker lined up perfectly where the labels are facing each other in a certain way; he'll have his potato chip bags specifically folded up at the corners; things are placed in his locker a certain way to where he will notice if they are moved. He will have an item leaning up against something, so it will fall when you move the item.

Even if your celly didn't tell you not to touch his stuff, he still may lay some traps for you just to see if you've been messing with his stuff while he's gone. So maybe it's just a good idea to not mess with your celly's stuff unless he says it's okay.

One Up, One Down

Since the cells are so small in jail/prison, there's a thing called "one up, one down." That means when your celly is on the floor - one down - you stay on your bunk - one up - until he finishes doing whatever it is he's doing on the floor. This is a prison rule that inmates established decades ago. But when two cellies is hella cool with each other, they might not follow this prison rule. Instead they will just squeeze past one another inside the cell. Cells are so small that the squeeze will be so tight they must brush butts together as they scoot past each other to get to the other side of the cell. You have to ask your celly whether or not y'all are going to be following the "one up, one down" prison rule.

Going to Someone's Cell Door

When you go to someone's cell door in jail/prison, don't just walk right up and look inside the cell through the cell door window. He could be doing something inside the cell that he don't want no one to see. The proper and respectful way inmates go to someone's cell door in jail /prison is to stand to the side of his cell door where he can't see you through his cell door window and knock 3 or 4 times. Then wave your hand back and forth in front of his cell door window so he can see it waving. Once he sees your hand waving back and forth in the window, he will come to the door and see what you want.

Unfortunately, I had to learn this the hard way. There was this inmate in my building that I'll just call RJ. I had just met RJ when I was trying to sell some CDs in the dayroom. He was interested in buying my Young Jeezy TM 103 CD. RJ said that he wanted to listen to the CD before he bought it to make sure that the CD didn't have any scratches on it. I told RJ that was fine and said I would bring the CD by his cell later so he can check it out. RJ said all right and told me what cell he lived in.

I went to RJ's cell with my Young Jeezy CD later that day. I walked straight up to his cell door, looked straight through his window and told him I got the Jeezy CD for him. As I looked through RJ's cell window, I saw him quickly get up from his bed and walk over to me. He looked at me like I had dodo on my face. When RJ arrived at the door, RJ said to me through his cell door, "What's wrong with you man?! Hey, when you come to my cell door, you knock first. You just don't look through my window."

After RJ was finished schooling me on the right and respectful way to go to somebody's cell, he told me to go ahead and slide him the Young Jeezy CD under his cell door so he can check it out before he buys it. So I slid him the CD and told him that I'll be back later for his answer. A couple hours later, I went back to RJ's cell and knocked on his cell door the way he showed me. RJ came to the door and said he'd buy the CD. As RJ said that to me, he looked down at his hand then looked back up at me. He told me to hold on for a minute, turned to the side and brought what he had in his hand up to his face and talked to it saying "Hold on baby...." I could see he was holding a cell phone. RJ then quickly grabbed some food off of his bed, walked back over to me and slid 3 packs of oysters under his cell door which was a total of $6 dollars, the price I was asking for my Young Jeezy CD. He said he'd holler at me later, so I picked up my oysters and walked away.

As I walked away from his cell, it started to make more sense to me why RJ had told me not to just walk up to his cell door and look right through his cell door window, explaining the right and respectful way to approach a cell door. It was because he had a cell phone and didn't want people just popping up, looking in his cell door window cuz they might see his cell phone. RJ was trying to be discreet. So when you go to somebody's cell door, out of respect for that man, knock the way I RJ taught me. This is the proper etiquette of going to somebody's cell door in jail/prison.

Don't Spit in the Sink

In the county jail and prison dorms, it's okay to spit in the sink. But in county jail/prison cell living, spitting in the sink is not cool.

Instead, inmates keep the germs down inside the cell by spitting in the toilet and not the sink. So when you're brushing your teeth and you need to spit the toothpaste out, spit in the toilet instead of the sink. Then flush the toilet. This is a cell living prison rule that you need to respect and follow. If you forget and spit in the sink, this could be a reason you and your celly end up falling out, becoming uncompatible.

Get a Program

To make your time in jail/prison go faster, you will need to create a program for yourself. Creating a program for yourself will also reduce your stress level, helping you do the time instead of letting the time do you. In other words, you'll be killing time doing things that you like to do throughout the day instead of just sitting around all day staring at the walls.

Here's how you create a program for yourself. Figure out all the things you like doing, and from the time you wake up and go back to sleep, you do them. This allows your mind to stay occupied doing other things instead of constantly thinking about the streets or stressing on being in prison. Once you get a program for yourself, your days will start to fly by so damn fast you won't be able to believe that it's already Friday again - or it's already a new month!

Here are some things you can add to your program to create a program for yourself: exercise, read religious material, meditate, write poems, write love songs or rap songs, do crossword puzzles or sudoku, make holiday cards, draw tattoo patterns or pictures, play chess or card games, play dominoes or board games, study, read a novel, listen to music, watch TV, write a book, go to self help groups, go to school...

Here's an example of what a program looks like:

6:30 a.m. wake up and get ready for breakfast (brush teeth, wash face)

7:00 a.m. breakfast chow (eat breakfast)

7:30 a.m. drink coffee and get ready to work out

8:00 a.m. yard-time (go workout)

10:00 a.m. come in from yard and take a shower

10:30 a.m. play some chess or card game

12:00 p.m. eat lunch

12:30 p.m. go to self help group

2:00 p.m. watch TV

4:00 p.m. read a novel or a book

5:00 p.m. dinner chow (go eat)

5:45 p.m. call family on phone

6:00 p.m. drawing while listening to music

7:00 p.m. read religious material

7:45 p.m. write a letter

8:30 p.m. watch more TV

9:30 p.m. winding down, getting ready for bed (brush teeth)

10:00 p.m. bedtime

Then wake up and repeat this program all over again.

If you're living in a cell, you need to quickly learn the program that your celly has. Pay attention to the time when he regularly does things inside the cell. That way you won't be in his way when he normally works out, cleans, etc. When that time comes around, you won't be on the floor and in your celly's way since you will already know his program. Try your best to remember. That way when the time comes around the next day, you'll be out his way. Hopefully, your celly will also be learning your program, too, by watching you and checking the time to see when you regularly do things inside the cell. Then he'll try his best to be out of your way.

So try to work out and do whatever you do on the floor inside the cell at the same time every day. Don't be one of those cellies who's not paying attention to their celly. You don't want to be getting in the way of your celly's daily program. There's nothing more irritating and annoying than somebody always getting in your way right before you're about to do something inside the cell. Don't be game goofy! Learn your cellies program and stay out his way and he'll be doing the same for you. This is part of showing respect for your celly.

Don't Bang Beats With Your Hands

A lot of time, inmates are bored inside a county jail cell with nothing to really do. So to entertain themselves, some will start banging beats on the cell door or desk as they rap to the beat. But banging beats will become annoying to your neighbors after a while. Plus, the banging could also be waking your neighbors up while they're trying to get some sleep. Don't do your neighbors like that! Instead, be courteous and respectful towards them. You just never know... your neighbor could be fighting a life sentence for murder and the last thing he needs is you driving him crazy with all that banging beats on the door or desk.

This applies for a prison environment, too, but it's even worse since a lot of inmates in prison have job assignments that they need to get to the next day. So they really need their rest so they can function well at work. Waking your neighbors up when he's desperately trying to get some rest will eventually bring trouble and animosity your way. I advise you not to start getting into the habit of banging beats on the door or desk, lowering your risk of creating unnecessary hatred towards you.

Workout

This next part applies to all inmates. It's crucial that you get yourself a workout program, working out at least 4 times a week. Not only does it help you stay healthy and preserve yourself, but it relieves some stress. It also helps you defend yourself, just in case you got to defend and protect yourself from an inmate that's charging at you during a race riot or in a one-on-one fist fight with another inmate.

Another reason why it's good to work out while incarcerated is because you got a lot of inmates that be walking around sizing other inmates up. They'll look at you and look at your shoulders, your chest, your arms, and your back. They'll try to figure out if they can beat you up if y'all were to ever fight, or will you whip him. And if you're frail looking, with puny muscles, then without a doubt that inmate is going to think that he can kick your butt in a fight. Once an inmate gets that in his mind, he will begin to feel more macho than you. So the chances of him getting at you or trying to check you in an aggressive manner is higher when he thinks he can kick your butt. Now, if you're walking around to where it looks like you work out, having that muscular build on you, it will not only raise doubt in the minds of those inmates that be sizing other inmates up, it will also cause those types of inmates to respect you more. They'll be more careful about what they say to you out of fear that you will kick their butt if they get at you foul or try to check you in an aggressive tone.

There's so much good that comes with working out in jail /prison - being better able to defend yourself, preserving yourself, gaining more respect from inmates, and making guys think twice before stepping to you or getting at you foul. So do yourself a favor and get a workout program. Always remember working out in jail/prison is more than just working out: IT'S SURVIVAL!

There are going to be days when you don't not feel like working out. On those days, do what I did: drink a little coffee and turn on some rap music. Your attitude is shaped by what you listen to. So if you're listening to some rap music and the rap artist is rapping about some gangster stuff, this will put you in somewhat of a war mode and amp you up a bit. And if the song that you're listening to gots a banging beat, this will motivate you even more.

But if you're in the county jail, then you won't be able to actually listen to music. But all hope ain't lost because you can have a friend or family member send you some rap lyrics to your favorite songs into the county jail. This will also do the trick of motivating you to work out. Your friends or family members can go on the internet and print the rap lyrics out for you. So on the days you don't feel like working out in the county jail, you can read the rap lyrics. And since you already know the song well, the beat will automatically pop in your head and the song will be stuck in your head which will now give you the drive you needed to get started with your work out.

Curl Bag

Inmates lift weights in their cell using a curl bag. There are two kinds of curl bags you can make. Being there's no mesh laundry bags in jail, you can only make the water bag one. But in prison, you can make both the water bag one and the mesh bag one.

You will get a laundry bag as soon as you get to prison. The mesh laundry bag is normally supposed to be used to turn in your dirty laundry once a week. You are to number the bag with your cell number on it and then throw your bag out in front of your cell in the morning. They will pick it up to be washed. You'll get a few laundry bags once you get to prison, so you could use one of them to make you a very nice curl bag.

For a water curl bag, ask the porter in your building for a big trash bag. Normally, the Porter (Porter - the inmate building janitor that cleans the dayroom, showers, tables and every other thing that needs cleaning inside the building. The Porter also mops, sweeps and wipes down tables in the bedroom.) will give you one. Once you get the bag, you will need to add water to it, enough for your desired weight. Once you got the weight that you feel is comfortable for you to curl, tie the trash bag real tight. Then get a t-shirt and put the water bag in it. Tie up the T-shirt so that the trash bag fits nicely inside the T-shirt. Now, cut a piece of sheet off to make a curl handle for your water bag.

To make a mesh curl bag, you will need to ask some of your homies if they have any old catalogs or old magazines that they don't need. The best time to stock up on these catalogs is at the end of the second and fourth quarter. This is when all new catalogs arrive at the prison and get passed out to all the inmates. That's when inmates will start throwing out all their old catalogs. You will need those old catalogs for the weight for your mesh curl bag. Once you get enough catalogs, stack the catalogs on top of each other in your mesh bag. When you feel the weight is good enough for you, tie it up. When you finish tying it up it should look like this:

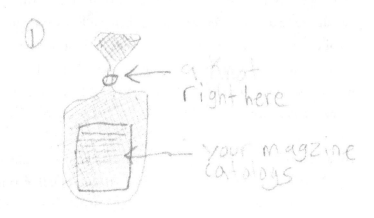

Now you need to start preparing the bag for the curl handle. Start by cutting off two strips from your sheet. The first strip should be at least eight inches long, and real thin like the size of a shoe string. The other strip of sheet should be at least ten inches long and wider like the size of a belt.

Next, roll up a catalog and take the skinny long sheet strip and tie the sheet around the rolled up catalog magazine. When you're finished, it should look like this:

Shoe string tied
around the
② catolog

Now, take a sock and put the rolled up catalog inside the sock. Then tie the sock up. When you're finished it should look like this:

③

Knot

the curled
up magazine
is now in the
sock

Next, make two little cuts at the top of your mesh laundry bag. Make sure the cuts are 6 to 7 inches apart from each other. Now, take that longer and wider strip of sheet that you cut off and string it through the holes on the top of the laundry bag like this:

Finally, take the sock handle and tie it on the mesh laundry bag like this:

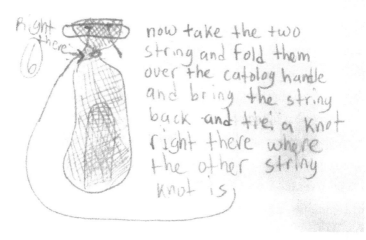

right here

now take the two string and fold them over the catolog handle and bring the string back and tie a knot right there where the other string knot is)

When you're finished, your completed mesh curl bag should look like this:

Respect

While doing time you will receive the utmost respect on a level four prison yard. A lot of this has to do with the fact that 95% of the inmates on level four yards have life sentences. A majority of them are walking around with an attitude like, "I already got a life sentence; what more can they do to me?" So when it's time to handle business, a majority of them are not trying to fist fight; instead, they're pulling out a knife with murder on their mind. Inmates that are on level four yards already know how the next inmate is likely to respond to disrespect. This is one of the main reasons why the respect level is so high on level four yards.

On a level three, two, or one prison yard, you do get respect, but just not as much as you would get from being on a level four. The lower the prison level yard that you're on, the lower the respect level. It's like that because being on a lower level prison yard, a lot of inmates already know that people are trying to stay out of trouble so they can get out of prison. See, it takes a lot to get in the lower level prison yards. You got to stay out of trouble. Some inmates take advantage of that. They know the chances are slim for someone pulling a knife on them or trying to fight them for disrespect.

They know the repercussions aren't as great on the lower level prison yards than it is on the level four yards. But don't get it twisted, because there are some inmates that will stab you in the lower level prison yards for disrespecting them. But the chances of running into one of those types of inmates in a lower level prison is like one out of fifty inmates. But on the level four prison yards, it's like one out of every one inmate that's likely to stab you for disrespecting them.

Being in the county jail is like being on a level zero yard, so the respect level is going to be the lowest. This has a lot to do with people coming to jail fresh off the streets and still operating the exact same way they were treating people on the streets which is with very little respect or no respect at all. Most of these guys just don't know any better, because that's just how the streets raise them. They're stuck in their ways of being rude and disrespectful to people. Fact is, once the county jail disrespectful inmates get sent to prison and get around inmates that demand respect, they'll get their act right - becoming respectful and polite to other inmates.

The main thing you need to have to survive prison is respect. When you show respect, you get respect. As long as you're respecting inmates, the lesser chance of you having problems, and the lesser chance of you getting into a fight. So when you're trying to pass another inmate and it's a tight squeeze, be respectful and say "excuse me" when you're trying to pass them. If you got to reach over an inmate for whatever reason, be respectful and say "excuse me." If you happen to fart loud out in the dayroom, be respectful and say "excuse me" and take a walk right after. If you're talking to someone and you just so happened to yawn in his face, be respectful and say "excuse me." If you're walking and you accidentally bump into another inmate, be respectful and say "excuse me." When you see two inmates talking to each other and you're trying to holler at one of them, don't just walk up to him and start talking to him, interrupting the conversation that he's having with the other inmate. Be respectful and walk up to the guy that you're trying to talk to and say "excuse me," Know that if you do just walk up and interrupt two inmates having a conversation without saying "excuse me", one of them is likely to turn to you and aggressively say, "Hey man! What the hell is wrong with you? Don't you see us having a conversation?!" Know that you would be out of pocket to match his aggressiveness, being you were in the wrong for rudely interrupting their conversation. So if you do happen to make the mistake of interrupting someone's conversation and they get aggressive with you, just say, "my bad." Don't say, "I'm sorry," because us inmates don't say "I'm sorry" in prison. We say "my bad."

I remember when I was at Calipatria, California, in the level four general population yard from November 1, 2006 to May 1, 2007. It was yard time, and a very very windy day. I was over by the pull up bars, waiting for my turn to go next. I was next in line, and there were 4 other inmates behind me. I had to spit, so I turned my head to the left and spit it downward. As soon as the spit left my mouth, the wind carried my spit behind me, landing on the chest of this guy that was behind me. "Mother f***er!", he yelled. As soon as those words left his mouth, I quickly said, "My bad, man. Excuse me, it was an accident." He stared into my eyes for about 5 seconds before he said, "Alright, man. But next time you got to spit, and it's windy like this, take your ass over there and spit," pointing towards an area where a trash can was located. Then he took his shirt off and began rubbing the spot that had my spit on it on the ground to rub the spit off. You see how powerful the words "my bad" is in prison? So add them words to your vocabulary to minimize your bumps on the road.

Lifer Cellies

If you got an out date, meaning you will be getting out of prison one day, and you happen to get a celly that gots a life sentence, don't be talking about the streets and your plans on what you want to do when you get out of prison. And especially don't be talking about women to him, unless he initiates this conversation with you first. If you do, most lifer cellies will think that you're trying to rub it in his face that you're getting out of prison one day and that he's going to be stuck in prison where he'll never get to see all the stuff that you're talking about. Talking about the streets and women to your celly can also mess with him emotionally and mentally, making him feel his life sentence all over again, realizing that the streets and women are forever gone from his life. By constantly making him feel hurt and painful, it's a possibility that he might reach his breaking point and flash on you one day.

I remember when I first started off doing my time, I didn't know nothing about prison life. So I didn't know that most lifer inmates don't like talking about the streets and women. I ended up getting a celly who had a life sentence. He was my first lifer-celly. He was in for murder. I told him, "When I get out of prison, I want to become a big rig truck driver so I could buy a 4 bedroom house and start a new family in it." I talked about finding a wife when I got out of prison, and having 2 more kids. I also talked about how I can't wait to go out and take a cruise trip to Hawaii. While I was talking to him about women, I talked about sex positions that I can't wait to try on a woman when I get out. "Like where I'm holding the woman up in front of me to where it looks like I'm giving her a piggyback ride, but in reverse; where I'm standing up and we're facing each other, and I'm holding her up by gripping her thighs. As I'm in the middle of the cell floor telling my celly this, he cut me off and said, "Come on man. Come on man! I got a life sentence. What makes you think I want to hear about what you plan to do with a woman when you get out of prison, or your plans for the streets?" He then went on to say that he's actually starting to think that I'm trying to rub it in his face that I'm getting out of prison one day and that he's not. After my celly was finished talking, I said, "Come on man, it ain't even like that. I had no idea that this was bothering you." That's when my celly angrily said, "Out of respect, man, can you stop talking about the streets and women? That's stuff I ain't never going to see again, and I'm trying to forget all about it. But your ass keeps bringing it up." I apologized to him, and told him that I won't talk about the streets or women anymore. And I never did.

So if you happen to get a celly that has life, don't be the first to talk about the streets or women. Let him initiate that type of conversation. And that goes for any inmate that you know that has a life sentence. Don't talk about the streets or women to them. Let him be the one that brings that type of conversation up first.

Babysitting

A majority of inmates that've been in prison 10 years or more normally won't accept a celly that hasn't done at least 5 years or more. Less than 5 years, they see it as having to babysit their celly, always having to correct them on the proper way to do things inside the cell. An inmate always having to correct their celly is agitating and annoying. Sometimes you get those knucklehead inmates that will feel like you're trying to punk them inside the cell, when all they're trying to do is show is the right way of doing things. As time goes on, tensions will rise if his corrections are taken as just being punked. Then the inevitable will occur, which is either a cell fight or a cell move. So they just won't accept those types of inmates as cellies. So listen and learn and don't be a burden making your celly have to constantly correct and babysit you. Listen and learn everything there is to know about cell living the right and respectful way.

Refusing a Celly

It's possible that there may come a time when you won't have an inmate assigned to your cell, so you'll be in the cell by yourself. But the day will eventually come when your cell door will pop open and you'll see an inmate standing right there with a cart full of his personal property saying they were just assigned to your cell. When that time finally comes and you don't want a celly right now, there is a way to go about this without receiving a 115-disciplinary action for refusing a celly.

If you flat out just tell him, "I don't want a celly!" and that's all you tell him, you will be getting a 115-disciplinary action for refusing a celly. Because when your potential celly starts pushing his cart away from your cell, the CO is going to ask him why he isn't moving into your cell. When the celly says that you just refused, or tells the CO that you said that you don't want a celly, or tells the CO that you said that he can't move in your cell, you will get a 115-disciplinary action for refusing a celly. And once you are found guilty, you'll get 30 days extra added to your sentence.

So the proper way to refuse a celly so that you don't get a 115-disciplinary write up is like this. When your potential celly is at your cell door trying to move in, you need to quickly tell him that you don't want a celly right now because you're stressing, that you're going through some things. After you tell him that, you need to tell him that you got nothing against him; it's just, right now, you can't handle a celly because you're stressing big time. Then once you tell him that, you need to ask him in a polite way if he can tell the CO, when they ask him why ain't he moving in, if he could tell them that you are not compatible as cellies. Think quickly. Explain to him that telling the CO "we're not compatible as cellies will avoid you getting the 115 write up. Once he tells the CO that y'all are not compatible as cellies, because of a "safety issue," the CO won't be able to force him inside your cell. If the CO tries to force him inside your cell after he was told that you are not compatible as cellies, this could be a lawsuit. And the CO knows this. That's why he won't try to force him inside your cell.

Of course, refusing a celly may hurt his feelings a little bit. But you either hurt his feelings a little bit, or you hurt your peace of mind that comes with being in the cell by yourself. I would advise you to only use this refusing a celly tactic one or two times in the same building.

On the flip side, remember that as you're pushing your cart to somebody's cell, it is a possibility that he might refuse you as a celly by using this celly refusal tactic. Don't get mad. Just respect the game and help keep him from getting a 115 disciplinary action for refusing you and just tell the CO that y'all are not compatible as cellies.

Credit Debt

You need to be very careful getting a credit in jail or prison, because the number one reason behind fights and stabbings in jail prison is an unpaid debt. And when it comes to racking up a credit debt, based on your family members or friends word that this week they will send you some money, I will advise you not to do it. Because anything could happen from now until then. For example, they could have car problems or some medical issues and now they desperately need to use the money they said they were going to send you. That now puts you in a situation where an inmate would have malicious intent towards you.

During my time in prison, I saw over 16 inmates roll up off the yard and go to protective custody, all because of the debt that they were unable to pay from getting credit. I also knew plenty of inmates that got jumped or stabbed due to an unpaid debt from them getting credit.

Suppose an inmate comes up to you, trying to give you something on credit and then tells you to pay him when you go to the store. I would advise you to tell him to just hold whatever it is that he is trying to give you on credit until you get the store, simply because it's not worth putting yourself in a situation where you might have to roll up and get protective custody, get beat up, stabbed, all because you thought you were going to be able to pay but we're unable to.

Door Blocker

If you want to keep your cell clean of the pincher bugs, roaches, spiders, crickets, mosquitoes, flies, rats and all the other weird looking bugs I don't know the name of, then you will need a door-blocker. Here are some things you could use for a door-blocker: rolled up newspaper, rolled up sheets, piece of blanket, pants, shirt, or a towel. Once you have your door-blocker made, jam it tight in the space underneath your cell door. All cells have about a two to three inch gap underneath the cell door.

I remember when I was at Ironwood State Prison in California from 2005 to 2006. One night I forgot to use the door-blocker, and that night I was awakened by a ruffling sound. I looked around to see exactly where the noise was coming from and quickly realized it was coming from up underneath the bunk. When I got off the bed to turn on the light, the ruffling noise stopped. I grabbed my shower shoe, and turned on the light. My celly woke up and asked, "What the hell you doing, man? Turn the light back off! I'm trying to sleep." I told him that something was making a ruffling noise under the bunk. My celly smacked his lips and told me that I was tripping. I pulled out the mesh laundry bags of clothes from under the bunk with my left hand, and held the shower shoe in my right. When I pulled out the third bag, a small rat ran out in the middle of the cell floor. My celly said, "Oh shit!! Kill that mother f****er!"

I slapped my shower shoe down, trying to smash the rat, but I missed. The rat shot straight to the door making it out. I looked at my store bag and saw exactly what that ruffling sound was. The rat had chewed through my mesh laundry bag and was trying to nibble through my chip bag.

I could tell a story for every insect or rat that made it in my cell whenever I forgot to put the door-blocker down, but I'm going to just tell you one last one. I was at a prison called Devel Vocational Institution, also known as Tracy Prison from March 2020 until June 8th, 2021, my parole date. Some nights I would forget to use the door-blocker. I would sometimes suffer the consequences by having thumb size roaches crawl inside my cell. When I would get up in the middle of the night and go take a piss, I'd spot a funsize Snicker shadow crawling either on the wall or on the floor. I quickly turned on the light to kill the roach, but it was like they all had nine lives;

cuz I would pick up a shoe and smash the roach and it would keep running. Then I'd hit it again and again, and the roach would still keep moving. Eventually I'd kill it. Some of them even flew, and every time they flew right at me, hitting me on the leg or torso. I always thought that the roach was trying to fight me back.

So to avoid these unwanted guests in your cell, put your door-blocker down. Also know that when mosquitoes come under your cell door, they like to hide underneath the bottom bunk. And when night comes, they come out looking for you. So when it is mosquito season, make sure before you go to sleep at night you hit up under your bottom bunk with a shower shoe to make sure no mosquitoes are hiding underneath there. Even if you got the door-blocker down, the mosquitoes can still sneak into your cell whenever you open up your door to go out or come in.

Cell Light

Light fixtures in the cell are on the ceiling. So when the light is on at night, the inmate on the top bunk has to deal with the light shining bright in his face. If you're on the bottom bunk and you need to use the light at night, your celly will get frustrated if you keep the light on for too long. He might not come out and say that the light is bothering him, because he don't want to argue with you. But the light is bothering him.

After having some of my cellys complain about the light shining bright in their face at night, I just stopped using the light at night. So during the day, while the sun is still out and shining, I would handle all my business for the day that required me needing light. When it got too dark in the cell to read, that's when my study time would be over and I would just kick back watching TV for the rest of the night. Yeah, I could have turned on the light to continue my studying; but I chose to not do it like that, being I knew how uncomfortable that bright light made him feel. With me, it was all about trying to make my celly feel comfortable. And it will be a good thing for you to be the same way too.

Making Your Bed

The normal way to make your bed is by lying your sheet down on your mattress and rolling your mat back some so you can tie your sheet together on your mattress like this:

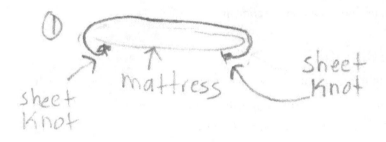

But, if you make it like that, your sheet will eventually roll off your mat from all the tossing and turning that happens while you sleep. So to make sure your sheets stay on your mattress while you sleep, you will need to cut three shoe string size pieces from your sheet. Put those pieces aside for later. Pull your mattress back a bit so you can tie your sheet together like this:

Then cut three little slits on both sides of your sheet. Next, take one of these shoe string size pieces and run it through the slices and tie the shoe string size piece together like this:

Do the same tie to the other side and the middle of the sheet. And now, you don't have to worry about your sheets sliding off your mattress at night time while you sleep.

Hooks Clothesline

This is the way you make the hook clothesline so you can hang your sheet up for privacy when you take a crap or birdbath. You can also make a separate line on the wall to hang your clothes up. Here's how you make it:

Cut two shoestring size pieces off your sheet. Another piece should be long enough to reach each side of your cell walls.

Now break apart your state-issued soap and drop it in your state-issued cup. Pour a little bit of water in the cup, just enough so that the water is level with the soap inside the cup. Next, let the cup of soapy water sit until morning. In the morning, the soap bar will be pasty.

Save your empty milk carton from your breakfast. You're going to need it to cut cracker-size squares off it. Once the soap has turned into paste and you have your empty milk carton and your long string size piece of sheet, you are now ready to make your lines. Cut out two cracker-size squares from the milk carton and put two slices in the middle of it like this:

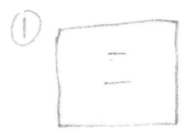

Now take the long string-size sheet that you cut out, string it through both sides and tie a knot. Next take the seven-inch shoe string size sheet and do the same with the other cracker size square hook. When you finish both cracker size squares, they should both look like this:

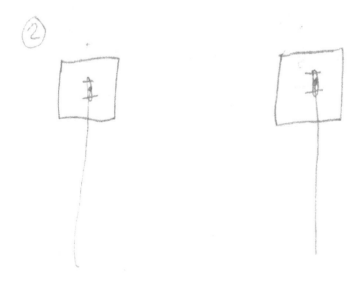

Now take your soap paste and rub some on the back of both crackers-size squares (hooks) and paste it on the wall where it needs to go. Let the hooks sit overnight so that the wet paste on the back of the hooks can dry, like how wet cement needs time to dry.

Once the wet pasty soap is dry, you can gently tie the two strings on the hooks together. Try not to pull hard on the strings or you'll tear the hooks right off the wall. Once you got the two strings tied together, you can now lay your sheet on top of the string creating a partition. You need this so you can have privacy while you take your crap or birdbath. When you finish your crap or birdbath, untie the strings and roll it up like you would a cord and just let it hang on the wall. Again, be gentle with it; that way you don't tear the hooks off the wall.

When you make your clothes line, do the exact same thing you did when you made the bathroom hook. But with your clothes line, you don't have to keep on tying and untying the two lines together like you do with the bathroom line. With the clothesline, you can leave it tied. The normal spot to hang your clothes line is along the wall next to the bunk.

If you feel like you're

losing everything,

remember that trees lose

their leaves every year and

they still stand tall and wait

for better days to come.

~ Unknown

3
Dorm Living

If the CO tells you that you're going to be housed in a dorm instead of a cell, some inmates that are the same nationality as you will approach you as soon as you walk into the dorm. They are going to introduce themselves to you and ask your name and where you're from. It's a possibility they will also ask to see your paperwork, so they can know what you're in prison for, to see if you're good or bad, or if you're a sex offender. You don't have a lot of personal property at the county jail, but you do in prison. Your homie will help you carry all your personal property bags to your bunk area. Your homie will then walk you around the dorm, showing you what areas are not cool to walk through and what areas you can walk through. He'll also show you what showers and phones you're allowed to use and which ones you're not to use. He'll show you what tables you're allowed to sit at and which ones you can't. He'll also show you what TV area is yours, if your dorm is the kind that has different TV areas for different races.

If you are a black inmate entering a dorm building, then things are done a little differently. When you enter a dorm building, a black inmate will approach you and ask you what your name is and where you're from. If you're not from the same city or gang as the inmate that just approached you, then he will let you know how many inmates are in the building that's from the same city or gang as you. He will then go get one of your homies for you. But if you don't have anybody in the building that's from the same city or gang as you, then that black inmate will be the one to show and tell you everything you need to know about the building, such as where you can walk through and where you can't, etc.

In cell living, you only have to deal with one person witch is your celly.. In dorm living, you're forced to deal with at least a hundred different personalities. You now in what I like to call a "fishbowl," where a hundred different fishes are all swimming around. It's inevitable that you will run into many different types of inmates with different personalities and characters.

Here are the characters that I'm talking about:

The bullshiter - the guy that says he's going to do something, but never does it or plays like he forgot.

The swindler - that guy that's always trying to work you for something, or always trying to get one over on you.

The deceptive type - that guy that will borrow your pen or swimsuit magazine etc., then end up telling you that someone stole it off the dayroom table when he got up to go take a piss...but the whole time he got it hidden somewhere.

The backstabbing type - the guy that will smile in your face, and the whole time he's trying to see what you got so he can later set you up to get it.

The instigator type - that guy that's always trying to get somebody to fight, saying things like "Man, you going to let him talk to you that way?" or "I can't believe you just let him disrespect you like that," and "You ain't going to do nothing about it?" The instigator will always try to get people to fight but will never do any fighting of his own.

The joker type - the guy that's always clowning around, constantly saying, "I'm just joking/playing" and thinks everything is funny. Even when something is not funny he still laughs.

The bully type - the guy that be going around trying to intimidate and pump fear into inmates by seeming like he's tough. Some county jail inmates act that way towards inmates so he can get what he wants from inmates. The bully knows from experience that when he acts that way some inmates will quickly give him what he wants such as honey bun, chips, or whatever, to make the bully more friendly towards them.

The begging type - that guy that will beg you for a shot of coffee, soups, or something one day. But once you give it to him, he keeps running back for more every few days.

The barking type - the guy that be barking, trying to seem hard. His bark is louder than his bite. He uses loud barking to try to pump fear into his opponent, praying that it works, because he really ain't trying to fight simply cuz he can't fight.

The playing type - the guy that talks crap a lot, but is only playing.

Hurry up and find out who these types are. That way when one gets at you foul, you will know that he's only playing. You can detect these types just by listening to how an inmate talks and talks crap to other inmates. He seems serious, but he's only playing. They'll say things like, "Man, you need to get the hell out of my way," or "I'm giving you two more minutes in the shower and if you ain't out by then we going to have a problem," or "Shut the hell up before I slap fire out your mouth." These types can quickly make you snap if you're unaware that he's the playing type. Normally these types won't play with you right from the start; it's when they start to know you that they begin playing with you. So if you never even introduced yourself to these playing types, chances are he won't even play with you.

It's important for your own good to do your homework and start figuring out the different types of inmates that are in your building. Knowing who's who will minimize your bumps on the road. Because now when the deceptive type, backstabbing type, or swindler type approaches you with something for sale, or a way for you to make money, you will know beforehand that he's not trying to look out for you but he's only looking to get over on you. You will know it ain't cool doing any type of business with him.

Still, be cordial and cool with these types of inmates; just avoid doing business with them. I say still be cordial and cool with these different types, not giving a clue that you really don't like them, because you don't need to create unnecessary tension and animosity between you and other inmates. If you act funny towards him by not saying "what's up" back when they say what's up to you, keep in mind that it just might be him that you got to call next after on the phone or shower. Or he might be who you need in case you're getting jumped by two inmates in a race riot.

So get on board with inmates you can't stand by acting like you cool with them when you really don't like them there's a lot of inmates that do this so they could keep their environment less hostile as they do there Time. You know the Bloods and Crips are enemies on the streets so if they can play it cool with they rival enemy up in prison then so can you if you don't gang bang if they can do there fake smiles and handshakes just to keep the peace with the enemy that is on the same yard as them then so can you to keep the peace. Know that if the other inmate is flat out acting funny towards you, not trying to speak to you or mess with you, then you got no choice but to fall back and stop messing with him too.

Suppose you find out that somebody is going to the store that week, and you go to ask him if he can get you a honey bun or whatever. He tells you, "Yeah, I'll get it." So store comes around and you see him carrying his store bag of food. You ask him did he get the honey bun for you, and he acts like he forgot all about it. A lot of times, it's not that people forget; it's just that they really didn't want to do it in the first place. So more than likely, he's the bullshiter type.

But let's just say he truly did forget. Now you know he's the forgetful type, and can't be depended on to always be 100% with his word. That's good information to learn about somebody's character. With that information, you will now know that he can't be 100% relied upon to handle some type of serious business for you, since you have seen he's capable of screwing things up.

Reading Inmates

The best way to figure out the different types of inmates is by watching and paying attention to how all the inmates are getting down inside your building. But almost as important is listening and remembering what each inmate says to you. Learn to "read" the other inmates.

Remember what each inmate says to you like you would remember what you were reading in a book. It's like you are reading lots of novels, but the novels are inmates. You "read" a few chapters of one guy, put that down and read the next guy. Pretty soon, you know who's who in your dorm, and you know how they're gonna act and learn how you need to respond to them.

Just like when you read a book, you get to know some things and put it down. You remember what you read when you pick up the book next time. But you add to what you read each time, making the story come together. Things start making sense. Now you read and remember just like that with all the different inmates that you talk to. Treat them all like a book you've been reading; but instead of reading words, you're listening to words. Try to remember what he said he's about to do, all he said he's going to do for you, all the stuff that he said he did in the past, and all the stuff he's saying he's going to do in the future. You try to remember the main topic of the conversation, so when you do end up hanging out and talking to him, you'll still remember what you "read" about him before. This makes it way easier to tell the real from the fake. If you catch inmates lying to you, then he's probably the backstabbing or swinder type. Lying is the number one thing that the swindlers and backstabbers do. When you do catch someone in a lie, keep it to yourself and just know that they can't be trusted and be very cautious when dealing with them.

And know that using drugs in prison is going to make "reading" inmates harder, because you're frying up your data (brain cells) that are storing all your vital information (memories).

I went seven years before I learned and began reading inmates, and was just messing with anybody and everybody without trying to figure out what type they were. Since I wasn't reading, I became a victim on numerous occasions to a deceiver, a swindler, and a backstabber. But once I learned to read inmates and began using the information I learned, I was no longer their victim. I could tell you multiple stories of encounters I had with each one of these different types of inmates, but I'm just narrowing it down to three stories, showing how it was with the deceptive types, the swindler types, and the backstabbing types.

This is how the deceptive types get down...

I was at Salinas Valley State Prison in California Level 4 from December 1, 2009 until August 1, 2010. I got deceived by this deceptive inmate who we'll just call Fred. My TV broke and instead of just ordering a new TV from the vendor catalog, I decided I would just hit the dayroom up and ask some inmates if they have a TV they're trying to sell. When it was dayroom time, I started asking around. After my fourth attempt at asking inmates, I found Fred who said he had a TV for sale. When I asked him how much he wanted for the TV, he said $25 in food. I told Fred I'd give him the food once I checked the TV out to make sure everything was good. If it was legit, I'll bring him the food. Fred agreed and we made plans for the exchange.

On the next cell unlock, he brought the TV over for me to check it out. I excitedly grabbed the TV and quickly headed to my cell to check it out. When I got to my cell, I plugged the TV in and pushed the power button. When the screen came on, it had a soap-size amount of green in the right upper corner. I shook the TV a little bit, hoping that this would make the green go away, but it didn't. I then decided to turn the TV off and back on again, hoping that this will make the green in the corner go away. But when I pushed the off button, it broke.It went down inside the TV.

I remember the three emotions hit me all at once: sadness, madness, and panic. Sadness because my hopes of quickly getting a TV back into my life were shattered. The madness was because I only had the TV in my cell for three minutes before the thing broke on me. And panic because I broke this dude's TV! I knew he was going to try to make me pay for it.

I looked down inside the TV again, where the on and off button had fallen. I could see that the TV had been worked on before. The TV circuit boards had tape on five different areas, and I also noticed that three of the TV buttons had some kind of homemade yellow glue holding the buttons in place, indicating that the buttons had broken off before. Then I took a closer look at the button that had broken off inside the TV and noticed that the button has some of that same homemade yellow glue on it, too. At that moment, I realized that Fred was trying to sell me a lemon TV.

On the next cell door unlock, I walked out to the dayroom with the TV in hand and went over to Fred. I told him about the green light that was in the corner of the TV, how the off button had broken off when I pushed it, and it fell down inside the TV. I then tried handing Fred his TV back, but Fred angrily said, "What you trying to hand me that back for? You broke it, you buy it! You can't break somebody's stuff and expect not to pay for it. You owe me $25 now. And I want my money!" I then told Fred how I saw the tape on the circuit boards and how some of the buttons had been glued on the TV. Fred said he didn't care about that, since everything was working perfect before he gave me the TV, and that he wants his money now.

I had none of my Seaside homies in the building with me, but two Oakland dudes that I was cool with must've heard the raised voice from Fred, because they came over and asked me, "What's going on? Is you straight?" I told my two Oakland partners what's been going on regarding the TV and Fred. One of them pointed to a table and told me to go over there for a minute. So I went and sat at the table. A few minutes later, he came over to me after talking to Fred and told me to give him back the TV. So I handed it to him and he walked back over to Fred and handed him his TV back.

I watched as Fred took the TV from him and walked away. Both the Oakland dudes then walked over to me as I sat at the table. One of them said, "I sure wish I would have known that you were about to do business with Fred, because I would have told you not to do any business with him. He's bad business." He went on to say how Fred was a meth head and that he'd been running around trying to work people. He told me a few of the fights that Fred had gotten into. He then told me that he handled everything for me with Fred and that I don't owe Fred anything. Fred was trying to work me and I was advised to not mess with Fred ever again. I thanked both of them for helping me out. "Don't trip man," one said as they walked away. "Right is right, and wrong is wrong."

Two days later I ended up meeting the inmate appliance repairman. As we were talking, I brought up the TV incident that I had with Fred. The inmate repairman asked me if the TV that Fred was trying to sell me had a Raiders sticker on it. I told him, "Yeah it did have a Raiders sticker on it at the bottom of the TV." He said that TV is on its deathbed, and that he worked on that TV four different times, including gluing some of the buttons back together!

Had those two Oakland dudes not come over to diffuse the situation I was having with Fred, there's no doubt that deceptive Fred would have messed up my out of prison date. Because, Lord knows, I wasn't going to pay nothing for it. So now you see how the deceptive types will mess up your out of prison date.

This is how the swindle types get down...

I was at Solano State Prison, on the Level 2 General Population side from March 2019 to April 2020. I was in a dorm building and I had a CD player that worked perfectly except that the volume knob was stuck on high. So whenever I went to play a CD it would continue to blast loud in my ear. I wanted it fixed, so I went to the inmate repair man in my dorm building and told him about my CD player problem. He said he could fix it, but right now he has got a lot of stuff lined up to work on. He told me to come back next week and he'd be ready for me.

I turned around to walk away and that's when I met a guy I'll just call Julian. Julian was standing right there and heard me talking to the inmate repairman about my CD player. He said that my CD player problem was easy to fix and that he could fix it in only an hour. I said, "Really?" I asked Julian how much he was going to charge me to fix it and he told me just $25. I didn't want to wait a whole week for the other repairman, so I told Julian, "All right, I'll mess with you." I then handed Julian my CD player. On several occasions I had talked to Julian in our dayroom and I had him down as being a righteous kind of guy, but that day proved me wrong. He ended up swindling me.

Thirty minutes after handing Julian my CD player to fix I decided to go over to his bunk area to see how things were going. When I walked up on him, he was sitting Indian style and facing his bunk. On his bunk I noticed he had my CD player guts out and right next to my CD player was another CD player with its guts out. I was going to ask him what was up with that other CD player, but I didn't. Instead I asked him how it was going. Julian responded by saying he should be done in about 15 minutes. I said all right and told him that I would be in the dayroom watching TV.

About 20 minutes later, Julian walked up on me with my CD player in his hand. He sat down next to me and said, "Do you want to hear the bad news first or the good news?" I said, "The good news first." Julian said the AM/FM radio still worked but the bad news was the

CD player motor stopped working completely so it wouldn't play any CDs. Julian then apologized, handed me my CD player, got up, and left. I got up to get some batteries and a CD so I could check my player. As I put the batteries into the back of the CD player, I began to notice that my CD player guts were no longer looking new like they used to. My CD player's guts were all dingy looking. I looked to see if my last name was engraved on the CD player. It was. Then I realized what had happened. Earlier, when I had gone over to Julian's bunk area, the CD player guts were being swapped.

I quickly got up to find Julian to let him know what I just discovered. I found him by his bunk area and told him about it. Julian said that I was tripping. He said, "Ain't nobody swap your CD player guts out." I held my CD player up again to look at the guts. I could clearly see that the guts weren't new. They weren't mine.

What I did next hurt my pride and ego a bit. I let it go. I told Julian, "All right man, it's all good." Then I walked away. Now I know you're probably thinking that I went out like a sucker for letting Julian get away with working me like that. But there are two reasons why I handled it like that. The first, was because I was looking at the CD player with Julian standing right there. I started doing something that I learned in one of my prison self help classes. Something that I now do ever since I learned about the consequences of my actions.

I was about to punch Julian in the mouth. But being I had a chance at getting out of prison two years early from my youth offender parole board, and my youth offender parole board was only 6 days away, I chose to remain disciplinary free. Punching him wouldn't help my chances. I had already scored a low psych evaluation when

I went to see the psych for the board, so things were already looking good for me. Without a doubt I could have kicked Julian's butt. But had I hit him, I would have been wanting to kick my own butt for having to explain to the parole board commissioner why I chose to get into a fight 6 days before my youth offender parole hearing.

The second thing that went through my mind while looking at the CD player guts with Julian standing there was the fact that the CD player was only worth $10 to me, being it was broken and the volume was stuck on high. Five years prior to this incident, I ended up becoming the type of guy that if you work me for $20 or less I was able to chalk it up to the game and accept the loss.

Fool me once - shame on you. Fool me twice - shame on me.

I learned from the experience to cut my losses and cut them off. $20 or less is just not worth facing my third strike from punching someone in the face, and possibly fracturing or breaking something on their face like my previous experience in prison. $20 or less is a small price to pay to get the swindler or deceptive type out of my circle, so I tell them it's all good and then from thereon, they're cut off.

This is how the backstabbing types get down...

I got backstabbed by an inmate when I was in the Mississippi Prison from September 1, 2010 to March 1, 2012. I don't want to say this backstabber's real name, so I'll just call him Andrew. Andrew and I lived in the same building. We would always hang out together in the building and play chess. I had no homies at this prison at the time, so Andrew ended up becoming my number one hangout partner.

In the prison canteen, Andrew's job was to bag the food that an inmate ordered from the canteen and tape their receipt to the bag. After stuff is rung up, Andrew would push the cart full of canteen to the different buildings at the prison. Andrew was able to see how much money all the inmates had in their prison canteen account when he taped the receipt to the bags.

I had dropped my canteen slip in the canteen box. When my store finally arrived to my building, I looked at my store receipt and there was $100 dollars extra taken from my prison trust account. I should have had $318, but now my receipt was showing that I only had $218. I quickly brought this issue to the canteen store staff attention and she said that it's an issue I would have to take up with my counselor.

When I finally got to the counselor's office, I told her about the $100 suspiciously missing from my canteen account. The counselor asked me for my CDC number and she pulled up all my prison trust account transactions. She then pointed to the screen and said, "Look here, last week you filled out a trust account withdrawal form slip and had $100 sent to this Mexican name in Los Angeles."

I then got up close to the screen to see what the counselor was looking at and sure enough there was a trust withdrawal form that was scanned in the computer slip with my name forged on it. I told the counselor that I didn't fill out that draw form. She said, "So what are you saying?"

I told her never mind and then asked her if she'd please print me out that trust withdrawal slip. She gave me a printout of the slip and I left her office. I was on my way to find my Mexican partner in my building to ask him if he could go around and ask some of his homies if they knew the name that's on the trust withdrawal form slip. When I finally made it back to my building I spotted my Mexican partner and waved him over to me. I told him about the $100 and asked him if he could go around and ask some of his homies if they know the person that's on the slip. My Mexican partner said yeah he'd help me out then asked to see the Mexican name that was on the trust withdrawal slip.

I pulled it out and showed him and when he saw the name he said, "That's my folks name." He then saw my last name up on top and said, "Oh, you're Bell?" I said, "Yeah, why, what's up?" He then said, "Wait a minute, you mean to tell me that your last name is Bell?" I again said, "Yeah, why, what's up?" He then said that Andrew told him last week he was going to send him a $100 check to pay off a debt that he owed and that the sender part of the name will be under Bell.

Hearing my Mexican partner tell me this blew my mind. I had considered Andrew to be my number one partner at that prison and now I'm hearing that he backstabbed me. My Mexican partner said we could go confront Andrew about this if I wanted to and I said, "Yeah, let's do that." He said, "Okay, when we see him we'll do that."

We were still out in the dayroom when Andrew finally walked in the building getting off work. I quickly went over and asked my Mexican partner if he was ready. I said, "Before Andrew can get to his cell, let me holler at him for a minute." Andrew said, "What's going on?" I said, "I heard you were the one that took $100 from my books."

Andrew denied it and that's when my Mexican partner stepped in and said to Andrew, "Didn't you tell me last week that you were going to send me a check for $100 to pay off the debt you owed me and that the name will be under Bell?" Andrew denied it and that's when my Mexican partner said in an angry voice, "So you didn't tell me that you were going to send me $100 and that it was going to be under the name Bell?" Andrew denied it again and that's when my Mexican partner got even more angry, and said, "So, you calling me a liar!"

Andrew then looked at me and then looked back at my Mexican partner and said, "All right man, that's what I told you." Andrew looked at me and said, "Yeah, I took your money man but I'm going to pay you back the $100. Just give me one week and I'll have your money." It took everything inside of me to keep from punching Andrew right then and there. I said, "All right man." Andrew walked away and went inside his cell.

I found out later how Andrew was able to take that $100 out of my trust account. He filled out a trust withdrawal form slip, forged my signature, and sent it through the mail to the counselor office that processed it. My Mexican partner must have told inmates about the $100 that Andrew took from me because different inmates were coming up to me asking me if it was true that Andrew took $100 from my trust account. I told them all that it was true but Andrew said he was going to pay the $100 back. Five days later Andrew ended up moving out of my building which now only allowed me to see him during chow time. So when the week was finally up for

Andrew to pay me my money, I walked up to Andrew at chow time and asked him if he had my money yet? Andrew said that he would need just one more week and I told him, "All right man, one more week." We both walked away. The week went by and at chow time I walked up to Andrew and asked him does he have my $100 yet? He said again that he's going to need another week. It took everything in me not to punch on him right then in there. But I told him alright and I walked away.

The next day at chow time, I packed up all my property. At chow time, I was gonna take off on Andrew. And afterwards, when the COs come to the cell to tell my celly to pack my bags up, they would already be right here on my bed. Ten minutes after I packed my property, our building was called out for dinner. On the way to dinner I didn't see Andrew; but on my way back from chow, I spotted him. I walked over towards him, and soon as I got up close to him, I heard him say, "I'm still working on..." But I didn't give him a chance to finish whatever he was trying to say, because I socked Andrew in the mouth and we began fighting.

So you see the deceptive type, swindler type, and backstabbing types are the worst of them all. Before I had my run-ins with those different inmates, I wasn't treating every inmate like a book by remembering what they say, say to me, or watching to see who's going around trying to hustle other inmates. I wasn't doing none of that because, at the time, I was clueless about it. It wasn't until way later on that I learned how to better detect deceptive, backstabbing, and all other different types by simply doing what I mentioned earlier. I believe if I had known about how to detect the different types sooner, I could have avoided my bumps in the road with each type, because I would have known who's who. So learn to read inmates so you can better avoid being deceived, swindled, or backstabbed.

The Disciplinary Action I got for the fight with Andrew for taking my $100.

ORIGINAL

STATE OF CALIFORNIA			DEPARTMENT OF CORRECTIONS AND REHABILITATIO	
PART A1 – SUPPLEMENT CDCR 837 – A1 (07/05)		PAGE 2 OF 6	INCIDENT LOG NUMBER COCF-TCCF-10-11-0434	

INSTITUTION COCF	FACILITY TCCF	INCIDENT DATE 11/11/10	INCIDENT TIME 1609 hrs

TYPE OF INFORMATION
☒ SYNOPSIS/SUMMARY OF INCIDENT ☐ SUPPLEMENTAL INFORMATION ☐ AMENDED INFORMATION ☐ CLOSURE REPORT

NARRATIVE:

On Thursday November 11, 2010 at approximately 1609 hours; Assistant Shift Supervisor L. Taylor was on the South hall monitoring E Unit inmates going to chow, when he observed inmates BELL, EMANUEL #V69940 who is housed in D9-108 approach _____ who is housed in E3-203, on the South Hall, and struck BELL in the facial area with his left and right fists. Inmates _____ and BELL began striking each other in the upper body and facial area with their left and right fists. Assistant Supervisor Taylor gave a directive for BELL and _____ to stop fighting and get down; they refused. Assistant Supervisor Taylor called via institutional radio for the Code 1 Responders to respond to D Unit Hallway (Inmate on Inmate). Assistant supervisor Taylor removed his chemical agents (Top Cop/OC) from his holster, and administered a burst of chemical agents to the facial area of BELL and _____ Assistant Supervisor Taylor gave the command for BELL and _____ to get down; they complied.

The Code 1 Responders arrived in the South Hall, ordered the inmates (non-participants) on the Hallway to get down; they complied. The Code 1 Responding Supervisor, Shift Supervisor Palmer instructed the responders to utilize the contact and cover procedures. BELL and _____ were placed in mechanical restraints (handcuffs) and escorted to the TCCF Medical Department for decontamination and an evaluation.

SUSPECT: BELL, EMANUEL #V69940 AND

VICTIM: NONE

USE OF FORCE: Assistant Shift Supervisor L. Taylor administered chemical agents (OC/Top Cop) in the facial area of BELL AND

ESCORTS:

Assistant Supervisor L. Taylor and Case Manager K. Jones escorted _____ from D Unit Hallway to the Main Building Medical Department for decontamination and medical evaluation. Correctional Officer L. Fonder filmed the escort.

Correctional Sergeant K. Johnson and Correctional Officer K. Cole escorted BELL from D Unit Hallway to the Main Building Medical Department for decontamination and medical evaluation. Correctional Sergeant R. Nelson filmed the escort.

MENTAL HEALTH DELIVERY SYSTEM: Inmates BELL and _____ are not a participants in the Mental Health Delivery System or in the Disability Placement Program.

MEDICAL STAFF INJURIES: Assistant Shift Supervisor L. Taylor was medically evaluated by Registered Nurse D. Farmer and noted the following, "No injuries noted."

MEDICAL INMATE INJURIES:

☒ CHECK IF NARRATIVE IS CONTINUED ON ADDITIONAL A1   Reviewed by:

NAME OF REPORTING STAFF (PRINT/TYPE) E Palmer	TITLE Captain	I.D.#	BADGE #
SIGNATURE OF REPORTING STAFF		PHONE EXT (INCIDENT SITE) 52066	DATE 11/11/10
NAME OF WARDEN / AGO (PRINT/SIGN) D. Phillips		TITLE Warden	DATE 11/12/10

Creating Animosity & Playing Tit-for-Tat

It's real easy to create animosity in prison. When you tell an inmate "No, you can't have none of my food," when he asks for some. Or "No, you can't borrow that." Each "no" grows animosity towards you, especially when the inmate knows you got it but you're just being stingy. So I advise you not to eat a bag of chips, cookies, or whatever when you are in the dayroom unless you plan on sharing some. Somebody you know is gonna ask for some. And when you tell him "no", he'll say, "Oh, it's like that."

That's when you know he just switched up on you. If he used to say, "What's up?" to you in the dayroom, he's likely to not be saying it anymore. If he used to ask you to play chess or cards with him, he's likely not to ask you anymore. Chances are that the inmate you just said "no" is now about to play, trying to make you feel the same way he felt when you told him "no". When you try to call the next shower after him, he may lie to you and say someone else already called next when really nobody did. Or if you try to call next on a chess or Domino's game that he's playing, he might lie and say that they're having a grudge match - meaning that he and the other player are playing continuous games back and forth - so you can't get next.

Eat on your bunk to minimize creating animosity towards you. I say minimize, cuz inmates could still come over to your bunk area and ask you for some of your food if they see you eating. But at least when you eat on your bunk, you're not in the dayroom where everybody can see you eating. Yeah, I know it's your food and you should be able to do whatever you want with it; but in prison, a lot of inmates be working with feelings. So to lessen animosity towards you, give a little when they ask.

If the same inmate is constantly coming back to you asking you for food, you gotta tell him that he's getting heavy. He'll get the message, realizing that he has been begging for stuff too much and that he needs to lighten up some. When you tell him that he's getting heavy, he can't get mad. Instead of animosity, he has to respect where you're coming from. He'll realize that all that begging that he's doing really ain't cool. If you don't let him know that he's getting heavy, he'll continue to be a leech on you, trying to suck you dry.

When I first got to prison, I was clueless on the tit-for-tat game. Most inmates play when you tell them no they can't borrow or have something that you've got. I used to tell inmates that they couldn't have any of the chips, cookies, or whatever I was eating. So for a while, I was getting hit with tit-for-tat games. If I had a dollar every time I got hit with a tit-for-tat game by an inmate, I wouldn't be rich but I would for sure have $23. I could tell you many tit-for-tat stories that were played on me while I was in prison, but I'm just going to tell you the one that impacted me the most. It caused me to become nicer and more giving when an inmate asked for something I was eating. This story opened up my eyes to see that I could avoid unnecessary animosity towards me by simply not being stingy and giving a little.

I was going into my sixth year in prison. I was in a Mississippi Prison. I was in the dayroom eating a bag of M&Ms. I had just told 2 inmates they couldn't have none of my candy when they asked.

Seconds later, an inmate that was the Porter in my building had come up to me and asked for some M&Ms. Instead of telling him he could have some, I told him, "It's all bad," and refused him my candy. The Porter then said, "All right, I see how it is."

Four days later, the Porter was going by all the inmates' cells telling them that new pillows are going to be passed out the next day. If anyone wanted a new pillow, he would write their name down on a piece of paper and they'd get the new pillow tomorrow. When the Porter finally made it to my cell and asked me and my celly if we wanted a new pillow, we both said, "yeah," and gave him our names. The next day when he was passing out the new pillows, he only put one pillow by my door and got ready to walk away. I called him and told him that we should have gotten two pillows, cuz me and my celly both gave our names yesterday.

The Porter then held up a piece of paper to my cell door window and pointed to my celly's last name and said, "Look right here. We only got your celly's name down to be getting a new pillow. We don't have your name down." I asked him how do I go about getting a new pillow, since my name is not on the list. He looked at me and said, "It's all bad for you right now," then walked away. As soon as he said it was bad for me, I knew what he was doing. He was getting me back for telling him "it's all bad for you now", when he had asked me for some of my M&Ms a few days ago. He used the same exact words I used.

I was about to get at the Porter for playing games with my pillow the way he did, but I thought twice. I decided to just leave it alone and obtain my new pillow by writing to clothing exchange, letting them know I need a new pillow. Two days later I went down to clothing exchange and I got my new pillow.

This situation impacted me the most and caused me to become more giving to inmates. I became nicer and more giving to inmates when they would ask me for something. I saw that just giving an inmate just a little piece or a little bit of what I'm eating when they ask would bring me less of a headache and less animosity in prison. Yeah, it's my food and I should be able to do whatever I want with it; but I learned some inmates be working with feelings and when you tell him "no" he might go out his way to make you feel the same way that he felt when you told him "no."

Plus I learned by giving you build good karma for yourself. No matter where you go in prison or in jail, the games are still the same. The only difference is the inmates change. I advise you not to be stingy with your stuff when an inmate asks. But if he's continually asking, then you have no choice but to tell him that he's getting heavy.

Ulterior Motives

You got to be careful when accepting a gift or food from an inmate out of the blue. A lot of time there's an ulterior motive when an inmate just gives you something that you weren't expecting. Some inmates will strategically give you a gift or some food to soften you up before he tries to get something from you. He knows you're more likely to say "yeah" when he asks you, since you will remember how nice he was to you a week or two ago when he blessed you with whatever it was he blessed you with. He thinks you'll feel guilty if you were to tell him "no," so you eventually give in to his request.

When an inmate has ulterior motives in his gift-giving, he's gonna bring up his generosity. You take his gift and then later on declined his request to get whatever it is he's trying to get out of you. He will probably bring up the gift that he gave you and might even tell you to give him back the gift. If I had a dollar every time I accepted a gift or some food from an inmate, only to find out that ulterior motives were involved, I wouldn't be rich but I'd for sure have $11. After that eleventh time, I was more reluctant to accept things for free from an inmate. I found myself telling inmates that "I'm good" or "I'm straight" whenever they would just offer me something out of the blue. Being that way, I'd avoid all the bull crap, lessening my bumps in the road while I did my time. The story here is what caused me to start being that way.

I was at Salinas Valley Prison Level 4 from February 10 2009, to October 10, 2010. I was in the dayroom watching TV, and this dude I had talked to a few times sat down next to me. I don't want to say his real name, so I'll just call him Jimmy. Me and Jimmy was talking, and he asked me if I wanted *Thizz* CD that he didn't want anymore. He said he didn't want the CD anymore because he was burnt out on it. I told him I'd take it. Jimmy handed me the CD and I thanked him for it. At the time, I had 31 CDs of my own. Two days later, I was sitting on my bunk by myself watching TV. Jimmy showed up at my cell door. I asked him what's going on, and he said he wanted to check out my CDs. I let him check 'em out. Then Jimmy asked me if he could have my Keyshia Cole, *The Way It Is* CD and I told him "no", since it is one of my favorite CDs. Jimmy said, "Come on man, don't be like that. I gave you my *Thizz Nation* CD last week." I told Jimmy that I can't do it since Keyshia Cole was my favorite CD. Jimmy got mad and said, "Man you acting like that? You got all them CDs and I can't even get that Keyshia Cole CD?" He then said, "Give me back my *Thizz Nation* CD that I gave you the other day." I just stared at him to see if he was serious. He then said, "I ain't playing with you man. Give me my CD back." I gave him his CD back without a fuss. And that was the day I stopped accepting free stuff from inmates.

Nothing for Free

You are in an environment where most inmates don't like doing anything for free. So if you're going to the store and find yourself needing help carrying some of your store bags back to your housing building, don't be surprised when nobody gives you a hand. When you're asking someone to help you carry your bags back to your building, add a little incentive like a honey bun, or soda for them. Inmates will be willing to help you out quicker doing that. Even one of your homies will be expecting a treat from you if you ask for help, even though he might not say it. It's part of the duties of the homie in your car to help you out with stuff like this.

I remember when I was at Solano Prison Level 2 from March 2019 to March 2020. I had just entered my building, coming from the law library where I was doing a little research. As I was getting ready for my new work assignment, I noticed my cup was missing. After searching my bunk area and locker, I realized I left my cup at the law library. I looked at my watch and saw that I only had 15 minutes left to get to my work assignment, and there was no way I was going to be able to go back to the law library to get my cup and make it to my work assignment on time. I decided to go to the dayroom and ask a few inmates that I knew if they could go to the law library for me to get my cup. None of them were willing to help.

I walked back to my bunk area, looked at my locker for something to give away to someone to go get my cup. I spotted a Snickers. I grabbed the Snickers, shut my locker, looked at my watch and saw that I now only had 7 minutes to get to my work assignment. I quickly went back to the dayroom with the Snickers in hand and went up to one of the inmates that previously told me "no". "If I give you a Snickers, would you go get my cup for me?" He smiled and said, "Hell yeah! I'll run to get your cup for a Snickers." I handed him the Snickers, told him what my cup looked like and where it should be located in the law library. Then I left for my work assignment. When I got back from work, my cup was on my bunk.

When you're trying to get an inmate to help you do something that requires his mental or physical energy, he will be hesitant to do it for free. But watch how greedily he'll accept your proposal as soon as you offer to pay him for the help.

Dorm Bathroom

In your dorm, you're going to be sharing the toilet and sink with everybody in your building unless your building has politics to where the toilets are separated by race. Even still, you will want to quickly find yourself an empty shampoo bottle so you can fill it up with the free disinfected that the Pod Porter give out in your building. Just ask the Porter in your building for some and he'll give it to you. Whenever you got to go take a crap in the bathroom you can disinfect the toilet seat before sitting on it. Also, before sitting on the toilet seat, take your shower shoes so you can put them on the toilet seat and sit on them to create for yourself a toilet cover. That way you're not sitting on the bare toilet seat. Yeah, you disinfected the toilet, but you just still want to take that extra layer of protection that your shower shoes will give you.

Also, after going number two, or number one, or just going to the bathroom to brush your teeth or wash your face, you would also want to disinfect the sink area. Inmates brush their teeth and spit right in the sink and a lot of times some spittle spray from the spit gets on the sink handles. Another thing that gets on the sink handle is snot from inmates that snot rocket right in the sink. A lot of times I would be at the next sink over when an inmate would snot rocket into his sink getting snot all on the handles and not even cleaning it up. I could have told them every time I saw them do that to clean that snot up off the sink handles, but everybody was allowing it to happen. For me to try to be the enforcer would have caused me to get into a lot of fights, and possibly a riot simply because inmates get pretty hostile when you try to make them clean something up that they don't want to clean. I minded my own business like everybody else did and just let the filthiness in the bathroom happen. It's a must to get yourself your own personal disinfectant bottle to keep the germs down when you go to the dorm bathroom.

Drawn to Same Likes

Just as birds of the same feather flock together, the same is true with inmates with the same likes. In jail and prison you will notice how an inmate that likes to play dominoes, chess, poker, or card games will gravitate towards another dominoes, chest, poker or card players in the dayroom. Because they are always playing one another in the dayroom, they'll start to become cool with one another. You'll even start seeing them hanging out in the yard together.

As humans we are drawn to people that are like ourselves. Basketball players are drawn to other basketball players. Cigarette smokers are drawn to other cigarette smokers. In prison, inmates who work out are drawn to other inmates that work out. So, if you're new in the jail or prison building and you see that you don't have any homies in your building to hang out with, don't trip cuz it's real easy to gain yourself some associates to hang out with. All you got to do is go to the dayroom and start playing one of the games you like playing, or sports you like playing in the yard.

Huddling Up

Try your best to be aware of any sudden huddling up that goes on around you, especially when it involves a different race. When you see 8 or more inmates just all of a sudden start huddling up, it's important that you stay vigilant and frequently dart your eyes back and forth to see what's going on. Normally when you see 4 or more inmates huddling up like that in a building or yard they're discussing an issue that needs to be dealt with within their car or outside their car.

To be on the safe side when you see this type of sudden huddling up going on inside your building, look around and make sure some of your race of people are nearby just in case the huddle is talking about an issue involving your race. When you're looking around and you don't see nobody from your race nearby, I will advise you for your own safety to get up and move by some of your race of people. The huddling up that you're seeing may be nothing but it's better to be safe than sorry. You don't want to be that animal that is separated from his pack getting viciously attacked by alliance. There's plenty of inmates that have lost their lives due to a 2-on-1 jumping during a race riot or a 2-on-1 stabbing during a race riot. Be smart and when you see this type of sudden huddling up going on inside your building, ease by your race of people.

If you're a Black man reading this know that the only time Black people move as a whole in prison is when it's time to participate in a race riot. Other than that, the Blacks are divided into many different cars. When you see Blacks hurling up like that it's not always a potential race riot going to jump off, it can also be them going to take off on another Black race car because like I said, the Blacks are divided into many different groups. Always remember to stay ready so you don't have to get ready.

Saving

A smart thing to start doing while you're in jail is to try to save up the money that your folks are sending you until you reach an amount of $500. I know the jail food is nasty being it's overcooked or undercooked a lot of time and you would rather want to eat honey buns, and meat spreads, and fish spreads everyday - but the sacrifice of holding off to do that right now until you have at least $500 saved up in your jail trust account will be well worth the wait and sacrifice. You've got to start thinking about the future just in case you do end up being found guilty and sent to prison. That way if the people that are sending you money right now end up doing you like most people's family and friends after their loved ones gets found guilty and sent to prison, which is to forget all about them, and leave them for dead to do their time all by themselves. But since you've been saving up your money now, once you get to prison you can order appliances and stuff to make your time go a lot smoother. Such as a $200 TV, a $50 CD player, MP3 player, headphones, rechargeable batteries, face trimmer, hot pot, fan, shoes, sweatpants, etc, etc, etc.

Be smart and start saving up now just in case. Don't be one of them inmates that spends all his money up at the jail store then gets sent to prison with no way to order a TV and other appliances. Believe me when I tell you it's a very sad look being in the cell without a TV. Your time will be harder without it. If you're in jail start saving up now and you'll be glad later on that you did.

Dorm Bunk Area

Your neighbors are watching you to see if you're cleaning up around your bunk area. To keep your neighbor from talking crap behind your back, telling inmates that you're a dirty neighbor, clean daily around and underneath your bunk area. You can find the broom, dustpan, and mop inside the mop room in your dorm building. Every dorm building has a mop room and if you need some disinfectant, just ask one of the Porters in your building for some. Your neighbor and other inmates are also watching you to see if you're showering, make sure you shower daily too.

Jail Withdrawal's

There are going to be a lot of inmates in your dorm building going through a withdrawal and I will advise you to minimize your interaction with the withdrawlers for now because they're going to be very irritable, moody, agitated, and pissed off due to them not being able to get their next high. The withdrawlers are also not working with a full deck right now, being their brain cells are all fried up from all that heroin, meth, or ecstasy usage while they were on the streets. They're not thinking rationally which makes them more likely to get at you foul or disrespectful to where you're going to feel like punching one of them.

It's pretty easy to spot the withdrawlers in your building. All you got to do is look around and see which inmates are walking around all sick like. I believe for the heavy meth, heroin, and fentanyl drug abusers that going to jail is actually a good thing. I say that because when you look at them strung out drug abusers that be running the streets all day chasing that next high, you'll see their nails and clothes be all filthy. Their brain is in a fog and their health is on a downward spiral to where that next high could be their last one. Not to mention neglecting their overall hygiene. But now, when those heavy drug abusers go to jail not only do they start gaining their health back, getting clean internally and externally, but they also start restoring brain cells, sense, and they began reflecting back on how they were out there doing bad running around in the streets, doing whatever it took to get that next high. They will start to see that all they were doing was pushing the fast forward button on their lives because without a doubt, they were heading to an early grave. They will start to see how going to jail has actually saved their lives from that moment forward. Some will begin to change their lives for the better, leaving the left track alone, and hopping on the right track.

Not all heavy drug abusers that go to jail are able to see how coming to jail actually saved their lives. Once they're released from jail, they continue abusing drugs, but for the ones that do see it and change their lives for the better - they are the lucky ones.

Jail has also saved a lot of gang bangers and robbers lives too. I say that because once they're in jail, going to court facing a life sentence, most of them will go into a deep depression. Once in that deep depression they will start looking back at all the stuff that's now been taken away from them. Things like not being able to watch their kids grow up or no longer being able to make love to their wives.

There will be no more barbecues, no more walks on the beach, no more driving a car, no more attending his kids birthday parties, no more riding on a boat at the lake with friends and families, missing their kid's graduation and wedding ceremonies. The list is endless.

But if he gets lucky and don't get sent to prison for decades or life, it's an experience equivalent to somebody getting shot 3 or 4 times and surviving the attack. He begins to realize how lucky he just got and just how precious life really is. From that day forward most of them turn their whole lives around - changing it for the better, realizing that if they don't, either one or two things will happen; an early grave or life in prison.

The court experience has also turned a lot of gang bangers into gang advocates that are out in their communities holding speeches trying to let the youngsters know that the gang banging life is the wrong way to go. During my time I ran across gang bangers who all told me the same thing but in different words. They say that prison life is not cool, and that they're going to make the necessary changes needed so that they don't ever come back to a hell hole prison again. Most say that they're going to just be a family man, getting a wife and kids, and just work a 9 to 5 job once they get out of prison.

Deep Car

When a race or a car is deeper than another race or car, most will start to think they run things and can do whatever they want simply because their car is deeper. I remember when I worked in the kitchen in an out of state prison in Arizona from 2017 to 2018. Damn near all the Black inmates in the kitchen were all from this one gang.

At the end of every workshift we were allowed to divvy up all the remaining leftover food. When it was time to divvy up the food, the black car that was deeper was always the one giving his boys the majority of the food and leaving just little for me and the other two inmates that were in idfferent cars.

One day I approached the inmate that divided up the food and told him that it ain't cool the way he's giving his homies more chicken and burgers then the rest of us. He said that those are his homies and they will always come before me. I just left it alone after that, realizing that I was way outnumbered. All together he had like 10 of his homies working in the kitchen from his car - and me none.

Know that when most cars gets deep they will feel like they have control of things and run things, and they will always put their car before you in any situation.

Most Hated

Most inmates all have one thing in common - they hate dorm living. There were two things we all hated most about dorm living. The first thing is you have no privacy. Somebody will always have their eyes on you whether intentionally or unintentionally. Unintentionally, because the way the bunks are set up in the dorm. A person can't help but to look at you either directly or in their peripheral vision. Being there is no privacy, it's hard for a man to get his rocks off except for uncomfortable, well-known spots. Inmates get their rocks off in the bathroom stall at night while everybody is asleep. They'll go to the bathroom and sit down on the toilet, put the stall up and fake like they're taking a crap.

The second most hated thing about the dorms is when you have loud neighbors. The ones who want to bring a bunch of his homies around his bunk - that's only 3 ft away from your bunk - and be talking loud and clowning around laughing while you're either trying to take a nap, study, read a book, or just relax. This can really become annoying, especially when your neighbor's homies who you don't really mess with are one foot away or closer.

I remember I found myself having to use every tool that I had in my anger management toolbox just to keep from snapping at my neighbor and his homies. My neighbor was the wild hyper type. He didn't have a job, nor did his homies. All they did all day long when there wasn't any yard was hanging out at his bunk area making lots of noise, playing music on a boombox, and clowning around with each other. On the weekends, my neighbor and his homies called it the party weekend because that's when they would drink pruno by his bunk area. I didn't have any backup, but my neighbor had not only his three homies that he hung out with in my building but he was from a gang that had at least 18 of his homeboys on the yard.

I was new to the dorm building, only having been in there one month until I finally said something about all the noise my neighbor was making. As I laid back on my bunk trying to take a nap after a long day, the boombox had to have been turned up to the max. When I finally asked my neighbor in a respectful tone if he could turn his radio down, his home boy responded by saying, "I know you ain't tripping on the radio being turned up, is you? It's program time so we can have the radio up as loud as we want to." I said I know it's programmed time. I was just asking out of respect, can you turn the music down while I take a nap. My neighbor's homie said, "Nah man, we can't do that. It's program time."

I could have stayed and just dealt with all that unnecessary loud noise and disrespect that my neighbor was constantly doing. But I decided to more. Not only was the noise messing with my nap time, it was also messing with my study time, reading time, and peace of mind. Within 2 weeks I found another dorm to move into. I wasn't the first one that moved out of that dorm cubicle where my neighbor was making all that noise. Four different inmates had previously moved out of that same bunk area before I had moved in all because of my loud neighbors.

There's no privacy in the dorms and you might end up with some bad neighbors but I will still pick dorm living over cell living simply cuz, when you're cell living you just can't get up and go get something like a CD, some soups from your homeboy, or whatever from another inmate. Whenever you want something outside a cell you've got to stand by your door and yell out, bang on the door to try to get a Pod Porter's attention to run for you to go pick up whatever it is you're trying to get or if you need to speak to an inmate about something important you can't just go over there and ask him. Most of the time the Porters are so burnt out from doing all that running around for the other inmates that when you do try to get their attention by yelling or banging on the cell door - they play deaf a lot and just keep walking like they didn't even hear you calling. When you're in a dorm you can always get up and go handle your business by yourself, moving around freely and not cooped up in a little cell. Another minus with cell living is you don't get that much dayroom or shower time.

Jailhouse Thieves

A lot of inmates that go to jail for stealing are still stuck in their ways. Being fresh off the streets, they had no time to change their ways as a person. These individuals sometimes become jailhouse thieves. They'll be doing their homework to see who has money and who doesn't. If you go to the store, know that these jailhouse thieves are watching you, plotting on when is the perfect time to catch you slipping, meaning take your store commissary from you without you even knowing. These jailhouse thieves are sneaky. Whenever you go to the yard, it will be wise for you toask one of your homies that stayed back from the yard if he could keep an eye on your stuff.

Asshole COs

No matter what jail or prison you're at you're always going to have at least one asshole CO that will talk to you crazy to try to push your buttons so that you will engage in a verbal or physical altercation with him so he can write you up and give you more time in prison. But you must be smart and not fall for the trap because if you engage in a verbal altercation with him and start talking about kicking his butt, that threat will most definitely get you a write-up. That type of write-up is a DA referral and the DA, without a doubt will pick that charge up and you will be getting life in prison. Plus, a strike because threatening someone is a strikeable offense. If you already got two strikes, you will now be receiving your third strike and you will be getting extra time added to your sentence. If you're only months away from going to the parole board hearing, know that an asshole CO knows this, and he may be trying to trap you.

When that asshole CO is around make sure that you lock up when it's time to lock up and be extra careful not to go out of bounds. You might have a good chance at getting found suitable for parole, but if you have a 115 disciplinary write up before your parole day, you will likely not get found suitable for parole. Just like identifying the different types of inmates in prison, you also got to quickly identify the asshole CO types and try your best to stay out of their way. You can quickly find out who the asshole CO are by simply asking somebody inside the building. So be smart and don't let that asshole CO trap you up and push your buttons. Stay focused on getting out of prison and home to your family.

Be thankful for

the hard times;

for they have made you.

~ Leonardo Dicaprio

4
Court

Attempted murder in the first degree is a life sentence but, second degree attempted murder carries a sentence of the lower term, 5 years or the midterm 7 years, or the upper term 9 years. They add all types of different enhancements to the sentence which ends up bringing the sentence to double digits. While doing my time for second degree attempted murder, I ran across a total of 21 inmates that all had the same charge as me. While talking to these different inmates I learned that 8 of them had paid lawyers and 13 of them had a free court appointed lawyer - in other words, a public defender.

The ones that didn't have a paid lawyer all had over 20 years or a life sentence. The most that the 8 inmates with paid lawyers got for their attempted murder charge was 13 years. In fact, a few of them told me that they were able to get their attempted murder charge dropped to a lesser charge of assault with a deadly weapon. Seeing the charges of the other inmates who didn't have a pay lawyer, let me know how lucky I was to receive 18 years for my attempted murder charge.

This also showed me how if your funds are low it can be really bad for you when going to court fighting a case. No wonder so many poverty-stricken people are incarcerated, they couldn't afford to pay a lawyer which would have put up a good fight in court for them. Instead, they were stuck with a public defender, a public defender that's still going to get paid whether he or she fights hard for you or not. And about 89% of the time, public defenders won't be able to put that necessary 100% of his or her time and energy into a client's case simply because the court system has him or her overloaded. With so many caseloads to carry, if they were to put a lot of time and energy on a client's case, they would fall behind on their other cases.

Don't get me wrong, some free Court appointed public defenders do put up a good fight in court for their clients . But just know that there's a reason why a lot of the celebrities are only getting slapped on the wrist for crimes they commit - it's 'cuz they got a good high paid lawyer.

Research

I would advise you to do a little research on your own case, that way, you won't be so ignorant on what's going on with you regarding your charges. Do some research so you know how much your charge carries. Doing research will also help you to decide what defense you want to use for yourself at trail.

Just in case you do end up going to trial, do some research at the law library to see how much time other people got with the same charges as you. That way when you get offered a plea deal by your lawyer, you will know whether or not it's a good deal or bad deal. Being ignorant to your charge is why so many inmates get railroaded. They don't know if what's happening to them is right or wrong. They don't know if the plea bargain deal they've been asked to sign is a good deal or bad deal, so they just hop on a bad deal not really knowing it's a bad deal.

Research begins by telling your county jail CO that you want to go to the law library to do some research. Once you tell him that, he will tell you what you need to do to get in the law library. You will need to fill out a request slip. When you're finally at the law library, the first book you would want to check out is called The Penal Code Book. This book will let you know how much time your charges carry, showing you the low term, middle term, and the high term.

Look up the penal code that you have been charged with along with all the enhancements, that way you will know what the max is. If you are in California, the second book I would advise you to check out is called West's Annotated California Codes. You can check this book out by telling the law library person that you need the penal codes for whatever charges you are facing. When you get the book, go to that penal code section in the West's Annotated California Codes and you're going to see a lot of different cases of people that went to trial with the same charges as you. You will need to write down all of the CAL.RPTR numbers for each case that you see in that section so you can look up those cases. You'll see people that got the same charges as you, so when the DA offers you a plea deal, you will know if it's a good deal or bad deal. Plus, you'll be able to read people's cases that went to trial so you can now see what defenses other people put up. This could give you an idea of what type of defense you might want to put up at trial for yourself.

Once you write down all of the CAL.RPTR numbers out of West's Annotated California Codes, start checking out the CAL.RPTR books for those codes. The CAL.RPTR books also tell the whole story of how a person's crime actually happened. Find cases that are similar to yours.

The last book I would advise you to check out is called the California Jury Instructions. This book is going to show you exactly what the jury has to look for to decide whether or not you're guilty, such as, was he in fear for his life. The jury instructions are different for each crime so read up on your jury instructions because it's always good to know exactly what the jury has to look at to decide whether or not you're guilty when you go to trial.

I was in the county jail facing life in prison for attempted murder in the first degree. I got arrested on October 19, 2003. I was 24 years old at the time. That Sunday morning the mother of my child and I were having an argument. Me, being emotionally immature at the time with no anger management skills, plus, being very impulsive with a fogged-out mind from all the PCP (sherm) I had smoked that morning , I lost my cool whal we got to arguing. During the argument I ended up stabbing her 13 times. The neighbor saw what was going on and called the police which resulted in me getting caught literally red-handed at the scene with blood on me and my hands.

I was booked in the Monterey County Jail on a first degree attempted murder charge. I was introduced to my public defender.

Later, he came to visit me at the county jail. As we were talking about my case, I asked him how much time I was looking at. My public defender said 32 years to life in prison. I then asked him what kind of plea bargain deal I have right now and my public defender said, "The only deal right now is 32 to life." I then asked him if there were any lesser charges that I could get other than first degree attempted murder.

My public defender said, "For what you did Emanuel, no, there are no lesser charges. You probably could have gotten a lesser charge of assault with a deadly weapon, if you hadn't stabbed her 13 times. If you would have only stabbed her one time, I could have gotten an assault with the deadly weapons charge." He went on to say that I would be getting a life sentence, but he'd try his hardest to get it down to 15 to life instead of 32 to life. At the moment it was the only plea bargain deal on the table.

I left the room and went back to my building. On my way back my neighbor asked me how my meeting with my public defender went. I told him that I'll holler at you later through the vent. In jail, you're able to holler at your neighbor through the vent. Once I got inside my cell, I quickly stood on the toilet and yelled out to my neighbor. My neighbor was an O.G. (refers to an older person). He was 50 years old and knew a lot about the law. I told him that it's looking like I'm getting life in prison and the only deal is 32 years to life. But my public defender is going to fight to try to get it lowered to 15 years to life. That's when my OG neighbor said, "What? That ain't no deal." He then asked me if this was the first time I've ever been arrested on a violent charge? I told him yes. He replied, "Look man, you need to get up in that law library as soon as possible and do some research for yourself." He then told me that he was going to write down some law books that he wanted me to check out - these were the books that I mentioned earlier.

I was able to get to the law library and the first thing I did was get The Penal Code Book. I read the attempted murder section and after reading it, I was a little happy and a little mad at the same time. Happy because I saw that there's not only a first degree attempted murder charge which is a life sentence, but there was also a second degree attempted murder charge which is not a life sentence. It had a sentence of the low-term 5 years, the middle term 7 years, or the high term 9 years, with no life sentence involved. In order to get convicted of the first degree charge the attack would have had to be willful, deliberate and premeditated.

To be convicted of second degree attempted murder there must not be any premeditation involved in the attack. It had to be in the heat of the moment or in the heat of passion. That made me a little happy. I knew I had not premeditated or plotted the attack on my baby mom. It was looking like I wouldn't be getting a life sentence after all. I would just need to prove that it wasn't premeditated. I was a little mad because my public defender had just told me that there was no other charges other than first degree attempted murder and that there is no other lesser charge other than assault with a deadly weapon. He failed to mention second degree attempted murder.

I then checked out the other books my OG told me about which was the West's Annotated California Codes book. I went to my charge section of attempted murder and wrote down all the CAL.RPTR cases. Then I checked out those CAL.RPTR cases starting from the top of my list. I began reading how some people were going to trial for first degree attempted murder and were facing life in prison but was able to come out of it getting charged with the lower charge of second degree attempted murder. One of them received 9 years and on another one of the CAL.RPTR case's, he received 11 years. As I read more of the CAL.RPTR cases, I saw that there was a thing called Involuntary Attempted Manslaughter. There was this guy who only got 5 years for his crime in which he stabbed somebody three times in the heat of the moment. I came across a case where a guy was charged with the first degree attempted murder for a shooting. He was facing life in prison but at trial his verdict came back not guilty of the first degree attempted murder. Instead, he was found guilty of assault with a deadly weapon and only received 3 years.

I began to realize that my public defender either lied to me about there not being any other lesser charges other than assault with a deadly weapon or it was just that he didn't know. After leaving the law library I went and laid on my bunk and started going over all of those CAL.RPTR cases in my head. I started to see that I can actually come out of this life sentence I was facing if I could just play my cards right and show the courts that there was no willful, deliberate premeditation involved in my case. I then made a mental note to call my public defender the first chance I got to tell him that I needed to talk to him.

When my public defender finally came to visit me the first thing I asked him was why did he tell me that there was no other lesser charge for me other than first degree. He said because there is no lesser charge for me other than assault with a deadly weapon. I then told him, "Yes there is. There's also a second degree attempted murder and an involuntary attempted murder charge. None of these carry a life sentence." I then asked my public defender if he had never heard of a second degree attempted murder charge or an involuntary manslaughter charge? He told me no, he never heard of it.

I asked him had he ever done an attempted murder case before or was I his first. My public defender told me that he never done an attempted murder case before and that I was his first attempted murder client. I then told him that I don't feel safe having you as my public defender and that my life is on the line here. I needed someone that's got experience. I told him that I will be filing a Marsden Motion to relieve him from my case. I then told him that he was fired. I then got up and walked out of the room.

Things worked out for me regarding firing my public defender and getting appointed another one by the judge when I filed my Marsden motion. My new public defender was a female. When she came to visit me for the first time, I quickly asked her had she ever done an attempted murder charge before and she said yes. I asked her had she ever heard of a second degree attempted murder charge before and she said yes. Then she went on to say that she's going to talk to the DA to see if we can get a plea bargain deal for second degree attempted murder because evidence clearly shows that my stabbing was done in the heat of passion and in the heat of the moment.

Our meeting lasted for about 10 minutes. The last thing my public defender said to me was that in two weeks she'd be coming back to visit me and hoped that she'd have a second degree attempted murder plea deal for me.

Two weeks later when she came back to visit me, she said she was able to make it happen but the DA is only giving me one week to decide. The plea bargain deal had a total of 18 years in prison. She then said if you don't have an answer within a week then the deal is coming off the table. She told me that I got the upper term of 9 years for the 2nd degree attempted murder, but with all the extra enhancements that got added to my charge it brought it up to 18 years.

My public defender said she would be back in a week to see if I want to take the plea bargain deal. I told her that I don't need to think about it. I'm ready to sign right now for the 18-year plea bargain deal. She asked if I was sure. I said, "Yes I'm sure!" She brought out some papers from her briefcase and told me to sign them, so I did. One week later I was brought to court to tell the judge I was guilty of the second degree attempted murder and agreed to take the 18-year sentence.

So you see, it's very important that you do some research of your own because Lord knows had I not - I pretty much would have ended up with that first degree attempted murder with a life sentence. My first public defender didn't even know that there was such a charge of second degree attempted murder. He was telling me that the crime I did fits the first degree attempted murder charge. So do some research for yourself to minimize the chances of you getting railroaded by the court system

Holding Tank Fights

When you're being transferred to court and back, be alert when waiting in the holding tank with all the other inmates. Really be alert if you're going to court for murder or any crime involving a victim because waiting in that holding tank with you might just be a friend or family member of your victim. Yes, every inmate will have ankle chains on plus a chain wrapped around their waist with handcuffs locked to the front of the waist chain. This way their hands stay secured in front of them. Even so, a fight can still happen.

I was going to court one day and the CO told all us inmates to go inside the holding tank. Once we were all inside, the CO walked away. I watched an inmate quickly approach another inmate, words were exchanged, and he simultaneously rammed the inmate with his shoulders and stepped on his ankle chain causing him to fall backwards and land on his butt.

I watched as he quickly shuffled over to the inmate on the ground and started getting some good golf swing hits to his face. His punches were looking like golf swings because of the way his hands were cuffed up in front of him and swung his upper body like a golf player, gaining momentum with every swing. Once he got a few good golf swings in, I watched as he got down on his knees, grabbed the inmate's hair and started making a dropping bowling ball sound with the guy's head by slamming it to the ground. After about 15 times of slamming the guy's head to the ground he got up and blended in with the rest of us inmates like nothing ever happened. So, be alert in the holding tanks.

You cannot have

a positive life

and a negative mind.

~ Joyce Meyer

5
Sentencing Anger

After you're finished with your court process and you finally get sentenced to prison you're going to experience some anger and emotional pain inside your chest. Depending on the amount of time you got sentenced to will determine that amount of anger and emotional pain you will feel. If you got sentenced to 20 plus years or a life sentence, the anger and pain you will feel will be similar to how you would feel if you just found out a family member has just died. The only difference is - you'll be mourning for yourself.

If you did just get sentenced to life in prison the advice I want to give you is don't give into hopelessness. Hopelessness can manifest itself into negative behavior and that negative behavior will be the reason why you stay in prison and get denied parole. Yes, you got sentenced to a life sentence but that don't mean you will spend the rest of your life in prison. It's all up to your behavior whether or not you're getting out of prison one day. You must start now, trying your best to stay out of trouble, especially violent behavior because that is the number one thing that the commissioners don't like and you'll get denied parole every time.

Trust me when I tell you that you will one day get out of prison if you got a life sentence - you just need to keep from getting any write-ups or disciplinary actions. I ran across plenty of inmates that had just got found suitable for parole and were just waiting to be released. I wanted to know how they did it. You know, got found suitable for parole.

I asked them all, "How did you do it?" They all said the same thing but in different words which was, "I stayed out of trouble. I haven't gotten a write-up disciplinary action for over 10 years or more." They went on to say that they participated in a lot of self help groups such as anger management, criminal thinking, family relationships, victims awareness impact, domestic violence. Plus, they were all able to speak on each group, they knew all of their stuff.

All those inmates that got found suitable for parole had to do like 25-28 years in prison and you too will have to serve that amount of time on your life sentence. Yet those inmates were all able to get out of prison when they had received a life sentence. It might not seem like it, but it's really easy to stay out of trouble in prison. All you gotta do is not put yourself in situations that can get you in trouble. Avoid those inmates that are full of deception and really think before you speak. Really think about what you're about to do before you act. Your thoughts determine your actions and your actions determine your destiny. Think about the long-term effects of your actions instead of just acting on impulse. That way you'll end up in less trouble in life and also end up with less regrets. Many inmates are in prison today because they gave very little thought, or no thought at all, to what they were about to do. They acted on impulse, resulting in a very lengthy sentence. Be sure to weigh the consequences of your actions and you'll see that the bad of your actions far outweigh the good of your actions.

While in prison I ran across 13 inmates that had over 26 years time under their belt. Each one expressed to me how when they first came to prison they were young and wild and didn't care about nothing. As the years went on they got into a lot of trouble for fighting, resulting in GBIs and some for stabbings. Once they were older and wiser they all said how they regretted it. These guys were in their 50s and 60s, and they all said they regretted their actions because they should have been out of prison by now. Their actions added extra years to their sentence. I remember one saying he got to do 26 extra years for a stabbing he did on the yard back when he was a youngster. Another said he had to do 17 years extra for the work he put in when he was younger.

I can go on and on about the extra time all these different inmates got for putting in work when they were younger but I'm going to tell you this last one about a lifer inmate that was tearing up as he expressed to me how he'd been in prison 36 years. The parole board just denied his parole, making it now a total of 4 parole denials. He went on to say how the board kept bringing up the stabbings and fights that he did in prison when he was younger. At 63 years old, now the parole board still wouldn't overlook the stabbings and fights that he did as a youngster.

Talking to all those different inmates over the years has shown me that a lot of youngsters rarely think about how their actions will affect them in the future. They fail to look that far ahead. Some believe that everything they know is correct and feel that nobody can tell them any different. Unfortunately, it takes them getting older, mature, and wiser in order for them to be able to look back and see that the way they were acting and thinking was all wrong. For most, it's too late to correct their younger ways of thinking because they have already dug themself a whole so deep that it's going to take decades in prison in order for them to climb back out.

The advice I'll give to an inmate that didn't get a life sentence, but got sentenced to 20 plus years or lesser, is to really think about what you want to be in life. Set that goal for yourself. It could be you wanting to be a big rig driver when you get out of prison, or a plumber, etc., etc., but whatever you want to be, make that your goal and stick to it. You can be whatever you want to be as long as you stay focused and not allow inmates to throw you off track. Making a goal for yourself will help you stay more focused on getting out of prison and achieving your goal. If you just so happen to get into an altercation with an inmate with your goal in mind you'll be more able to put your pride and ego to the side and say to yourself that you're not going to let this asshole mess your goal up, that you got planned for yourself.

Being focused on your goal in life helps you to be able to try to diffuse a heated conversation. Walk away from a hostile situation with an inmate, and realize that he's just not worth the setback, especially if the goal you've set for yourself involves you possibly becoming a millionaire one day.

Your goal can someday come true and you can earn that million dollars that you visualize. Start training yourself to think like you already achieved that million dollars. Let me elaborate more on what I'm trying to say here. You ever wonder why you don't see too many millionaire celebrities on the news for punching someone? It's 'cuz they know people are out to get their money by trying to set them up to make them lose their cool. If they punch that person, that person will try to sue him or her for hundreds of thousands of dollars. It's kind of the same thing con artists do when they hop in an old rusty beat up car and get on the highway searching for an expensive luxury car like a BMW or Mercedes to get in front of so they can start pumping their brakes, hoping that expensive luxury car that's in back of him hits his rusty old beat up car from behind. That way the con artist can get paid both ways. First, from the guy's insurance company, the second, by suing him claiming that his neck and back got injured during the accident.

Just like people will try to get a celebrity to punch them so they can sue for money, or how them con artists in their rusty old beat-up cars try to get an expensive cars to hit him from behind, know that some inmates in prison will also try to bait you in by trying to push your buttons so that you lose your cool and hit him. The reason behind this is 'cuz of jealousy. Jealousy because you're going to be getting out of prison soon, or out of prison way before him. They will hate on you to try to mess your out of prison date. Jealous because you're doing a lot better than him financially by going to the store spending $240 every month. Getting fat packages every quarter when he doesn't get any packages and don't even know where his next deodorant or toothpaste will come from. He'll be mad at you out of jealousy and he will be trying to take some of his jealousy out on you.

Start now with having the mindset as though you've already achieved your million dollar dream goal that you got planned for yourself once you get out of prison. That way you'll be more aware of the bait traps and bait setups people will try on you to sue you or bring you down. Stay focused on getting out of prison and don't let your haters bait you in so easily. Don't give them the satisfaction of keeping you in prison longer. Don't allow inmates to throw you off your game.

Let It Out

I also advise you to go ahead and let it out regarding the tears you're fighting back. When you hold your tears back, you're holding in all that hurt and pressure, but letting it out releases a lot of the hurt and pressure that's built up inside of you.

When you're mourning for yourself, don't fight back the tears. I want to tell you at a time like this it will be a good thing to let it all out instead of holding it all in. It's not good to be walking around with all that build up anger and pain inside of you 'cuz it's a possibility your pipes might burst, causing you to take your anger out on innocent inmates. If you're worried about other inmates thinking you are weak because you're crying a little, then when you get back on your bunk to avoid inmates from seeing you cry, lay on your stomach with your arms crossed up by your head and cry silently into your arms.

Most men today are too afraid to cry because as a little boy their dad wired them up like that. That little boy will be trying to learn how to ride his bike, with his dad standing nearby when all of a sudden the little boy falls off his bike and begins crying. An average dad will run over to his son and tell him, "Stop all that crying - men don't cry. Crying is for sissies. Men are supposed to be strong and tough. So, toughen up boy, and stop all that crying. People are going to think you're weak if they see you crying."

When a little boy hears a message like this, the message the little boy receives is he will be weak if he cries and that he should never show that he's hurting by crying. That he should always hold back his feelings and tears. But know that blocking out your feelings, or blocking out feelings for another person will breed a violent psychopathic person.

And as a little boy, you probably watched your little sister learn how to ride a bike with your dad standing near by. When she fell off her bike, crying, your dad ran over there and began comforting her, rubbing her back saying, "It's okay princess, let it all out. It's okay to cry." The message the little girl receives from dad is that it's okay to cry and show your feelings. It's okay to cry when she's hurting or feeling pain. I believe this is one of the reasons why there are more men in prison than there are women - simply 'cuz women don't let their build up hurt, anger and pain build up inside of them because they release the steam by crying. Unlike men, who will hold on to all that built up anger and hurting pain until eventually, one day, their pipes burst. Reaching their breaking point, they end up snapping in a violent rage. After you get that lengthy sentence I will advise you to go on and let it out. Release some of that build up pressure in your pipes.

Anger Control

It's very important that you learn how to control your anger while doing time, that way, you don't get baited in so easily by the COs and inmates that will inevitably piss you off. If you let them piss you off to the point you snap and take off on them causing GBI, such as, a fracture or broken nose, stitches, or you knock him unconscious. Not only will you get one year added to your prison sentence by the prison system but you will also be getting a DA referral. This means the prison that you're at will notify the local DA's office in the county letting him or her know that you just committed a felony crime of assault with GBI. If they want to pick the case up they can. If they do, you'll now be facing additional time added to your sentence. This is a penal code 4501 case and charge.

PART 3. OF IMPRISONMENT AND THE DEATH PENALTY [2000 - 10007] *(Part 3 repealed and added by Stats. 1941, Ch. 106.)*

TITLE 5. OFFENSES RELATING TO PRISONS AND PRISONERS [4500 - 4758] *(Title 5 added by Stats. 1941, Ch. 106.)*

CHAPTER 1. Offenses by Prisoners [4500 - 4504] *(Heading of Chapter 1 amended by Stats. 1943, Ch. 173.)*

4501. (a) Except as provided in Section 4500, every person confined in the state prison of this state who commits an assault upon the person of another with a deadly weapon or instrument shall be guilty of a felony and shall be imprisoned in the state prison for two, four, or six years to be served consecutively.

(b) Except as provided in Section 4500, every person confined in the state prison of this state who commits an assault upon the person of another by any means of force likely to produce great bodily injury shall be guilty of a felony and shall be imprisoned in the state prison for two, four, or six years to be served consecutively.

(Amended by Stats. 2015, Ch. 303, Sec. 401. Effective January 1, 2016.)

You'll also be getting an extra 3 years for GBI enhancement added on to that.

PENAL CODE - PEN

PART 4. PREVENTION OF CRIMES AND APPREHENSION OF CRIMINALS [11006 - 14315] (*Part 4 added by Stats. 1953, Ch. 1385.*)

TITLE 2. SENTENCE ENHANCEMENTS [12001 - 12022.95] (*Title 2 repealed and added by Stats. 2010, Ch. 711, Sec. 5.*)

12022.7. (a) Any person who personally inflicts great bodily injury on any person other than an accomplice in the commission of a felony or attempted felony shall be punished by an additional and consecutive term of imprisonment in the state prison for three years.

(b) Any person who personally inflicts great bodily injury on any person other than an accomplice in the commission of a felony or attempted felony which causes the victim to become comatose due to brain injury or to suffer paralysis of a permanent nature shall be punished by an additional and consecutive term of imprisonment in the state prison for five years. As used in this subdivision, "paralysis" means a major or complete loss of motor function resulting from injury to the nervous system or to a muscular mechanism.

(c) Any person who personally inflicts great bodily injury on a person who is 70 years of age or older, other than an accomplice, in the commission of a felony or attempted felony shall be punished by an additional and consecutive term of imprisonment in the state prison for five years.

(d) Any person who personally inflicts great bodily injury on a child under the age of five years in the commission of a felony or attempted felony shall be punished by an additional and consecutive term of imprisonment in the state prison for four, five, or six years.

(e) Any person who personally inflicts great bodily injury under circumstances involving domestic violence in the commission of a felony or attempted felony shall be punished by an additional and consecutive term of imprisonment in the state prison for three, four, or five years. As used in this subdivision, "domestic violence" has the meaning provided in subdivision (b) of Section 13700.

(f) As used in this section, "great bodily injury" means a significant or substantial physical injury.

(g) This section shall not apply to murder or manslaughter or a violation of Section 451 or 452. Subdivisions (a), (b), (c), and (d) shall not apply if infliction of great bodily injury is an element of the offense.

(h) The court shall impose the additional terms of imprisonment under either subdivision (a), (b), (c), or (d), but may not impose more than one of those terms for the same offense.

(Amended (as added by Stats. 2010, Ch. 711, Sec. 5) by Stats. 2011, Ch. 296, Sec. 226. Effective January 1, 2012.)

But if you already got 2 strikes on your record, you will now be facing your third strike because this penal code 4501 is a strikeable offense. Take a look at this real case right here called People versus Robinson 2010 cal.

He decided to jump another inmate leaving the inmate unconscious. The DA ended up picking up this case and struck the man out.

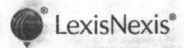

1 of 1 DOCUMENT

REARENCE ROBERSON, Petitioner, vs. TIM VIRGA, Warden, California State Prison, Sacramento, Respondent.

No. 2:11-cv-00386-JKS

STATED STATES DISTRICT COURT FOR THE EASTERN DISTRICT OF CALIFORNIA

REARENC...

1. Dist. LEXIS 109191

August 2, 2012, Decided
August 3, 2012, Filed

PRIOR HISTORY: *People v. Roberson (Clarence),* 2010 Cal. LEXIS 11059 (Cal. Oct. 27, 2010)

COUNSEL: [*1] Clarence Roberson, Petitioner, Pro se, REPRESA, CA.

For People of the State of California, Tim Virga, Respondents: Craig Steven Meyers, LEAD ATTORNEY, Office of the Attorney General, State of California, Sacramento, CA.

JUDGES: JAMES K. SINGLETON, JR., United States District Judge.

OPINION BY: JAMES K. SINGLETON, JR.

OPINION

MEMORANDUM DECISION

Clarence Roberson, a state prisoner appearing *pro se,* filed a Petition for a Writ of Habeas Corpus under *28 U.S.C. § 2254.* Roberson is currently in the custody of the California Department of Corrections and Rehabilitation, incarcerated at the California State Prison, Sacramento. Respondent has answered, and Roberson has replied.

I. BACKGROUND/PRIOR PROCEEDINGS

Following a jury trial, in November 2008 Roberson was convicted in the Sacramento County Superior Court of assault by force likely to produce great bodily injury *(Cal. Penal Code § 150J),* with two prior strike convictions *(Cal. Penal Code § 667(b)-(i)).* The trial court sentenced Roberson to an indeterminate prison term of twenty-five years to life. The California Court of Appeal affirmed Roberson's conviction and sentence in an unpublished decision,[1] and the California Supreme Court denied review on October 27, 2010. [*2] Roberson timely filed his Petition dated November 16, 2010, in this Court on February 11, 2011.

> [1] *People v. Roberson,* No. C060546, 2010 Cal. App. Unpub. LEXIS 5657, 2010 WL 2806257 (Cal. Ct. App. July 19, 2010).

The factual underpinning of Roberson's conviction as recited by the California Court of Appeal:

> About 1:30 p.m. on January 7, 2006, California State Prison Correctional Officer Juan Cantu saw, from 30 yards away, two inmates, David Sarente and defendant, push another inmate, Michael Rhinehart, to the ground and kick him.

The kicks were to the upper torso and head. Rhinehart appeared to be unconscious. Officer Cantu ordered Sarente and defendant to stop and to move away from Rhinehart.

Correctional Officer Michael Key also witnessed the assault. Officer Key's attention was drawn to the area when, 10 to 15 yards away, several inmates quickly dispersed. Officer Key saw Rhinehart's motionless body on the ground. Defendant and Sarente were kicking Rhinehart above the waist. All inmates were ordered to get down on the ground.

Correctional Officer Alice Link-Lopez responded to the area and saw a group of inmates on the ground. Rhinehart was bleeding from his mouth and was unresponsive, appearing to be unconscious. Rhinehart [*3] was transported on a gurney to the medical clinic, where he regained consciousness. He was slightly confused and disoriented. He suffered lacerations on his lip and chin and received stitches to his lip. He also had abrasions on his neck and arm.

At trial, Rhinehart was called by the defense to testify. He was in prison for murder. He claimed that he and [Roberson] had been friendly. Rhinehart grew up with Sarente's father. Rhinehart claimed that on the day of the incident, he threatened to stab [Roberson]. When they approached one another, Rhinehart landed on the ground. Rhinehart denied that either [Roberson] or Sarente knocked him down. Rhinehart denied that he had been knocked out or kicked. He claimed he was on the ground with his eyes closed and was resting. He denied that [Roberson] was at fault. Rhinehart acknowledged that [Roberson] may have punched him. Rhinehart would not "testify to that in court."

Sarente testified and denied having been involved in the incident. Sarente denied seeing [Roberson] kick Rhinehart.

[Roberson] testified. He claimed that Rhinehart called him over and threw two punches. [Roberson] blocked the second punch and then punched Rhinehart in the mouth, [*4] causing Rhinehart to fall backwards to the ground. [Roberson] denied that he or Sarente kicked Rhinehart.

Defense investigator Andrew Saucedo was called to testify in rebuttal. He interviewed Rhinehart on June 13, 2008. Rhinehart claimed that he had been hit from behind and did not know who had knocked him out. Rhinehart also claimed he had been kicked but did not know who had kicked him.

A district attorney investigator also interviewed Rhinehart. Rhinehart stated that inmates will not testify against each other after a fight. [2]

2 *2010 Cal. App. Unpub. LEXIS 5657, [WL] at *1-2.*

II. GROUNDS RAISED/DEFENSES

In his Amended Petition, Roberson raises four grounds: (1) the trial court failed to exercise its independent judgment; (2) there is insufficient evidence to support the conviction; (3) the trial court improperly denied a motion for a new trial in refusing to re-weigh the evidence; and (4) the trial court failed to investigate Roberson's competence. Respondent does not assert any affirmative defenses. [3]

3 *See Rules Governing Section 2254 Cases in the U.S. Dist. Courts, Rule 5(b)* (2011).

III. STANDARD OF REVIEW

Under the Antiterrorism and Effective Death Penalty Act of 1996 ("AEDPA"), *28 U.S.C. § 2254(d)*, this Court cannot grant [*5] relief unless the decision of the state court was "contrary to, or involved an unreasonable application of, clearly established Federal law, as determined by the Supreme Court of the United States" at the time the state court renders its decision or "was based on an unreasonable determination of the facts in light of

I too, had my own run-in with that penal code 4501 while I was in prison and here's the story of how I caught my penal code 4501. I was at the California City Correctional Facility in Kern County. I fought an inmate and gave him a fractured nasal and a fractured orbital, better known as the lower eye socket. No, I don't want to say the inmate's real name so I'll just call him Ernest.

Ernest was housed in the same building as me. Ernest was known to be an inmate bully. He was the loud and aggressive type. Nobody in my building really liked him. He was known for just getting up and changing the TV channel in the dayroom as all us inmates sat and watched a TV show. He was also known for taking people's time on the phone and turn in the shower. Because of his size, which was 6'5" and 260 lbs. of all muscle inmates gave very little argument to his wrong doing.

A few times, Ernest even got at me foul. I spoke up on him taking my turn on the phone, but I ended up letting it go, figuring the phone just ain't worth fighting over. Not long after me and Ernest had that argument over the phone it was breakfast time and Ernest had got at me, hella aggressive and loud in the chow line by saying I was cutting him. That morning I had had enough of Ernest's shit when he yelled at me. I lost my cool and I punched him below his left eye. The punch caused him to drop his breakfast tray and fall backwards landing on his butt. As Ernest started to get back up from his fall I ran over to him and started landing solid punches to his face, left, right, left, right, until the CO that was standing only about 20 feet away ran over and started spraying me all in my face with pepper spray. He was yelling for me to get down! I stopped punching Ernest and got down on the floor as the CO said to. I proned out (proning out is when you're laid out flat on your stomach with your hands straight out in front of you). As I lay proned out on the ground not able to see from all the pepper spray, all I could do was hope that Ernest don't get up and come kick me in my mouth. Ernest didn't.

The CO came over to me and told me to put my hands behind my back. I did as he told me to and he put handcuffs on me and then told me to get up and start walking. I still wasn't able to see, so the CO guided me to the program office where I was put in the refrigerator-like cage and told to strip out. My vision started to come back to me slowly but the pepper spray still burned like hell all on my face.

I saw when they brought Ernest into the program office and also put him in a refrigerator-like cage and told him to strip out. Our cages were only about 8 feet apart. After I was stripped out the CO told me to squat, cough, and lift both my feet up so he could see the bottom of them. He then looked inside of my mouth to see if I had anything in there. After I was finished with the embarrassing search, he gave me my boxers and socks and told me to put them back on. The CO did the same type of search with Ernest. He then asked Ernest and me why the incident occurred. Ernest and I didn't say nothing so the CO moved on to the next question which was, "Is this issue resolved with the both of you and would you be willing to sign a Marriage Chrono? By signing a Marriage Chrono you're saying that the issue is resolved and that there will be no further incidents between the guy you just fought.

Ernest and I both agreed to sign the Marriage Chrono but before we can leave out of the program office we would both have to get a medical clearance from the nurse. The CO called the nurse and she came with a clipboard in hand. There was a piece of paper of a man's body sketched on it attached to the clipboard. The nurse used it to indicate where marks or bruises were located on our bodies. As we stood there in just our boxers as the nurse looked over us, the nurse said I had no markings or bruises on me and told the CO that I was okay to leave. I was medically cleared.

When the nurse examined Ernest though, she said that he will need to go to the outside hospital to get an X-ray done to his face due to the massive swelling underneath the left side of his eye. Both Ernest and I were handed back our clothes and was told to get dressed.

Once me and Ernest got dressed the CO said that one of us would have to get moved out of the building even though we signed the Marriage Chrono. He would still need to separate us. I said I'd move. The CO told me my new building and cell number and I was told to go back to my building and start packing. I said okay, and was let out of the program office refrigerator-like cage and headed to my old cell.

Ernest was headed to the outside hospital to see what was going on with the massive swelling underneath his left eye. As I walked inside my old building heading to my old cell to go pack my property up and move, a few inmates came up to me smiling saying how glad they were because I beat Ernest, the inmate bully, up the way I did. I just gave them all a little grin and kept walking towards my cell. I told them all that the CO got me moving to another building. Once inside my old cell I quickly started splashing water all on my face in hopes that this would take away some of the fire that was happening on my skin from all that pepper spray. All the water did was reactivate the pepper spray to where it started to feel like I just freshly got pepper sprayed.

It took about 25 minutes before I was all packed up and moved to my new building. My new celly was cool but we didn't stay cellies for long because 7 hours later as I sat on my bunk watching TV I started hearing the inmates in the dayroom making siren calls. A call that inmates do to let others know that the COs are coming or are walking the floor. I got up to look out my cell door window but my celly beat me to the door. I asked what's going on out there and he said it looks like the COs are headed this way. My celly then said, "Yep they're coming this way." The CO stood outside the door and said he needed to speak to Mr. Bell. My celly stepped back and I went to the door and said, "I'm Mr Bell. What's going on?" The CO said he'll explain everything to me once we get inside the program office. He ordered me to step back and turn the other way so he could open up the door. When he opened up the door he walked up behind me and put handcuffs on me. He then escorted me to the program office.

As I'm leaving the cell being escorted to the program office I remember counting 10 COs that all came to get me. Once inside the program office I was put back in that refrigerator-like cage and then one of the COs came up to me and started reading something. Ernest had just got back from the outside hospital and the doctor at the hospital said that Ernest was diagnosed with a nasal fracture and an orbital fracture and that I am now going to the hole on the charge of assault and battery with GBI. He then went on to say that I would be getting a DA referral and not to worry about my personal property because he will go back and get my property and will have my celly pack it up for me.

I was then handed an orange jumpsuit and was told to put this on and I did as he told me. I got the orange jumpsuit on and was handcuffed and escorted to the hole. The DA picked up my case and I spent 13 months going back and forth to court while I was in the hole in a segregated housing unit. I already had one strike, I was now facing my second strike - and if I got convicted, my maximum exposure was 16 more years in prison due to them doubling up my time. Only because Ernest was not gonna press charges on me and had already made a statement that his face was already swollen before I hit him - I was offered a good plea bargain deal and the DA struck the strike. Meaning the GBI enhancement would be taken off. It was the GBI part of it all that made the battery charge a strikeable offense.

When it was all said and done I received a total of 5-years extra added to my already 18-year sentence. The cold part about this is

I was about to be getting out of prison in just 10 months from the day I took the plea bargain deal for 5 years. Now, I had to do more time in prison.

Yeah, I know you're probably saying that's double jeopardy being I got double charged by the prison system and the court, but that's just the way it goes when you catch a new charge while you're doing time. The prison will give you time and the courts will give you time. This is a letter that my lawyer wrote me after I wrote her:

LAW OFFICE OF THE PUBLIC DEFENDER
COUNTY OF KERN

PAM SINGH
Public Defender

DOMINIC EYHERABIDE
Chief Assistant Public Defender

PETER KANG
Chief Deputy Public Defender

1315 Truxtun Avenue
Bakersfield, California 93301

Telephone: (661) 868-4799
Fax: (661) 868-4785

June 13, 2017

Attorney-Client Privilege

Mr. Emmanuel Bell, V-69940
Cell yd-126
La Palma Correctional Center
5501 N. LaPalma Road
Elroy, AZ 85131

    Re: People v. Bell, MF012056A

Dear Mr. Bell:

I am writing in response to your request for modification pursuant to Penal Code Section 1170(d). I am receipt of all correspondence sent to the court, including your certificates. As noted in your motion you were facing maximum exposure of 16 years and you decided to enter a plea for 5 years with the understanding if your alleged prison prior was not valid you would receive 4 years.

Prior to the date of the plea, the offer from the DA had been 8 years and you made a counter offer of 4 years. The District Attorney took into consideration the certificates you provided and the potential self-defense that would be raised at trial in reaching the plea agreement. All factors were known to you at the time of the plea. You ultimately received a sentence of 4 years. There is no basis for a modification of sentence given the above stated factors.

I hope this letter addresses your concerns.

Sincerely,

+

Gloria J. Cannon
Deputy Public Defender

CALIFORNIA DEPARTMENT of
Corrections and Rehabilitation

ADMINISTRATIVE SEGREGATION UNIT PLACEMENT NOTICE

INSTITUTION NAME	INMATE'S NAME	CDC NUMBER
CAC-Facility B	BELL, EMANUEL	V69940

REASON(S) FOR PLACEMENT (PART A)

☐ PRESENTS AN IMMEDIATE THREAT TO THE SAFETY OF SELF OR OTHERS

☐ JEOPARDIZES INTEGRITY OF AN INVESTIGATION OF ALLEGED SERIOUS MISCONDUCT OR CRIMINAL ACTIVITY

☐ ENDANGERS INSTITUTION SECURITY   ☐ RETAINED IN ASU AS NO BED AVAILABLE IN GENERAL POPULATION

DESCRIPTION OF CIRCUMSTANCES WHICH SUPPORT THE REASON(S) FOR PLACEMENT:
On June 29, 2015, you, Inmate Bell V69940 are being placed in Administrative Segregation for Battery on an Inmate Resulting In Serious Bodily Injury. Specifically, on today's date during the morning breakfast meal, you battered Inmate   AF0322 by striking him repeatedly in the face with your fists. Due to injuries received, Inmate   was transported to Palmdale Regional Medical Center where he was diagnosed as having a fractured nasal process and fractured left orbital.

As a result of your conduct, you are deemed a threat to the safety of other inmates. You will remain in Administrative Segregation pending administrative review of this incident. Your credit earning status, visiting privileges, and privilege group are subject to change. Inmate Bell has a TABE score of 9.0 and is NOT a participant in the Mental Health Services Delivery System.

☐ IF CONFIDENTIAL INFORMATION USED, DATE INFORMATION DISCLOSED:

DATE OF ASU PLACEMENT	SEGREGATION AUTHORITY'S PRINTED NAME	SIGNATURE	TITLE
06/29/2015	Jay Manges	J. Manges	Lieutenant

DATE NOTICE SERVED	TIME SERVED	PRINTED NAME OF STAFF SERVING ASU PLACEMENT NOTICE	SIGNATURE	STAFF'S TITLE

☐ INMATE REFUSED TO SIGN	INMATE SIGNATURE	CDC NUMBER
		V69940

You were identified with a disability of:
☐ Hearing ☐ Vision ☐ Speech ☐ Learning Disability ☐ TABE under 4.0 / no TABE ☐ Developmental Disability ☐ CCCMS ☐ EOP ☐ Foreign Language Speaking

Method
☐ BELL, EMANUEL reiterated in his own words, what was explained

☐ BELL, EMANUEL provided appropriate, substantive responses to questions asked

☐ BELL, EMANUEL asked appropriate questions regarding the information provided

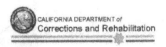

CALIFORNIA DEPARTMENT of
Corrections and Rehabilitation

SHU TERM ASSESSMENT WORKSHEET

Inmate Name:	BELL, EMANUEL	Date: 01/28/2016
CDC#:	V69940	Date of Birth: 11/19/1970
Prepared Date:	07/07/2015	Prepared Time: 07:04:40
Facility:	CAC-Facility A [CAC-A]	
Staff:	J. Christensen	
SHU Term Type:	Determinate	
Status:	Assessed and Imposed	As of Date: 01/28/2016

Related Rule Violation

Log Number: B15060012R   Violation Date: 06/29/2015

Specific Offense: Battery on an inmate with a weapon capable of causing serious or mortal injury; caustic substance or other fluids capable of causing serious or mortal injury or physical force causing serious injury

Attempt (1/2 term): No   Conspiracy: No

Offense Term-Lowest: 12   Expected: 18   Highest: 24

Total Determinate SHU Term Assessed

Expected SHU Term	18 Months	0 Days
Mitigating Factors Time	2 Months	0 Days

☑ The inmate has no serious RVR's within 12 months of the behavior or no disciplinary history during the first year of his/her incarceration.

☑ The inmate has not been involved in prior serious misconduct of the same or similar nature, as listed in subsection 3341.9(e), within the last five calendar years.

☐ The serious misconduct was situational and spontaneous, as documented and referenced.

☐ The inmate was influenced by others to commit the offense, as documented and referenced.

☐ The serious misconduct resulted, in part, from the inmate's fear for safety, as documented and referenced.

☐ The serious misconduct resulted, in part, from the inmate's mental health, as documented and referenced on the CDCR Form 115-MH.

Aggravating Factors Time +	0 Months	0 Days

☐ The inmate has been involved in prior serious misconduct of the same or similar nature, as listed in subsection 3341.9(e), within the last five calendar years.

Prior Offense:

Prior Violation Date:

☐ The serious misconduct was planned and executed, as documented and referenced.

☐ The serious misconduct was committed on behalf of an STG, as documented and referenced.

☐ The inmate influenced others to commit serious misconduct at the time of the offense, as documented and referenced.

☐ The serious misconduct directly resulted in injury to more than one victim, as documented and referenced.

Maximum SHU Term	16 Months	0 Days

V69940

SUPERIOR COURT OF CALIFORNIA, COUNTY OF:
KERN

PEOPLE OF THE STATE OF CALIFORNIA vs.
DEFENDANT:
EMANUEL BELL
AKA: MANUEL BELL
CII NO.: A11540134
BOOKING NO.: SO 2157990 ☐ NOT PRESENT
DOB: 11/19/1978

MF012056 A — -A
— -B
— -C
— -D

ENDORSED
FILED
KERN COUNTY

DEC 16 2016

TERRY McNALLY, CLERK
BY_____DEPUTY

FELONY ABSTRACT OF JUDGMENT
☑ PRISON COMMITMENT ☐ COUNTY JAIL COMMITMENT ☐ AMENDED ABSTRACT

DATE OF HEARING	DEPT. NO.	JUDGE
12/15/2016	1	JOHN S. SOMERS

CLERK	REPORTER	PROBATION NO. OR PROBATION OFFICER	☐ PRIVATE REFERENCES
A. RALLS	D.BAUMRUK	HEATHER SALAZAR	

COUNSEL FOR PEOPLE	COUNSEL FOR DEFENDANT	☐ APPOINTED
KEN GREEN	GLORIA CANNON	

1. Defendant was convicted of the commission of the following felonies:

☐ Additional counts are listed on attachment
_____ (number of pages attached)

COUNT	CODE	SECTION NO.	CRIME	YEAR CRIME COMMITTED	DATE OF CONVICTION (MO./DATE/YR.)	CONVICTED BY JURY	CONVICTED BY COURT	PLEA	TERM (L, M, U)	CONCURRENT	CONSECUTIVE FULL TERM	INCOMPLETE SENTENCE (REFER TO Item 5)	654 STAY	MISDEM FELONY	VIOL EXE FELONY	PRINCIPAL OR CONSECUTIVE TIME IMPOSED YRS.	MOS.
1	PC	4501(B)	ASSAULT BY PRISONER	2015	11/18/16			X	L							4	0
					/ /												
					/ /												
					/ /												
					/ /												

2. ENHANCEMENTS charged and found to be true TIED TO SPECIFIC COUNTS (mainly in the PC 12022 series). List each count enhancement horizontally. Enter time imposed, "S" for stayed, or "PS" for punishment struck. DO NOT LIST ENHANCEMENTS FULLY STRICKEN by the court.

COUNT	ENHANCEMENT	TIME IMPOSED, "S," or "PS"	ENHANCEMENT	TIME IMPOSED, "S," or "PS"	ENHANCEMENT	TIME IMPOSED, "S," or "PS"	TOTAL

3. ENHANCEMENTS charged and found to be true for PRIOR CONVICTIONS OR PRISON TERMS (mainly in the PC 667 series). List all enhancements horizontally. Enter time imposed, "S" for stayed, or "PS" for punishment struck. DO NOT LIST ENHANCEMENTS FULLY STRICKEN by the court.

ENHANCEMENT	TIME IMPOSED, "S," or "PS"	ENHANCEMENT	TIME IMPOSED, "S," or "PS"	ENHANCEMENT	TIME IMPOSED, "S," or "PS"	TOTAL

4. Defendant sentenced ☐ to county jail per 1170(h)(1) or (2)
☐ to prison per 1170(a), 1170.1(a) or 1170(h)(3) due to ☐ current or prior serious or violent felony ☐ PC 290 or ☐ PC 188.11 enhancement
☑ per PC 667(b)-(i) or PC 1170.12 (strike prior)
☐ per PC 1170(a)(3). Preconfinement credits equal or exceed time imposed. ☐ Defendant ordered to report to local parole or probation office.

5. INCOMPLETE SENTENCE(S) CONSECUTIVE

COUNTY	CASE NUMBER		
MONTEREY COUNTY	SS033129A		

6. ☐ TOTAL TIME ON ATTACHED PAGES:

7. ☐ Additional indeterminate term (see CR-292).

8. ☐ TOTAL TIME: 4 | 0

Attachments may be used but must be referred to in this document.

Form Adopted for Mandatory Use
Judicial Council of California
CR-290 [Rev. July 1, 2012]

Page 1 of 2

FELONY ABSTRACT OF JUDGMENT—DETERMINATE

Penal Code,
§ 1213, 1213.5

INMATE COPY

In a way catching that pc-4501 charge in prison was a gift and a curse to me. A curse because I had to do 5 extra years in prison and a gift because it was that experience that woke me up and got my attention, showing me that I really needed to start working on my anger before it's too late and I do end up catching a life sentence one day from lack of anger control. Not once, but twice, my anger has put me in two different court situations where I ended up catching prison time; once for stabbing the mother of my child and another for fracturing an inmate's face by punching him. From that day forward after receiving that five extra years in prison, I began my journey on gaining anger control skills and knowledge. Everything that I learned in my prison self help anger management class helped reshape my way of thinking. I still use it to this day. It has kept me from reaching a 10 (anger explodes into violence) on my anger meter scale for over 8 years. The anger management knowledge that I'm going to share with you has been working for me and I know it will work for you, too.

Anger Management Tools

There's a thing called the"anger meter scale"and this is used to see where you're at with your anger at the present time. This is what an anger meter looks like:

10 - anger explodes into violence

9 - pissed off

8 - fuming

7 - hostile

6 - physically distressed

5 - frustrated

4 - stressed

3 - annoyed

2 - irritated

1 - bothered

0 - humble and at peace

The way this Anger Meter Scale works is when you wake up in the morning your anger meter scale is at a zero, humbled and relaxed. As you go about your day and encounter people and things that trigger your anger, the needle on your anger meter scale goes up a notch or two depending on how bad your anger was triggered. If you fail to put a stop to the climb on your anger meter scale by using some of your coping skills to bring your anger meter needle back down, then it will be just a matter of time until you finally reach that 10 and explode into violence.

I know that some people don't wake up in the morning with their anger needle on a 0 - humble and relaxed. Some people wake up with their anger meter needle already on a 3 or 4 or even higher due to them not lowering it before they went to sleep. These people got to be more careful as they go about their day because their anger meter needle is already up from the start of the day. They're not too far away from reaching that 10. That's why it's important to check in with yourself throughout your day to check your inner feelings and mood to see how these things are with yourself at the present moment. As you're checking your inner feelings and mood, if you feel like your anger meter needle is up a bit - or a lot - try to find some time for yourself so you can begin using some of your coping skills to bring your anger meter needle back down.

A lot of people make the mistake of ignoring how they feel inside. They go about their day continuing to let their anger meter needle rise, failing to use any coping skills until they finally reach that 10. They end up taking their anger out on innocent people that really didn't deserve the aggressive tone or aggressive behavior they gave. They give into violent physical attacks. When a person takes their anger out on innocent people that is called displacement of anger. Here's an example of the Anger Meter Scale in use, plus an example of displacement of anger all wrapped into one story.

You wake up with your Anger Meter Scale on 0-relaxed and humble. You go to breakfast chow and after the CO tells you that your quarterly package is here and to go down to R&R to pick it up. The CO writes you a pass to go pick up your package and on your way the alarm goes off indicating for all inmates to get down on the ground due to a fight or man down code that just happened in your building. After sitting on the ground for about 15 minutes the CO announces for all inmates to return back to their cells and lock it up.

On your way to lock up in the cell you go ask the CO that wrote your pass and you ask him if you can still go pick your package. The CO tells you that you're not going no more and that you'll have to wait till tomorrow. Now this triggers your anger meter needle to rise up 3 notches to annoyed. Being you know nothing about using coping skills to bring your anger back down, you're now walking around with your anger meter needle on a 3.

Later on that day, the program gets back to normal so your building is running dayroom and as you're out in the dayroom you call next on the phone. The inmate that was already on the phone told you, "Yeah, you could get next." When the inmate hangs the phone up and you begin walking towards the phone, you notice another inmate that's also walking towards the same phone. You quickly tell him, "Hey, I already called next on the phone." He tells you the same thing and you end up calling the inmate back who just got off the phone. That inmate ends up saying, "Oh my bad man, I forgot you did call next but I ended up telling this guy too."

As soon as he finishes saying that, the other inmate quickly walks over and grabs the phone and dials. This causes the needle on your anger meter scale to go up, landing on a 5 - frustrated. When that inmate finally gets off the phone you hop on and end up hearing some bad news about your favorite cousin dying. Hearing this news causes your anger meter needle to rise some more, landing on either an 8 - fuming or at 9 - pissed off. Still, you do not have the coping skills to lower the needle on your Anger Meter Scale. So you do nothing about your built up anger and continue on with your day.

You go back to your cell and end up washing one of your t-shirts, and then you sit down on your bottom bunk and watch some TV. As you're watching TV, your celly starts pointing to a pancake size amount of water that you left on the ground by the sink where you was washing your t-shirt, and says, "Hey man, you just going to leave that puddle of water right there on the ground?"

You tell your celly it's nothing but water man, it's going to dry up. That's when you hear your celly say under his breath, "Weirdo." Being you're already at 9 - pissed off from all the previous stuff that happened to you throughout your day, hearing your celly call you a weirdo triggers your anger, causing you to go up a notch reaching that 10 - exploded to violence. You stand up and ask your celly, "What did you just call me?" and then your celly says it again , "I called you a weirdo", and that's when you rush him, throwing blows.

Had you been using coping skills before your celly called you a weirdo, you would have probably only been at a 3 or 4 on your Anger Meter Scale. When your celly called you a weirdo, your anger meter needle would have raised 1 or 2 notches, but you wouldn't have been to a 10! You would have only been on a 5 - frustrated or a 6 - physically distressed. You would have pretty much just brushed him off for calling you a weirdo. You were in the wrong in the first place for leaving water on the ground and you would have just cleaned it up when you're celly asked you to. You would have prevented your celly even calling you a weirdo in the first place.

Coping Skills

Here are some things you could do to keep your cool and to keep your Anger Meter Scale under control which are known as coping skills. These will help lower your anger meter needle whenever you feel that it is up.

Picture a beautiful place or event - this is when you go to a happy place inside your head. I got two different places I would go to inside my head to begin lowering my anger meter needle. The first one is being on a cruise ship cruising the sea on a hot summer day, relaxing in a beach chair by the swimming pool area, sipping some wine. The second place I imagine which helps with lower my anger is picturing a Christmas morning with my wife and our little kids and I sitting around the Christmas tree opening up our Christmas presents in my nice 4 bedroom house. Picturing beautiful events or places in your head like this is not only a calming feeling but it also helps with keeping you focused so you don't lose your cool. You can make what you're picturing inside your head come true one day.

Talking positive to yourself - this is when you tell yourself positive things to keep you on track when you feel your anger rising. When I feel my anger rising, I use this coping skill. I tell myself that I'm finally on the right track in life and if I continue on this track I will one day reach all my goals in life. I can't allow this person that's triggering my anger to throw me off track and cause a setback for me. I must keep my cool. This guy is not worth it.

Take a time out for yourself - when you feel your anger rising take a time out for yourself and go for a walk and as you're walking to calm yourself down, count to 10 and take deep breaths while you're figuring out the best way to handle the situation at hand. It's always good to take a time out for yourself to calm yourself down when you're having a heated conversation, 'cuz when you're angry like that, you're not thinking clearly so you're more likely to say, or do, something that you'll regret later.

Exercise - exercising is one of the best ways to lower your anger meter needle because you'll be releasing steam as you sweat it out.

Listening to soothing music - it can relax you and lower your anger. If you're an inmate without a girlfriend then hearing female artists singing to you, talking about making love tonight, or kissing your soft lips, or licking my body all over; hearing a woman singing like that when your anger meter needle is up will trigger something in your head to remind you that you need to stay focused on getting out of prison so you can one day be with a woman again. If you lose your cool and snap on the inmate it will only prolong that amazing event - sex with a woman. Listening to female R&B singers is known to lower an inmates stress and the meter needle.

Venting - venting is talking to somebody you trust about what got you angry. It is a good way to let out some steam.

Meditate - As you sit with your legs crossed and eyes closed, each deep breath you take in and hold, you're breathing in calmness and strength that's soaking up all that anger inside of you. Once you finally blow out the air, you're blowing out some of that built up anger and steam that was inside of you. When you do this enough you eventually blow out most of the anger and steam inside of you which will lower your anger meter needle scale causing you to be in a relaxed and peaceful state.

Praying to your higher power - as you pray to your God, connecting yourself with Him - this tends to bring inner peace within you knowing that He's looking down on you and would want you to keep the peace. As you pray to your God to lower your anger meter needle, your faith in a higher power knows He will do just that.

Looking at family photos - looking at family photos when you're angry will do the trick with bringing your anger meter needle down. When looking at your loved ones you'll begin to see that you need to stay focused and out of trouble so you can one day get back in their lives. When you start to see pictures of your kids, this doubles the effect of keeping you focused and trying to stay out of trouble, knowing that your kids really miss you and really needs Daddy back home to protect and help guide them. If you're a father with a little girl, she really needs Daddy back home. If you're a father with a little girl - she really needs your fatherly presence 'cuz without you there to show her how a man is supposed to treat her, she won't know any better and she'll put up with the disrespect and mistreatment that her boyfriend is doing to her.

The more coping skills you use the lower your anger meter needle will go.

Development Strategy

Another tool that's good with controlling your anger is what I call the *development strategy*. The way this tool works is whenever something is repeatedly getting you angry, develop a strategy to go around it. For instance, let's say there's an inmate that at chow always likes to rush out first like you do to be the first one in the chow hall. When going to chow in prison, the way it works is called control feeding. Once you enter the chow hall you must sit in an orderly fashion, controlled by the CO. You can be eating at the table with the 3 inmates that are in front of you in the line or in the back of you in line.

Let's say every time you sit down at the table with that other guy, he constantly be yelling to the other inmates at the other table, saying things like, "I got an apple for your cookies," or "I got a cake for one of your hot dogs." A lot of times while he be doing all this yelling across the table, little pieces of food from his mouth be flying out, barely missing your food tray. This is really getting on your nerves making the needle on your anger meter needle rise. With the development strategy, you can develop a strategy for yourself so that your anger will stop being triggered. Instead of rushing out first for chow like he does, wait a minute or two and let other inmates go first. Then you won't be positioned near him in the line.

Another scenario is let's say you're in the cell at night and it's now mail pickup time. You put your mail under the door for the CO to pick up but in the morning you notice the CO forgot to pick your mail up and this is the third time he forgot. This is starting to get you mad, but the development strategy that you could develop for yourself is at night before you lock up, grab your mail and go drop it in the mailbox yourself.

It's a must that you learn how to develop strategies to go around situations that trigger your anger. Not only are you going to need it for prison but you're also going to need it for when you get out of prison. Know that it might be impossible to develop a strategy for everything that gets you angry. For the ones you can, develop a strategy for it.

Core Beliefs

Another thing that will help control your anger and violent behavior is to start rooting out all of the negative core beliefs that've been installed in you as a youngster. Maybe it was an uncles or your big OG homie who you look up to. They may have wired you up to think that if you feel you can't whoop a person, you can pick up a brick and bust him upside the head.For many years you may have been operating on that negative core belief. Instead of picking up a brick, you picked up a gun. You may have begun running around in the streets, and believed the only way to get money is to sell drugs or rob people. Or you were taught that if somebody disrespected you, you need to quickly take off on them, no questions asked.

Until you take the necessary timeout to begin weeding out all the negative core beliefs, you will continue to behave violently. You may think that that type of behavior is normal simply because you really don't know any better. Thinking that because your uncles are big homies that you looked up to, and laced you up like this it's got to be the proper way to behave. Once you root out the negative beliefs, replace them with positive core beliefs. You can get a lot of positive core belief knowledge by enrolling yourself in some self help prison classes.

Dig Deep Within Yourself

Another thing you can do to help control your anger if you continually find yourself engaging in violent behavior is to dig deep within yourself to try to find the root to what got you burning inside. Problems just don't go away like most people think, like when they try to drink or smoke the memories of the past and present hurts away. The problem must be worked out and once you finally get to the root of your problem, that burning inside of you which is causing you to act so violently goes away.

You must start ASAP working on it by either taking self help classes, seeing a counselor, or seeing a psychologist. Know that hurt people, hurt people. Until you seek help, that fire that's been burning inside of you for so many years will continue to burn. If you don't act quickly by putting that fire out, it will be just a matter of time until you burn your temple down.

Your problem may also be coming from being raped or molested by your uncle as a kid, or bullied all the time when you were younger, or abandoned by your parents, or your mother dying years ago, and you're still holding on to all that hurt and pain. You mustn't let something that happened to you in the past destroy your future life. You mustn't give somebody that much power over you to where they not only got you burning inside for decades, but also got you destroying your life. The anger and the pain they caused is constantly getting you in trouble with the law. Seek some help so you can win this battle inside of you by permanently putting out the fire.

If I had a dollar every time an inmate expressed to me how pissed off they were because all the people that he thought would be there for them had all left him for dead, I wouldn't be rich but I'd for sure have $31.

From my personal experience and from talking to other inmates, I learned that this type of hurt and pain inside of you can last up to 3 to 4 years. The reason why it lasts that long is due to the shock of finding out that the people who you truly thought were loyal to you are now showing you that it was all an act. They were never loyal to you in the first place. The realization of this hurts tremendously. These were people who you helped out big time when you were on the streets, letting them stay at your house when they needed a place to stay, or when they called you asking for money, or whatever it was, you never hesitated to help them out. But now, here they all are dodging your calls and not responding back to any of your letters.

The advice I want to give to you is if you're experiencing this type of let down by your friends and family members, stay strong and know that time heals all wounds. It may take up to 3 to 4 years to finally get over the hurt and pain, but as you're going through the let down, know that you are waking up everyday with your anger meter needle at like a 2 or 3. Being you're not waking up with your anger meter needle starting on a 0 - relax and humble, you're more quicker to reach a 10.

For those of you that are going through this type of let down, know that in 3 or 4 years you'll finally be able to wake up with your anger meter needle starting on a 0. Until then, just keep using your coping skills and you'll be alright. Don't get on the inmate statistics list of not being able to control the hurt and pain inside of you from being abandoned by all of your people, to where you end up taking it out on the innocent inmates. Be smart and stay focused. I promise you it will get greater later.

There's one thing that comes out of this. You know the real you when you get out of prison. You now know that all of the friends and family that you thought you had before you went to prison - you now know that they were never really your friends in the first place. They were just opportunists. This is a good thing to know because had you not gone to prison or jail, you would have still been blind thinking that your friends truly were your friends - not even knowing that once you go to jail or prison they will leave you for dead to do your time all by yourself. Now you know that they really didn't have your back. The good thing is you're not blind no more.

Being violent in prison will only keep you in prison longer. Being violent on the streets will only bring you right back to prison. That's why it's important to have your anger under control. One of the main reasons why so many inmates come right back to prison less than a year after being paroled is because they failed to see that the way that they behaved was meant only for prison not society. They failed to work on themselves, or change their behavior to fit the ways of society. They got out on the streets, acting the same way they did when they were in prison, and having a prison mentality on the streets will eventually land you right back in prison. Until a person takes the necessary timeout to make the changes within himself, the prison doors will continue to remain a revolving door for him.

I remember when I was at DVI (during the covid-19 pandemic from April 4, 2020 until I was paroled from prison on June 8, 2021. I ended up getting a celly fresh out of the reception center and he said that he had never been to prison before. I don't want to say my celly's real name so I'll just call him Luger. Luger had only been locked up for 1 year and most of that time was done in the county jail. Luger said he used to smoke heroin and meth when he was on the streets. When I explained my cell rules to him, he said he understood them. As time went on, I found myself having to correct him on things all the time. Damn near everyday I had to keep correcting him to not spit in the sink, wipe the toilet rim after you finish pissing, to do a courtesy flush when taking a crap, and not leave stains on the sink. It was obvious that Luger fried up a lot of his brain cells when he was on the streets and being he was still kind of fresh in prison, he still needed a lot more time to restore his brain cells.

At the time, I only had 2 months left to do until I was finally going to be released from prison after serving 17 and a half years. Daily, I found myself using every single coping skill I knew just to keep from turning into the old me, the young and impulsive me, that would have blown a fuse and taken off on Luger. I was now older, and understood that there are truly slow minded people in the world who actually forget things an hour after you tell them something, and mentally ill people with mental illness. It would be very silly of me to fight a person such as Luger for not respecting my cell rules.

I learned that fighting these types of inmates is pointless, and that there's a better way to deal with these types of arrested development, slow minded, mental health issue inmates. So instead of fighting Luger, I just told him that this ain't working out and it took three days for him to find a new celly. Some people are able to get it right with themselves within a year. With others, it may take even longer. Unfortunately, it took me until my late 30's to get my anger under control. Yes, in prison you got to stand up for yourself and keep inmates from trying to run all over you, but you don't always have to use violence to get your point across. You can use your words in a calm, respectable way, always remembering that your feelings are your own. The same way your actions are your own - nobody can make you react violently, you react violently on your own.

Warning Signs

As your anger meter needle begins to rise, know that your body is trying to help you out by giving you warning signs to let you know that your needle is too high. You have to start doing something about it before it's too late! So when the following happens know that your body is giving you warning signs:

Your heart starts beating faster than what it normally does.

Your body starts getting hot.

You start clenching your jaws or your palms start to sweat.

You find yourself pacing back and forth (pacing back and forth can also be from nervousness).

Your nose wrinkles up (this can also mean that something is disgusting or strange to you).

Talking in a higher voice than you normally do or talking fast.

Butterflies in your stomach.

You start to shake.

Your muscles tense.

Pay attention to your body because it can prevent you from reaching a 10.

Not only is it crucial to keep your anger meter needle low so that you don't explode to a 10, but it's also crucial to keep it low to minimize the effects that stress hormones have on your physical well-being. As stress hormones get released throughout your body from you getting angry and staying angry, it can do damage to your health and cause your face and hair to age way faster than it normally would.

Life is 10%

what happens to you

and

90% how you react to it.

~ Charles R. Swindoll

6
Words That Can Help Control Your Violence and Anger

Don't take everything personally - I used to be that guy that took things personally. You could say I was stupid or weird and I would be ready to fight. Thanks to my self help groups, I learned not to let a person's opinion of me become my reality. Just because someone says I'm stupid or weird doesn't mean I'm weird. I know I'm not stupid. If those name callers were to really get to know me, better they would see I'm nothing like they thought I was.

Don't be working with feelings - I will admit I used to be one of those inmates that would get mad when someone would tell me "no" when I would ask for something. Thanks to my self help groups I came to realize that there's nothing to get mad over. It's not like the guy is really my homeboy anyway. In fact, I should be mad at myself for not having enough self-control to not want what he has. He has the right to do whatever he wants with his stuff. It's not like the dude cares anything about me anyway. So what's the point of getting angry over somebody that don't care nothing about me, telling me no?!

You don't got to prove nothing to nobody - I know what I'm capable of doing. I work out 5 days a week. I know from experience that if I got a good solid punch in I can fracture a lower eye socket or knock someone out. Just like I know what I'm capable of, I'm sure you know what you're capable of if you were to lose your cool and attack the guy that's getting at you foul. Sometimes it is best to just let it go and save yourself a new charge or case.

We know what we're capable of, but we don't always got to prove it to that person that's getting at us. A lot of times it's better to defuse the situation by remaining calm and respectful. By simply saying, "My bad man, you're right, I apologize." or "My bad man, it won't happen again." Do whatever you got to say to try to diffuse the situation and walk away. A lot of times it's best to just be the bigger man and handle the situation like that because it's just not worth the inevitable setback or financial cost that's going to come after your attack on him. This doesn't make you no punk by trying to defuse the situation. What it does is make you smart. Smart that you're staying focused on your goals and getting out of prison.

In one of my self help groups an inmate opened up to the group, talking about how he ended up in prison on a manslaughter charge for killing a dude. He punched a dude in the face, knocking him out cold and causing the guy to fall down like a tree. He hit his head on the ground fracturing his skull, causing hemorrhaging inside the skull. In other words, internal head bleeding. When the other guy ended up dying from his injury he received his third strike - life in prison. He went on to say how the other guy was the aggressor that started the fight between them. All he was doing was defending himself from the guy's punches.

Like I said earlier, sometimes it's best to just be the bigger man and put your anger and pride to the side and just say to him "you know what man, you right," and then walk away.

Lord, give me the serenity to accept the things I cannot change, the courage to change the things I can and the wisdom to know the difference.

There is going to be stuff happening in our lives that we have no control over and can't do nothing about. You might be in prison when you hear the bad news from friends or family. There's no need to hold on to that anger or lose your cool over a situation you've no control over. Instead, give the problem to your higher power and let him handle it for you and work it out. It might be a death in the family. No need to lose your cool and snap on innocent people. Snapping on somebody would most definitely make your deceased turn over in their grave. Your deceased would want you to succeed in life and become successful, but now if you fight and get in trouble, that would be something that your deceased most definitely don't want you doing, all because of their death. Dying is a part of life. We all must die one day, it's out of our control. So accept it, and know that they are now in a way better place than we are where there's no more hurt, pain, or crying.

Worse than you are - Even though you might not have much stuff at the moment, there's still a lot of inmates doing worse than you are, so be thankful for what you got and still count it as a blessing.

Mind playing tricks on you - A lot of times we are thinking stuff that's not even accurate. For example, I turn my head and see an inmate looking my way with a mug on his face and I start thinking he's mugging me (staring at me with a frown on his face). I'm ready to go over there now and ask him, do you got a problem with me? Why you keep staring at me? In all actuality he maybe wasn't even looking at me, he might have been looking past me and he only had the mug on his face because he didn't have his eyeglasses on so he was squinting to see. We should never act on impulse. We should always second-guess ourselves to see if what we're thinking about someone else's action is true or false.

Forgiveness - Eventually you got to be able to forgive the person that did you wrong. Walking around with all that built up hate and anger inside can rob you not only of your joyful laughter, but also your inner peace - causing you to be somewhat bitter inside. As hard as it may be, you should forgive to get rid of the emotional baggage that you've been carrying around with you for so long. Then you can restore the old you and be back being that jolly high spirited person. Don't allow someone to have a hold on you like that because 9 times out of 10, the person that caused you hurt has moved on happily with their life. Now it's your time to do the same.

Hard times - If you believe in God, know that God does everything for a reason. You were created for a purpose. Your life has already been scripted by God and all you're doing is playing out the role that He gave you. God knows what you are about to do before you even do it. He will never put too much on you that you can't handle. Everything that's happening in your life, God has His hands in it. God will purposely put you in a bad situation so you can learn from it and to draw you closer to Him. God sees you haven't been paying Him any attention. God sees that you are weak in a certain area and now He wants to strengthen you and make you a better person. So God will take you through trials and tribulations to strengthen you.

You need to pray to God as you're going through your trials and tribulations. Ask God, "What are you trying to show me?" He will put you through those trials and tribulations because there's a blessing He wants to give you. He knows if He was to give you that blessing right now, you would only mess it up. He knows that you are not ready for it.

The blessing God may have in store for you might be him bringing your kids back in your life, but God knows that if He does this right now, you would only hurt your kids emotionally or physically cuz you're still a drunk and a violent person. God will take you through hard times to get you right. The blessing God may have in store for you might be you winning a $270 million dollar lottery ticket, but God knows that if He gives you this blessing right now, you will only spend the money frivolously on expensive cars, women, and drugs.

There's a lot of different reasons why God will take you through a hard time in your life. The hard time that you're going through won't last forever. The day will come when God will feel that you've been molded enough to his perfection and it is time to take you out of your hard time situation and give you the blessing that He's been holding for you. It should be easier facing hard times in your life when you know why they are occurring. A gem cannot be properly polished without friction. A man cannot be perfected without the hard times in this life. So welcome the hard times in your life with open arms. Know that something good is going to come out of it in the long run.

Empathy - For every action there's a reaction. That's why it's good to always put yourself in the other person's shoes to see how you would feel or react if the action that you're about to do towards that person happened to you. How would that thing you're about to say make you feel if that was said to you? By doing this, you can see how it made you feel and understand how it might make the other person feel. We're all wired with the same emotions inside and by doing this, you will be more considerate, lessening your rudeness and disrespect towards other individuals.

Dodged calls and packages - This could be very frustrating when you're trying to call somebody back that told you a week ago that they were sending a package. You're trying to call them back but they're not picking up. When they do finally answer the phone, they tell you that they ordered the package for you. As a few months go by, you're still waiting on the package and now as you're trying to call the person again, they're not picking up. You never received the package they said they ordered for you 2 months ago. This can cause all types of emotions to run through you. Feeling unloved, worthless, crushed, depressed, unappreciated, abandoned, broken-hearted, and rejected all at the same time. To avoid going through all those emotions, try not to get your hopes up too high. Try to have the attitude that if they do it, they do it. But if they don't, it's all good. This way, if they do let you down, you weren't really expecting it anyway. After 2 days of trying to call them and you still can't get a hold of them, chill out. Wait 4 or 5 days, then try again. Constantly calling someone everyday and not getting an answer can cause your anger to build up. Trust me, I know from experiance, don't allow people to play games with you and kick you while you're down. That will not only anger you, but will also lower your self-esteem, making you feel less than a man - which can cause depression.

*Everything comes to you
at the right time.
Be patient.
Your time will come.*

– Anonymous

7
Reception Center

After you receive your prison sentence from the judge, you will have 2 to 3 weeks before you leave the county jail and get transferred to a prison reception center. A reception center is a place that determines what prison you're going to be sent to to do your prison time. The day before you leave the jail, the CO is going to give you a big brown paper bag. You will put all your personal belongings inside the bag and in the morning the CO will announce for you to come to the front podium. There, he will take your property bag and mark your name on it, if it's not already marked. You will then get handcuffed and ankle cuffed and told to line up next to the other inmates.

Once all the inmates are cuffed, you'll be escorted down to the holding tank where you'll wait for the bus to take you to the reception center. Once the bus finally arrives and y'all are all on it, the bus driver will tell you no talking allowed. Whoever he catches talking will get written, in other words a disciplinary action. Normally, the bus driver will play the radio station softly as he drives but you got some bus drivers that don't play any music, and would rather ride in silence. It's going to be a while until you get to see cars and society again so enjoy the views as you are riding to the reception center.

Once you arrive at the reception center and are off the bus, your handcuffs will come off and remain off the whole time as you're getting booked into prison. You will then be told what number holding tank to go into. There will be like six different holding tanks lined up next to each other along the wall. Find the number which will be located above the cell and go inside. You're going to go through the same new arrival process that you went through upon arriving at the county jail. One by one, you and all the other inmates will be called out to see the nurse and have a picture taken like you did at the county jail. You must wait until everybody that's in the holding tank with you finishes with their new arrival process. Then you will all leave together to get housed.

You will arrive at the reception center in the morning, but will not be housed in your cell or dorm until night. Inside your holding cell will be a toilet and a sink, and a long bench lined up against the wall. Being there's so many inmates in that holding tank, it's a 50/50 chance you will get a seat on the bench. If you're one of those unlucky inmates that can't find a seat on the bench, you must stand for hours or have a seat on the filthy floor. There's nothing to do in the holding tank so there's going to be inmates in there talking for hours and hours to entertain themselves. Be prepared to have to tell one of them talkative inmates that's talking you to death, that you're tired and you're about to take a nap. The way inmates normally take a nap while sitting on the bench is by leaning forward with arms on knees and face resting on arms.

Depending on what reception center you go to, a CO or inmate will come by your holding tank and ask you what size you wear. You will get your prison blue clothes right then and there, or you will remain in that paper jumpsuit that they gave you before leaving the county jail. Once you get housed, if you don't already have your blue clothes, fill out a clothing slip. Shortly, you will receive all your prison blue clothes from the clothing room.

Once everybody in the holding tank is done with their new arrival process, the CO will come by and call all y'all out by your last name. You'll be lined up and be handed a bedroll and a fish kit the same kind that you got when you first arrived at the county jail. The CO will then tell all of you where you're going. Try your best to remember where he told you - but even if you forget, you can ask him later. You will all walk in single file. As you're walking, inmates will be dropping out of the line and going in different directions, to different buildings. If it's a dorm that you are going to be housed in, then just follow everything I told you regarding dorm living and you'll be fine. If it's a cell you're going to be housed in, follow everything I told you about cell living and you'll be alright.

Being you're in a prison reception center and not the actual prison yet, you won't be able to order your TV, CD player, hot pot, hair trimmer, or fan. There will be a TV in the dayroom. In your dorm living, there will be either 2 or 3 different TVs. In the dayroom, the TVs will be divided up by races such as Blacks and Northerns will share one TV, the white and Southerners or Surenos will share another, the Piezas and Asians will share another.

Depending on what reception center you're at will determine what races will be sharing a TV. If you're cell living, you will have to stand up the whole time and watch TV through your cell door window. You're not going to be able to hear every word from the TV clearly because of the echo the TV makes as the sounds bounce off the walls. Being that there's only one TV for cell living, the TV control gets switched up daily. For instance, one day the Blacks will have control of it then the next day the Southsiders will have control over it, then the whites. The race rotation will keep switching up until it comes back around. Each week the librarian will come around to drop off books from a push cart. You can read books when you're still living at a reception center.

If you're on a 23-hour a day lockdown, your program will be 1 hour of yard or 1 hour of dayroom. You can go play basketball or work out. Then the next day you'll get dayroom for an hour. You can shower and it switches up like that. It's hard to get a shower at the reception center cuz as soon as the cell doors open up, inmates sprint to the shower and a lot of them automatically put their homeboys next after them even though their homies didn't call next on the shower.

The average stay at the reception center is 4 to 6 months and once you see your counselor and go to committee, all you're doing is waiting on your bus ride to take you to the prison that was chosen for you. From the time you leave your committee hearing it should take no longer than 3 to 4 months for your bus ride to prison.

Committee determines what level prison you will be going to based on your placement score. The length of your sentence, having prison priors, and the type of crime you committed, all determine your placement score. If your placement score is between 0 and 19, you will be going to a Level 1 minimum security prison, or a fire camp, or even a ranch. A placement score of between 20 and 36 then you will be going to a Level 2 low security prison, a fire camp, or ranch. A placement score between 37 and 60 then you will be going to a Level 3 medium security prison, but if your replacement score is 60 or higher you will be going to the highest level prison which is a Level 4 max security prison. If you stay out of trouble at your prison then yearly your placement score points will drop and you will eventually get your placement score down to a lower level score and will be moved accordingly to the lower level prison.

Reception Center Dayroom

It's no longer how it used to be with having inmates from only your county incarcerated with you, now you're incarcerated with inmates from all different counties. I thought when I got to the reception center that everybody knew about my city Seaside, but when inmates would ask me where I was from and I told them, nobody even knew where Seaside was. They had mistaken it for Riverside or Oceanside.

When you're out in the reception center dayroom keep in mind that everybody out there with you has just recently received their prison sentence. The hurt and pain from the sentence is still very fresh inside of them, especially the ones that received a life sentence, as they're still mourning. Remember, hurt people - hurt people. Know that there are inmates walking around like ticking timebombs just waiting for the first inmate to say or do something crazy so they can finally release some of that freshly built up steam. To make matters worse, some of those inmates in the dayroom with you are also dealing with sentencing anger, mourning for themselves, and the recent breakup with his girlfriend or wife, who is now treating him like "out of sight out of mind".

When you are out in the dayroom with inmates that are freshly mourning for themselves and freshly heartbroken, you need to be very careful. I'm pretty sure a majority of inmates that are going through this type of hurt and pain have no anger management knowledge or coping skills. The only way they know how to bring their anger meter needle down is by displacing anger, taking it out on innocent people by fighting.

Don't be out in the dayroom complaining to other inmates about your problems, especially not the amount of time you got. The guy you're probably complaining to about the 5 or 6 years you got to do, he might be one of them inmates with a life sentence. Hearing you complaining about the little 5 to 6 years will make him even angrier being he's serving a life sentence or 20 plus years. Let's hope if you do end up complaining to him that his anger meter needle ain't already on a 9 - cuz hearing you complain about something so small could be the thing that brings his anger needle up a notch reaching that 10, exploding to violence. Even if your family only put $40 on your books, don't be complaining about that either. The inmate you're complaining to might not have anybody at all putting money on his books, which will make that inmate angry. He will now start feeling the pain of being left for dead by his folks. You don't want to do that. you don't want to go around sparking ill feelings inside of inmates, especially the feeling of trying to seem bigger and better then them.

What I mean by trying to seem bigger and better than them is, let's say you and 3 other inmates are all out in the dayroom sitting down at a table when one of the inmates begins talking about how before he got arrested and came to prison. He tells you he had a 2020 hardtop BMW on some 18-inch stock rims, but then you jump in and say, "That ain't nothing man. I had a 2021 convertible candy painted BMW on some 28-inch Ashanti rims with Vogue tires and four 15-inch speakers in the trunk, and five 6x9 speakers inside the car. Trying to be bigger and better than the next man means that what you're really doing is trying to get above him. You're being combative. You may be impressing the people that are standing around, but you can best believe you're creating low-key animosity inside the man you're trying to seem bigger and better than. Nobody really likes to feel below the next man or mediocre to him.

You'll see this type of behavior happening a lot when there is a beautiful single woman around 3 men that are also all single. Each man will try to seem bigger and better and smarter than the next man in hopes of impressing the attractive woman and making her fall for him. Don't be that inmate that other inmates be trying to avoid 'cuz you're always trying to seem bigger and better than the next man. Instead, when you're out in the dayroom and an inmate gets to talking about how before he came to prison he was out there on the street corner selling $20 rocks making $300 a day and you know you were making double that amount of money a day because your street corner was really cracking - as the inmate tells you how much money he was making on the streets you don't have to compete. You could just be modest and just be like, "Damn you was out there getting your money, you are a real Hustler." Or you can say, "Damn, your street corner was cracking." Believe me when I say there's nothing wrong with being modest. In fact, being modest alleviates the hate and animosity that comes with trying to seem bigger and better than the next man.

Now there's also those other types of inmates that try the same bigger and better but they do it in a different way. These types of inmates are worse. They will have lots of money. And just cuz they got a lot of money, they walk around with an arrogant and cocky attitude, treating and talking to other inmates that barely got any money or no money at all, as though they are slaves and he the slave master. As though they're below him and him being superior to them as though they ain't even worth talking to because they have little money or no money at all. If he does decide to talk to them, it's in a condescending way.

Not all, but most inmates that go to the store every month and get fat packages every quarter, will also act that way. This bigger and better attitude will be turned up a few more notches if he also got a cell phone. If you just so happen to be one of those lucky inmates that got your money up like that, try to remain humble and treat and talk to all the inmates as though they're equal to you and not below you. The inmates that are broke are already dealing with the stress of being broke. When you're out in the dayroom or yard, most inmates don't really like being asked how much time they got sentenced to, especially if the time they got to do is a lot. Being asked that question reminds that inmate of their prison sentence, especially if it's a long sentence. This makes inmates begin to feel uncomfortable. They would rather avoid it and try to push it out of their mind. If you're trying to find out how much time an inmate got, do like I used to do - when you're talking to him, tell him how much time you got sentenced to and in return, if he feels like it, he will tell you how much time he got. Normally, an inmate will respond right back, but if he doesn't, then you will know that he's one of them inmates that don't like talking about how much time he got to do.

Showers

The only time you can shower is at dayroom time and you've got to find out who's next on the shower and call next after him. If you don't already know who got next in the shower, then you will need to go and ask the inmate that's already in the shower who got next after him. He will tell you the inmate's name. If you don't know who he's talking about, just ask him to point the inmate out. Once you finally see the guy, you go ask him can you get next in the shower. If he says an inmate already called next after him but you don't know who that inmate is, then once again you will need to ask that inmate to point out the inmate. Keep doing that until you finally find out who the last inmate is for the shower. Once you find him, call next after him. It's likely that somebody will be walking up on you asking you who got next after you in the shower.

To avoid an inmate getting at you aggressively in the shower area, you need to give all the naked inmates around you at least an arm's length of space. If I had a dollar every time I saw an inmate aggressively bark at another inmate for being too close to him in the shower, I wouldn't be rich, but I will for sure have $16.

This is how those aggressive situations occur. An inmate will be already drying off when another inmate tries to reach past to grab his towel. As he's reaching, he ends up getting too close to the inmate drying off and the aggressive barking occurs. Other times are when one inmate will walk up too close behind another inmate while they both are naked. Only once did I see an inmate get physical and push an inmate for being too close to him. The inmate that got pushed down quickly got back up and they both started quckly putting back on their boxers. Then they started fighting.

While you're in the shower area naked, give everybody at least an arms length of space to avoid an inmate barking at you aggressively and saying, "Back the fuck up man! You too close." or "Hell, what's wrong with you man? Back the hell up."

Mind Your Business

I can almost guarantee you that you're going to see a fight and when you do, don't be running over there to watch like you used to do when you were in high school or middle school. If it don't concern you or your car, and it don't look like it's your race fighting another race, then you need to mind your business. When the fight is over, do the same and mind your business. Don't be walking around asking inmates, "What were those inmates fighting for?" One of the rules for surviving prison is to mind your business and stay out of other people's business. You'll go a long way in prison if you can do that, believe me - I know. If you do happen to look over and see an inmate from your car getting into it with another inmate, it's a must that you run over there to have your homies back to see what's going on. If you end up finding out that the whole argument is all over an unpaid $15 or $20 debt, then help your homie out by trying to defuse the situation by stepping in and telling the other inmate that you will pay the debt if you do got the money. Even if your homie is telling you not to pay the debt, still pay it and get that mess over with.

If this situation ends up coming to blows, think about what awaits you which is 90 days extra added to your sentence. If you give the other inmate GBI during the fight, now you're looking at a whole other charge and a possible life sentence. If you already got 2 strikes, you'll be going to the hole. Plus, getting 8 extra points added to your placement score and now might bring your placement score to a higher custody level and you'll be getting transferred to a higher level prison. Trust me when I say going through all that ain't worth no $15 to $20 unpaid debt!

Don't be afraid to start over. This time you're not starting from scratch, you're starting from experience.

~ *Anonymous*

8
Observant

Being observant in prison is a must. If you're not already an observing person, now will be a good time to start training yourself to be so. It will be even better if you can train yourself to be super observant. What I mean by super observant, is the ability to pay attention to the things and stuff that's around you, making a mental note of it all and then being able to recall what you've seen with accuracy. Even hours later from the time you were at any particular spot throughout your day if needed.

Let's say you and I were cellies and at yard time we went to the yard and started walking some laps. After we went back inside our cell, I started asking you questions about the yard, like, "Did you see that photo album on the yard and where it was located?" You should be able to tell me, "Yes, I saw the photo album and it was lying down next to the basketball pole on the Mexican basketball court." If you and I were in the dayroom together and after dayroom time we went back in the cell and I asked you how many tables do you think are in the dayroom? Your response should be, "I know how many tables there are in the dayroom because I counted all of them when

I was out there and there were 13 tables. The table that's in the far right corner is missing one of the four seats. I even counted all the cells and all the showers and all the ceiling lights in the dayroom and would you like to know how many there were?"

That should be your response because you were being super observant. If you're still using drugs in prison, being super observant like this might be a hard task for you to accomplish simply cuz you're killing thousands of brain cells with each hit of the drug. Brain cells which are needed to accurately store all your mental notes in your memory bank so that you'll be able to recall the information back later. With each hit of the drug, you're frying valuable data.

Being super observant like this and having that high level of awareness of your surroundings, helps you with detecting danger when it's lurking. Because you're always paying attention and noticing all things around you, you'll be able to better pick up on bad vibes in the area. You'll sense when something seems out of the ordinary or just not right. Being super observant like this is a lot easier in prison than it is on the streets. In prison, there's not as much stuff to look at and remember then it is on the streets. Another part of being super observant is paying attention to inmate's body language.

Body Language

Being able to pick up on nonverbal signs, such as, if you see an inmate walking around with his head down, you'll know that something is either really bothering him or he's sad, depressed, or stressing.

If you're talking to an inmate and he's blinking a lot, it could be an indication that he's probably lying to you.

Seeing an inmate roll their eyes as you're talking to him could be an indication that he's probably getting tired of listening to you talking or might think that what you're telling him is a lie or stupid.

When the bridge of an inmate's nose is pulled up or wrinkled between their eyes, you know that they're either disgusted, mad, or confused about something.

An inmate walking with his chin tilted up and his chest poked out could mean that he thinks he's hard.

An inmate not looking you in the eyes when he's talking to you could mean he's nervous, scared of you or lying.

Seeing an inmate wink at you or somebody could mean he's thinking something slick or mischievous.

Seeing an inmate raise and drop his eyebrows quickly could mean he's just seen something surprising, weird or strange.

An inmate sitting down bouncing his leg up and down fast could mean he's nervous or anxious about something.

Seeing an inmate press the side of his mouth to the side as you're talking to him could mean that he's subliminally saying, "yeah, right, whatever" as if he don't believe you.

An inmate drumming his fingers on the table as you're talking to him or tapping his thigh with his hand could be an indication that he's getting impatient with you.

Seeing an inmate rubbing his chin with his hand could be an indication that he's having deep thoughts about something.

When you see an inmate raise only one corner of his mouth as he's smiling instead of both corners of his mouth, could be an indication that he's fake smiling or laughing.

An inmate who is pressing his head between his two palms could be an indication that he's either disappointed, frustrated, exhausted, or sad.

Seeing an inmate just all of a sudden snap his fingers one time could be an indication that he just remembered something or just thought of something he needed to do or forgot to do.

Hearing an inmate all of a sudden clear his throat could be an indication that he's trying to direct your attention to something that he sees and he's trying to get you to look and pay attention.

Hearing an inmate cough as you're talking could be an indication that he's trying to cut you off.

Peripheral Vision

If you haven't already been paying attention to stuff in your peripheral vision, now is a good time to start doing so. Get familiar and be aware when an inmate is walking towards you. That way if an inmate tries to cause you harm by side stepping on you, or creeping up on you, you'll be able to see the attack coming, allowing you to better stop the sucker punch or sneak attack.

Have a peripheral vision space set for yourself so when it gets crossed, it gets your attention causing you to quickly turn your head to see who just invaded your space and see who's coming towards you. A good way to get in tune with your peripheral vision is by extending your right arm all the way out to the right side to where you can still see your hand. Now play with your peripheral vision by moving your hand side to side. Then bring your hand towards your face and away from your face. Next, extend your right hand out and bring it back to where you can't see it in your peripheral vision and then slowly move it into where you can see it again.

Keep doing this exercise until you become aware when something is moving towards you in your peripheral vision. Do the same thing on your left side using your left hand so you could get familiar with your left peripheral vision as well.

*What you think of yourself
is much more important than
what others think of you.*

-Seneca

9
Making Games

Like I mentioned earlier, you're unable to get a quarterly package while at reception center you won't be able to order any board games, like Dominos or card games. However, all hopes of playing all those games are not lost because you can make games yourself to kill time by simply following these easy directions. It's a total of 4 games you can easily make and 3 of the games require you to save up some of the cardboard that your lunch comes in. You can make a chess set, Dominos set, and a deck of cards. The last game you can make only requires toilet paper. With the toilet paper, you'll be able to make some very hard dice to shoot craps.

Chess set - take two cardboard boxes from your lunch and flip them both upside down. Bring them together so that the boxes are touching each other like this:

Now take your pencil and draw out the chessboard squares on the cardboard. Make sure that you have 64 squares total and when you finish it should look like this:

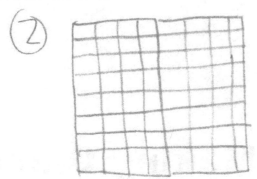

Now take some of your state issued coffee packs, about 13 of them. Open them up and pour them in your state issued cup. Add just a little water in the cup and stir it with your finger. You might need to add a few more drops of water in the cup to make the coffee syrupy looking.

Once you have the coffee all syrupy looking, start rubbing the coffee on the chessboard like you would water paint - skipping a square every time you color a square with the coffee. Once you finish it should look like this :

Now to make the chess pieces for the chess board. All you do is get a cup of water and a toilet paper roll. Tear one sheet of toilet paper square off to make your pawn pieces. Dip the one sheet of toilet paper in the cup of water, remove it, and begin molding the pawn piece together. You're going to need to make a total of 16 pawns.

Once you're finished making the pawns, set the pieces to the side and let them dry overnight. In the morning your pieces will be dry and very hard. Take eight pieces of the pawns and color them with some of that syrupy coffee like you did the chess board, set them to the side to dry.

To make the Kings, Queens, Bishops, rooks and knights, you'll need to use 3 or 4 strips of the toilet paper squares. Repeat the same process you did when making your pawns.

Remember you're going to need: 4 Bishops, 2 Queens, 2 Kings, 4 Rooks, and 4 knights. Once all those chess pieces are dry, paint half of the chest pieces with that same syrupy coffee and allow to dry. You are now ready to play

Making Dominos- to make Domino's you're going to need to neatly cut off dominos size pieces from your cardboard lunch box. Now take your pencil and on each Domino piece mark the necessary dots on each one. You should have a total of 28 domino pieces when you finish.

Making a deck of cards-to make a deck of cards you're going to need to save your lunch boxes and neatly cut off card size pieces and neatly cut off 52 card pieces.

Now take your pencil and on each card mark the necessary numbers on them and draw the spades, hearts, clubs, and diamonds on the cards. There should be a total of 13 of each set and one big and little joker. You could also make a set of pinochle cards by using the same method.

Making dice-to make some dice you need to take four pieces of squares off the toilet paper roll for each dice, then wet the four pieces of squares and begin molding the dice by pinching it using your thumb and index finger. Once you mold the dice let it sit overnight to dry and then in the morning put the necessary numbers of dots on all sides.

To make these games more fun with your celly, set a rule that whoever loses got to do 30 - 40 push-ups straight.

*You can't go back
and change the beginning
but you can start where you
are and change the ending.*

— C.S. Lewis

10
Prison

Know that upon entering a prison environment you're now going to be around a lot of guys with arrested development issues. Meaning, guys who came to prison when they were young like 18-22 years old but are now 30-40 years, and some closer to 55 years old. They're still acting and thinking with that same young mindset that they had back when they first got to prison simply because as the decades passed by, they chose not to educate themselves. Instead, all they chose to do was get high and drunk everyday to help pass the time away and help ease the pain of having to do decades in prison.

You're also going to be around a lot of inmates taking psych pills due to mental illness problems. Some of these inmates are very slow-minded. There are also inmates that are slow due to them being a slow learner. You're going to have to very quickly learn not to take everything personally and you're going to have to be able to overlook certain things that some of them do simply because some of them are truly slow-minded and just don't know any better.

Also, be prepared to have to dummy down and get on some of their levels so that you can try to diffuse a situation before it escalates. Talking normal to some of these inmates, your words will just go right over their heads and they won't fully comprehend what you're saying. And as you well know, lack of communication can lead to bloodshed.

I remember when I was at DVI institution AKA Tracy Prison in 2020. There was this one inmate that I'll just call Kasheff. Kasheff liked my French Montana CD and he wanted to make a CD trade with me. I asked him what CDs he had for trade? As he started telling me one caught my attention, it was a Mozzy CD. So We ended up making the CD trade.

A month went by and I started missing my French Montana CD so I approached Kasheff and told him that I'd give him two CDs for that one French Montana CD back. He asked what two CDs I'd give him and I told him I'd give him a Little Boosie CD and a Keyshia Cole CD. He agreed to the trade. The next day I got a kite, a brief message on a little piece of torn off paper, from Kasheff telling me that I forgot to give him his Mozzy CD back and for me to send it to him with a Porter right now. I looked at the kite thinking to myself, Is this guy serious? What the heck is Kasheff thinking? That Mozzy CD had nothing to do with our second trade. I really didn't know what Kasheff was talking about but I did know that he was on psych meds and he was pretty slow-minded. I ended up writing a kite back telling him that he was tripping and that Mozzy CD belongs to me.

About 10 minutes later I get another kite from Kasheff talking about, "So you ain't going to give me the Mozzy CD back? Alright then, I'll see you at yard time." Finally the bell rang for yard and I went to yard . I walked over to the water fountain to get some water when Kasheff and two of his homies that I knew were in his car, all approached me. Kasheff said to me in an aggressive tone, "Hey man - that Mozzy CD's mine! You need to give it back to me."

So being that I knew Kasheff had mental illness problems and was slow-minded, I dummied down and started speaking slower than what I normally speak to make sure I didn't lose him. I told Kasheff our initial trade was my French Montana CD for his Mozzy CD. Then one month later, I offered two CDs which was my Lil Boosie CD and my Keyshia Cole CD for my French Montana CD back. The Mozzy CD had nothing to do with this second trade of ours. What makes you think I owe you the Mozzy CD?

Kasheff said, "Oh, my bad. Okay, I see it now that you broke it down better to me. I get it." He went on to say that he thought I still owed him that Mozzy CD. I said, "Why would you think that? That was our first trade. The second trade had nothing to do with the Mozzy CD." Kasheff then said "Yeah I get it now." One of his homeboys grabbed him by his shirt, pulling him away and said, " Man let's go. You tripping." And all three of them walked away.

Some might think Kasheff knew exactly what he was doing and that he was trying to pull a fast one on me by saying I still owed him that Mozzy CD. I took it like he was slow-minded and handled the situation accordingly. There's a lot of inmates walking around prison just like Kasheff, slow-minded, slow learner, with arrested development issues that will see a situation for what it really is not. They'll get at you, and be verbally aggressive, but for you to match his verbal aggression will be a very silly thing to do, especially when you know what he's saying is way off. Matching anybody's verbal aggressive tone could easily cause y'all to be fist fighting. Don't match his aggressive tone, it will be best to just remain calm and dummy down so you can straighten this mess out.

Equip yourself with this dummy down tool by speaking slowly and not using big words. When you know that an inmate is slow-minded and they're getting at you wrong, don't be foolish and end up in the hole over one of these slow-minded slow learner arrested development types. I know this may be a hard pill to swallow - trying to remain calm when an inmate is getting at you wrong and verbally aggressive, but it truly would be foolish of you to end up in the hole and get 90 days added to your sentence because of one of those types. Be smart and avoid getting into a wreck with those crash dummies that pretty much don't even know where they're headed in life. You've got your goals planned for your life when you get out of prison, so stay focused and on course and don't get derailed.

Educate Yourself

Going to middle school and high school, I'm sure you heard the same thing I heard - if you got good grades and paid attention in school you were considered a geek, nerd, or a square. Nobody really wanted to be labeled as that when you're trying to fit in with the popular crowd, the cool crowd. And because of not wanting to be labeled a nerd, geek, or square, what did most of us do? We chose not to take our education seriously, wanting to be the class clown instead and ditch school, and now today, most of us are paying for it by being an adult with lack of education.

By not taking our education seriously back then, in today's world, you must be educated in order to get that good paying job. Unfortunately, I had to learn this the hard way. By acting up in class and not taking my education seriously, I ended up getting expelled from high school when I was in the 10th grade. Today, I know that education is everything and that being labeled a geek, nerd, or square really ain't that bad of a label. When you really look at it, it be the geeks, nerds, and squares with all the high good-paying jobs, making six figures or more a year. A nerd, in other words being brainy, puts a person on a higher scale to succeed in life and become successful. You could be a nerd (brainy) and still have swagg and thug to yourself, "I'm sure you were just like me before you came to prison - got high and drunk for breakfast, and got high and drunk for lunch, and got high and drunk for dinner." Educating yourself was not on the agenda, but now that you're in prison, doing prison time is wasted time unless you choose to use that time wisely. What's wiser than educating yourself? Start educating yourself on all the knowledge that you plan to have as a career for when you get out of prison. Educate yourself by building your vocabulary so you can learn new words. Invest in a dictionary if you don't have one.

Pick up a novel, and as you come across words that you don't know, write them down and look them up in your dictionary. Write the meaning of the word out on paper and every night before you go to sleep, study the words. Study the words until you become familiar with them.

Educate yourself by enrolling in some self help groups. The prison self help groups are good because pretty much everybody in the class is doing the positive thing, and trying to better themselves.

Ideas, beliefs, and philosophies get bounced around by all the different inmates in the group, and you can learn a lot. You're not only learning about the self help group material that was designed for the class, but you're also getting valuable knowledge from all the different inmates in the group which is knowledge that will better help you succeed in life. One thing you don't want to do is leave prison the same way you came in. You leaving prison operating on the same ideas, philosophies, and core beliefs that landed you in prison in the first place will just lead to you getting in trouble with the law again, landing you right back in prison.

If you're a Black man reading this, know that back in the slavery days black people would get killed by their slave owner if their slave owner found out that the black slave was trying to educate himself or herself by trying to learn how to read and write. Yes, this is true history. See the slave owner wanted his black slaves to be ignorant and dumb so that he could take advantage of them and keep them in a mediocre position an oppressed state. Those was the old days of slavery but today, being locked up in this modern day slavery (prison) the good thing about this modern-day slavery that you're now in is you won't get killed by your slave owner for trying to educate yourself.

This modern day slavery you wasn't sold to a slave owner, the difference is you put yourself in slavery by doing your crime. Always remember that knowledge is power and without knowledge, you're more than likely to remain in a lower class, getting underpaid for your back breaking work.

Milestone Credits and Rehabilitation Achievement Credits (R.A.C.)

Not only is it good to educate yourself in prison to become smarter, but it's also good to educate yourself in prison so you can get milestone credits and rehabilitative achievement credits also known as RAC credits. By getting milestone credits and rehabilitative achievement credits, you get time off your sentence. They both act in different ways.

To get milestone credits-you will need to get enrolled in either an L-top class school , e-learning course, transitional class, college class or an education class. Then you complete the course and get your certificate of completion. Depending on which one you took, you will get either 14-21 days off your sentence. If you get your GED, you will get a total of 6 months off your sentence.

To get RAC credits-you will need to get enrolled in a self help group such as, Alcoholics Anonymous, Narcotics Anonymous, Al-Anon and a whole lot of other classes. Once you reach 52 hours worth, you will get 10 days off your sentence. Your hours will start all over again, allowing you to be able to get another 10 days off your sentence. You will be able to take as many self -help groups that you want at a time and yes, the hours that you get in each self help group counts as your hours as a whole. During the week if you get 2 hours from your N.A. group, 1 hour from your AA group, and 3 hours from another RAC credit self help group, that means in one week you will have achieved 6 hours worth of RAC credit. The next week after going to all your self help groups, you will now have 12 hours of RAC credits and so on, until you finally reach that 52 hour mark to get another 10 days off your sentence.

With Milestone Credits, you'll only be able to get a total of 12 weeks off your sentence per year. With RAC credits you're only allowed to get 40 days off your sentence a year. If you go over your Milestone Credits or your RAC credits within that same year, then it will all get stored away for you so when next year comes around your Milestone Credits or RAC credits will automatically get rolled over for you. See, educating yourself in prison is a win-win situation.

Clicked Up

Every time you arrive to a prison or jail and walk inside your new building, you should start doing your homework immediately. The type of homework I'm talking about is being observant and paying attention so you can quickly learn who's clicked up with who. This is a good thing to know just in case you happen to get into it with an inmate one day, you will know what car he's from and know all the inmates that's likely to come to his aid, If you did decide that you wanted to take off on a particular inmate. Inmates take their car seriously. So seriously, that if you were cool with a particular inmate but ended up falling out with an inmate that's from his car, chances are that inmate that you were cool with might switch up on you and start acting funny towards you, distancing himself from you, simply cuz he's siding with his homie from his car.

I remember when I was at an out-of-state prison in Arizona in 2017. There was this one inmate that I was hella cool with every time we saw each other. We would always say, "What's up?" to one another. One day, I ended up getting into it with one of his homies from his car because his homie was trying to take my turn in the shower. Me and the homie from his car got into a little argument behind the showers and it ended with his homie being angry at me and me getting the shower before him.

The next day I was chilling by the basketball courts with three other inmates when I spotted that inmate that I was hella cool with walking towards me with his homie, the one I fell out with behind the showers. When they both finally reached me, and the three other dudes I was chilling with by the basketball court, I stuck my hand out like we normally did. But this time, he left me hanging and only gave dap to the other three inmates that I was chilling with. It bothered me a bit, the way he left me hanging but I didn't show it. Instead I asked them how everything was going, but they both ignored me. That's when it hit me that his homie from his car, the dude that I had fell out with, was standing right there with him must have told him about the argument that we had over the shower. He must have told him that I ain't cool, which now caused him to stop messing with me too. As the days went on, I came to realize that I was right because a few more times I said, "What's up?" to the dude I thought I was cool with and he still didn't say what's up back. He just kept on walking like he didn't see me.

I remember this other time when I was at a California prison named California City Correctional Facility Level 2, there was this inmate who used to always come by my cell to borrow CDs from me. He used to always ask me to play chess with him which I always did whenever he would act me. One day, I was in the dayroom when this one inmate was getting at me aggressively saying I needed to stop sweating him over the $2 that he owes me. I wasn't really sweating him. I hit him up on Friday like he told me to do on Monday. When I hit him up on Friday he turned and looked at me like I had do-do on my face and said, "Man, you sweating me over 2 funky little dollars. I ain't got your money yet. Imma need more time." I said to him, "You told me on Monday you'll pay me on Friday. Today's Friday so what's going on with my money?" He got loud and aggressive and repeated himself. "You sweating me over 2 funky little dollars?"

The inmate that be always coming to my cell asking to borrow my CDs heard his homie loud voice and came running over there asking his homie was he straight. That's when the dude told the inmate. "Hell no, I ain't straight. This dude right here sweating me over 2 funky little dollars." That's when the guy that borrowed CDs from me started tucking in his shirt and pulling his pants up which clearly told me that he was ready to help his homeboy from his car jump me. I was not willing to go to the hole over $2. I told the inmate that owed me the $2, "Don't even trip on the $2 man, you could go ahead and keep it. It's all good."

See when a person is giving me the runaround, I become that type of person that would tell him, "Don't even trip on it. You can keep it." I figure that's a good price to pay to get a person that's not a man or woman of his word out of my circle. Besides, if they're trying to play me out of that little sum of money I could just imagine what they'll try when $1,000 is involved. When I tell that person they can keep that little sum of money from that day forward I'm still be cordial with them, saying, "Hi." But they will be cut off from me financially, never to ever get a cent for me. You see, it doesn't really matter how cool you are with an inmate because due to prison politics, he gots to side with his homie from his car regardless of the situation. Do your homework and find out who's all clicked up and who runs with who.

Get Back To Them

Know that when you go to the dayroom or yard talking crap behind an inmates back - know that the chances of it getting back to him is very high. It's possible the inmate who you're talking to might like the inmate that you're talking about, or the inmate who you're talking to might just be in the same car as him. That's why it's good to be cool with all inmates, because once they begin to take a liking towards you - nobody likes to hear somebody talking crap about somebody they like. Chances are high that he will come to let you know about the crap somebody was saying about you, or the harm that he heard that's about to come your way.

Not being stingy and being cordial with inmates, blessing an inmate out of nowhere with some candy chips or food will gain you some extra ears and eyes on the yard. I remember when I was at Solano State Prison the Level 2 side from March 2019 to March 2021, there was this one inmate that used to come by my bunk area from time to time and asked me for a shot of coffee or some ramen soups. I would give it to him even though he wasn't from my Seaside car. I gave it to him and other inmates that used to ask me for stuff as well. I gave to not only build up good karma, but I also gave freely when I had it because I knew by helping an inmate out in a time of need will go a long way. It will keep the animosity and hate down as I do my time. Nobody likes to be told, "No." I know once an inmate took a liking towards me, if he heard somebody talking crap about me, chances are higher that he will come and let me know what he heard.

One day I was on the yard doing my normal workout routine when that inmate I was looking out for with coffee and soups walk up to me and said, "I need to holler at you after you finish working out." I said, "What's going on? What is it? You can holler at me now?" Me and him walked over towards building 16 and he started saying that he heard earlier today in our dayroom that my bunky was telling some inmates that I was a weirdo and how me and him wasn't getting along. He also told me how my bunky also said that a few times he thought about socking me up cuz he can't stand me. I said, "Is that right." Then told him how me and my bunky in fact, wasn't getting along. I then told him, "Good looking out with the information." I proceeded to walk back to the workout area to get my workout on and that's when the guy I be looking out with with coffee and soups stopped me and said, "Hey EB, keep this between me and you." I yelled over my shoulder, "For sure! I ain't going to tell nobody."

I could tell some more stories on how some inmates I was blessing with food and stuff all came to let me know about some trash talk some other inmate was saying about me behind my back. If you feel you want to talk crap about somebody, know that there is a high chance that it will get back to him unless the person you're talking to is from your car. A person in your car will not go back and tell somebody in a different car what you said about him. But if you're talking crap about somebody that's in the same car as y'all both, then it is a possibility that it will get back to him if he took a liking towards that other individual in your car.

Cool with Different Races and Cars

You might be one of those antisocial type of guy that don't like talking much, but at least try to be cool with at least one inmate from each car and cool with at least one inmate from each race. This is good for several reasons. The first reason is, let's say you got an issue or a problem with that inmate that's not in your car or it's not your race, you can now handle this situation a whole lot better by telling the inmate that you're cool with that's in the same car as the inmate you got an issue with. He will go back and talk to that inmate for you to try to resolve the issue that you have with his homie from his car. He may even make him come and apologize to you if what he did was disrespectful or wrong.

If it happens to be an unpaid debt that he keeps giving you the runaround with, then his people will get on him and make sure he pays you what he owes you. If he doesn't, his car will discipline him by jumping him when you bring it to his car's attention. If the inmate that owes you money really don't have any money, then his car will pretty much pay the guys debt. After his car pays you, they will turn around and beat the dog mess out of the guy that owed you the money. This lessens your chances of getting into a fight with a different race by just going to that inmate that you're cool with that's in the same car as the guy that owes you and ask him to help you handle the situation with the guy that's in his car.

The second reason why it's good to be cool with at least one inmate from a different car and race is when the dude you're cool with car is about to go handle some business on the yard (stabbing or jumping) either that day or sometime that week, it's a high possibility that he will let you know what's going to go down. He won't just come looking for you to tell you the news, it will just happen randomly as you're walking to yard, or on the yard, and he runs into you. It will normally happen like this; as you're walking to the yard, you see the guy that's in a different car or race from you and you say, "What's up?" Chances are he will walk over to you and tell you in a quiet voice that his peoples has to take care of some business on the yard today and to avoid a certain area.

The third reason why it's good to be cool with at least one inmate from a different race and car is, when you're trying to sell something like a hot pot, CD, shirt, or whatever you're trying to sell, you can get the word out there way faster by simply going to that one inmate that you're cool with from a different car or race and ask him can he go ask some of his people's are they interested in buying what it is you're trying to sell. When he goes back to where his car or race is hanging out on the yard or dayroom, he will broadcast it to everyone there. When I was in prison, no matter what I had for sale it was gone within a week because I would go to every inmate that I was cool from each car and each race and ask him if he could go ask his folks are they interested in what I had to buy. Being cool with different cars and races widens your range of inmates you can sell stuff to and gets the word out there faster.

Ear Hustle

When you're out on the yard or in the dayroom talking to someone and there's other inmates that are able to hear you talking, it's a high possibility that those inmates are all in your conversation. There's been plenty of times when I would be talking to an inmate, then an inmate who was on the side - who I wasn't even talking to - hops right in my conversation. He'll say something like, "Oh yeah, I seen that too on TV last night. That show was hella funny, huh."

A lot of inmates got this bad, that's why when you're conducting business with an inmate, trying to buy something from him, I would strongly advise you to take the inmate that you're conducting business with to an area where nobody can hear. I can almost guarantee you that if what that inmate is selling is a bargain deal, or is something that the ear hustler really wants, he will hop right in your conversation and begin to step on your toes. If I had a dollar every time an inmate overheard me conducting business then tried to jump in to step on my toes, I wouldn't be rich, but I'll for sure have $7.

I remember when I was in a Oklahoma Prison from 2012 to 2014, I was in the dayroom watching TV and there was an inmate sitting next to me listening to his CD player. I asked him what was he listening to and he said, "50 Cent, Get Rich or Die Tryin.'"

I told him that that was one of my favorite CDs and that I used to bump that CD in my ride before I came to prison. I had told him that I would give him $7 in food for the 50 Cent CD right now. I then asked him if he wanted to sell the CD. He said, "Not really, but I am out of soups right now and can use some." He then asked me if I had $7 in soups inside my cell. There was another inmate sitting on the other side of me who was listening to our whole conversation. He jumped in and said, "You trying to sell that "50 Cent CD for only $7. I'll give you $9 for it." That's when I turned and said, "Hold on man! Why is you all in my conversation? I'm going to buy the

CD so you need to back off." That's when the inmate with the CD said to the other inmate, "You got $9 in soups?" He replied, "Yep."

I knew I only had $7 in soups in my cell that's why I didn't even bother trying to higher bid the guy. Instead, I just looked at the inmate and shook my head side to side, got up from the bench and walked away.

Avoid a situation like this happening to you by simply going over to an area where nobody can really hear y'all talking business. If you can't find an isolated area, just talk low.

Inmate Twitter

Inmate Twitter is not actually a website. Inmate Twitter is the gossip that's spreading throughout the inmates. The way things get started up or posted on Inmate Twitter is by one inmate telling another inmate about some good or bad news that he said he heard. Then that inmate who he just told about the news tells another inmate about the juicy or bad news and before you know it, the news is spreaded throughout the whole prison. For it to get spreaded like this, there has to be some very good or some very bad news. The thing about Inmate Twitter is that it's a 50/50 chance that what you're hearing is fake news - so don't fully believe what's being posted on Inmate Twitter. If you do, it's a high pssibility that you're only setting yourself up for disappointment. For example, the good news that you got all juiced up thinking all inmates will be getting 4 months off their sentence soon for being good through the year, then finding out later it wasn't real at all. When it comes to Inmate Twitter, wait till you see it on paper before you fully believe it - that way your emotions won't get played with.

Subliminal Messages, Hints, and Innuendos

Constantly inmates are throwing subliminal messages, hints, and innuendos at you. If you're not listening carefully to every word he's saying to you, chances are the subliminal message, hint, or innuendo will go right over your head. A lot of times inmates would rather say something indirectly opposed to directly. For instance, say you're in the dayroom sitting on the benches in the TV area. You're talking to another inmate when an inmate comes up and sits down right in front of ya'll. Now the inmate that you've been talking to makes a statement to you like, "You smell that? It smells like onions." You start sniffing the air, trying to smell that onion smell, but you don't smell it. What you do smell is musty, funk that seems to be coming from the inmate that just sat down in front of y'all. In this case, the subliminal message that the inmate you were talking to threw at you, was the dude who just sat down in front of y'all - is very musty.

Here's are some examples:

Say you're at the workout pal on the yard when you decide to take your shirt off. As soon as you do, an inmate starts making bird call noises. You know you got a small chest with little muscles, so know that when you hear those bird call know that the innuendo he is throwing out there is - you got a bird chest.

You're about to get in the shower, you start hanging up your boxers and dry towel on the shower rail when an inmate asks you, "Is that your floor towel?" the subliminal message - your towel is filthy looking being a floor towel is used to clean the filthy dirty floor in your cell

Another example..

You're leaving the store, carrying a bag of food on your way back to your building when you're stopped by an inmate and you begin talking to him. He makes a comment like, "Damn I sure wish I had a couple of soups to eat tonight. They're serving us that nasty vegetable stew for chow tonight I hate that vegetable stew" The hint he just threw at you was pretty obvious, he's asking you for a few soups.

There are inmates that be sex playing a lot of times also. They use subliminal messages, hints, and innuendos frequently. You're at breakfast chow and you ask an inmate if you can have his banana? If he responds with a grin on his face saying, "Oh, I got a banana for you all right." Know that you just been sex played subliminally.

Be aware of inmates that subliminally tell you they don't like you by extending their left hand out to shake your hand, or by extending their left fist out to greet you. The proper and respectful way to shake a man's hand in prison is by using your right hand and right hand only. Pay close attention to an inmate when he's talking to you so you can pick up on all the subliminal messages, hints, and innuendos that he's throwing at you.

Patience

In prison you must be equipped with patience. Not having patience can easily make your prison time hard. Also You will constantly get into arguments with inmates from trying to rush them to do something. Or trying to rush them to finish up something for you. Not having patience could also get you cut off from your friends and family members that's trying to be there for you whal you do your prison time. By constantly trying to rush them to order your package, or handle some other type of business for you, will cause them to get very frustrated and annoyed. To rid themselves from the unnecessary annoyance and frustration that you're causing them, they'll throw their hands up and eventually cut you off. Nobody likes to be rushed. They figure why put up with your annoyance when they really don't have to.

When your package is finally ordered and shipped, don't be asking your building CO every day to call down to R&R to see if your package has arrived. When you're impatient and begin annoying and frustrating to the CO like this, he or she is likely to call R&R and instead of asking R&R has your package arrived yet, the CO will play games with your package and tell the R&R staff to push your package box all the way to the back of the line in retaliation for you bugging him like you been doing about your package, causing you to have to wait 2 to 3 more weeks extra to get your package. If you would have just been patient from the start, you would have gotten your package sooner. So it's essential to equip yourself with having patience.

When you're going about your day in prison, don't be impatient by running to your destination. In prison, you got some inmates walking around spooked about an unpaid debt that he owes someone and is unable to pay the debt. So he's spooked thinking that any minute the guy that he owes might run up on them and by you running past him, his natural reflex kicks in and he takes flight on you first so don't be running past inmates.. You also got them inmates that be on meth and have been up for like 4 or 5 days and they're now walking around thinking that everybody's out to get them. When you're impatiently running to get to your destination and you zoom past those types of inmates - you can easily spook and startle him causing his natural reflexes to kick in and punch you. This will cause you to be in a riot if it was another race that hit you or a one-on-one fight.

Even if you see that you're going to be late to your prison self help group or educational class, still don't run. Have you ever heard the story about the man that was speeding in his car, trying to arrive to his destination on time. He sees that if he don't speed on the highway, he will be late to his destination. So the man is doing 15 mph over the speed limit when he finally gets pulled over by the police. The police officer makes the man do a sobriety test, making him walk a straight line, touch his nose, and blow in the breathalyzer. The man passes all the sobriety test's but the amount of time that it took him to do all the sobriety test's, plus the officer writing out his ticket for speeding, took about 40 minutes . Now the man is going to be even more later than he would have been had he not sped. Had the man just drove normally without speeding, he would have probably only been 4 or 5 minutes late.

The point I'm trying to make here is the man speeding in his car - could be you when you're impatient and in a hurry. The only difference is you will be on foot, running...and your ticket will be coming from a CO for fighting another inmate. A fight that you cause by running past another inmate where you spooked and startled him causing his natural reflexes to kick in. That caused him to punch you in the face. You too will be arriving at your destination late or maybe not at all cuz you might just end up in the hole. If you're not already a patient person, now will be a good time to start training yourself to be one. Always remember, if you don't take your time to do things right then be prepared to find time to do it all over.

Desperate

Every now and then there will be an inmate walking around trying to sell something. Whether it be a hot pot, TV, fan, whatever it is that you're thinking about buying from him - try not to let him see how desperate you really are. Try to hide your excitement. When an inmate sees just how desperate and excited you really are to buy what he's selling, he just might raise his price up some on you. Instead, try to control the tone in your voice so he can't hear the desperation and excitement. Control your face too. Don't allow your eyes to get big with excitement. If he's a super observant person, like most inmates are, he will notice it. Act like you don't really need what he's selling at all and can live without it. When you act that way, it tends to switch the desperation role on him. He's selling what he has because he needs money. When he sees you begin to lose interest in buying what he has, he will start trying to negotiate a better deal for you - even coming down on his price.

When an inmate is selling something, he normally starts with a price that's higher than what he's really asking for it. He does this because he already knows that inmates are going to try to talk him down on his price. When he does come down on his price, it might seem like he just showed you some love, but really, all he did was lower the price to what he wanted all along. If you're desperate and excited from the start to buy what he's selling, he will leave the price high like he had it. He will begin to play his little game with you, being firm and not willing to budge or lower the price. He knows from past experience that any second now you will give in and pay the high price. When you become interested in buying something that an inmate has for sale, play your cards right so you can get a lower price.

Human Chess Game

There are inmates that will play a human chess game with you, using you as a chess piece in his little game. They will act friendly towards you, coming with smiling faces, so it will be hard to tell when you're actually in the game. When you're doing better than other inmates and have a job that other inmates would love to have, this is when you have to be more cautious of being played in someones human chess game. The move that he asks you to make, could actually be a setup play. Your opponent is looking 3 or 4 moves ahead and hoping that you move the exact same way he set you up to make where he later on checkmates you.

I remember when I was in California prison called California City Facility Level 2 from 2014 to 2016 general population in the county of Kern, there were two kitchen job positions that had just opened up. The interviews were going to be held on Friday and Saturday. There were 49 inmates interviewing for the same job. I guess you could say I got lucky for being one of the guys that got picked.

My first day at work my job position was a line server where I stood side by side with four other inmates and put food on the trays as the trays got pushed down the line. The inmate that was working next to me was pretty mad because his homeboy from his car didn't get picked to work in the kitchen. I remember him telling me that he was praying for his homie to get the job position that I now had.

The next day I went to my work area where all the other line servers for my line were. That night for dinner, the main course was chicken breast. The cooked chicken breast was locked up in a refrigerator so that one side of the door was locked, the other side could open enough to squeeze your hand through and pinch out food. The inmate that wanted his homie to work in the kitchen told me that if I sneak all of us some chicken breasts today, then tomorrow on burger day, he'll sneak us all out some burgers. He went on to say that this is what we all do in the kitchen and every day, we take turns sneaking out food so we can all have something extra to eat.

I said, "I'm cool man, I ain't trying to do that." He then said, "Come on man - we do it all the time. Don't be scared. You can't be scared working on the line with us. This is what we do over here - we take turns sneaking food out. Come on and hurry up before we get started serving chow." He went on to say that right now was a perfect time to sneak the food out. I said, "All right man, let's do this." He got me a tray to pile the chicken breast onto and then told me that he will look out for me.

I opened up the other side of the cart and began squeezing my hand through the 3-in opening and started pinching out chicken breasts. I was on my fifth piece of chicken breast when the CO walked up on me and saw the tray full of chicken breasts in one hand and my other hand squeezing through the side of the cart trying to pinch out another chicken breast. The CO said, "What in the hell are you doing Mr Bell? Get your filthy hand out of that food and give me that tray." He told me to get out of here and that I was fired. I did just what the CO asked me to do and as I turned to look at my fellow ex co-workers, they were all laughing. The one who got me to do it was laughing the hardest at me. When I walked past him, I asked him, "What happened man? You were supposed to be my lookout." That made him laugh even louder.

When I finally got back to my house building, inmates were wondering why was I back so soon. When I told them I got fired, they all started laughing too. They couldn't believe I got fired from my kitchen job because I had only been working there for 2 days.

The next day at yard, I ran into a kitchen worker that I had become cool with in those 2 days. He was the kitchen cook and he told me that the reason why those 2 kitchen job positions had got open up in the first place was because those two inmates had got caught sneaking food out. He then went on to tell me that the word in the kitchen was I got set up to get fired. A few days later at yard time, I ran into the kitchen cook again and he told me that the guy who set me up was able to get his homie my old job position working as a line server.

Till this day I still can't believe I allow that dude to use me as a pawn piece, sacrificing me so that he can get his homeboy to fill my work position in the kitchen.

Wants vs. Needs

Controlling our egos through discipline is a lot easier on us than trying to satisfy the ego all the time. By giving your ego what it wants you might get a quick relief from its craving and demands. Your ego is always wanting something that will help it feel good and better. The ego always wants to be kept happy, so we tend to react to the ego's every want. Because you always want to satisfy your ego, you could be putting an unnecessary strain on the people who are looking out for you with packages and money on your books.

You already have the new style of Nike shoes that just came out last quarter and they're still in good shape, but being next quarter you see a newer version of the Nike shoes your ego now wants the newer style Nike shoes. You already got a $250 package on the way, but your ego wants more stuff. You're now out in the dayroom trying to find two more inmates that will let you use their name to order a package. You already got all of your appliances working perfectly but because your ego always wants the newer version of things, you constantly upgrade your appliances. Be happy with the old version appliance that you have as long as it works good, you're straight. Some inmates act that way because they want to seem special in the eyes of other inmates. They want to be looked at as a prison baller so they can get the praise that comes with being a prison baller, and some act that way because they don't got their ego in check. They allow their egos to constantly chase after wants instead of checking their egos to go after just their needs.

I will advise you to get your ego in check. Training it to go after your needs and not always what it wants. Training it to be happy with the last year version of things that you got, that still works perfectly fine. Not always trying to satisfy your ego by upgrading to the newest and better style. Once you get out of prison if you're still allowing your ego to chase after it's wants and cravings you could easily find yourself in a financial mess. That kind of ego can easily get you living above your means.

When you get out of prison even though you can't really afford to set yourself up to pay that $600 a month car note for that

Mercedes-Benz your ego wants, you do it anyway. You really can't afford to set yourself up to pay that $600 a month note for the 28-inch rims to put on the Mercedes-Benz but you do it anyway to satisfy your ego. There you are, struggling to make ends meet, living paycheck to paycheck. See, not getting your ego under control can have you out there putting a major strain on your mental health. The worry and stress that comes with having a high monthly car note, bills, and not being completely sure if you're even going to be able to make ends meet, weighs heavily. It could drive you to the point where you go into panic mode and do something that puts you back in prison. Get your ego in check so that you can lessen your stress level and not be in a financial mess.

Know When Your Being Used

In the jungle the mosquito gets eaten up by the spider, the spider gets eaten up by the raccoon, the racoon by the snake, the snake by the hyena, and so on. The animals and insects feeding off one another in the jungle do it to survive. Us as human beings, we don't try to eat the other person's fleshly meat to survive, instead, we try to eat their pockets. In other words, eat them up economically or financially to survive.

That's why you have so many people that's so quick to try to sue someone because they're hungry and they want to eat his pockets up. In the bars and steel jungle - also known as prison, you will have plenty of inmates acting as real life jungle animals. They'll see the next inmate as prey and will try to feed off him financially. You will have inmates that will be watching you like a vulture to see if you get store or packages. If you do, the vulture will try to befriend you so he can begin feeding off you, constantly asking for your food. If the vulture sees that you got stuff like CD player, good books to read, hot pot, he'll also try to befriend you to try to use your stuff. He could try to borrow them from you. Also these vulture inmates are good at seeming like they're truly your friend but really, they're only after the things you got.

When I was in prison I always kept a lot of CDs. I always stayed with 40 to 50 CDs because I had a good hiding spot for them all. I had to get rid of all the CD cases to be able to hide them good. Even when I was being transferred to another prison, the CO still couldn't find my CD hiding spots. I don't want to put it down on paper exactly where my CD hiding spot was, but if you ever see me and ask me - I will tell you if I feel that you're cool.

I didn't mind letting inmates use my CDs whenever they would come by my cell and ask me, until one day my lifer celly that was in prison for murder said to me, "EB, I want to make a bet with you." I said, "What kind of bet you talking about?" My lifer celly said, "You know you got a lot of inmates always coming to our cell asking to borrow a CD from you? I bet you that if you were to tell them all that you stopped loaning out your CDs because they've been coming back scratched up and you don't want to take the chance anymore - I bet you that they'll stop coming by to ask you how you're doing and to see if you're alright. I bet you that most of them - if not all - will stop even messing with you because they were only using you for your CDs." I told my lifer celly that he was crazy if he thought he would win a bet like that. I then asked him what are we betting for and he said, "Let's bet a week's worth of dinner dessert." I said, "All right, it's a bet."

One by one as the inmates came by my cell I told them all that I stopped loaning out my CDs. Even in the dayroom, when inmates ask to use my CDs I told them the same thing. A week went by and finally I was finished telling them all that I stopped loaning out CDs, and to my surprise only two out of the 14 inmates that I used to let use my CDs still came by my cell to check on me to see how I was doing. When I was in the dayroom or yard, most of them now just walked right on by me without even speaking. This was real strange to me because before I stopped loaning out my CDs, they used to always say, "What's up?" to me whenever they saw me.

This messed me up a little bit cuz I started to see that my celly was right, most of them were just using me for my CDs. Out of the 14 inmates, only 2 of them didn't switch up on me. I went on and told my lifer celly that he won the bet. That night at dinner chow, I began paying off my debt by giving him one week's worth of dinner dessert. Every time I gave him my dinner dessert he had to rub it in my face by saying, "Mmmmmmm," to let me know that my dessert tasted good.

I eventually opened back up with loaning my CDs out to inmates, but I only lent them out to those two inmates that kept it solid with me. I guess you can say what my lifer celly helped me out with was weeding out the real from the fake. Seeing who was just using me for my CDs and who wasn't. So know that with your food, appliances, and CDs there are inmates that will try to be cool with you only to get or use what you got. I would advise you to do some type of test of your own so you can weed out the real from the fake.

When you do loan out a CD to someone that's not in your car, they're likely to try to lock up on your CD, meaning once they borrow a CD from you they won't return it until you ask for it back.

They do this in hopes that you will forget all about the CD so they can keep it. That's why when you do loan out a CD to somebody that's not in your car you should do a one for one, meaning you get a CD from him just to hold for collateral, or to borrow a CD that you like from him to listen to. Also, to make sure it is returned, I used to attach a note on my CD cases saying, "5-day return policy - please respect."

Constantly paying $15 to $20 for a new CD out of the prison music catalog can get pretty expensive. The best way to save up money with your CDs is once you get burnt out on one of your CDs, let inmates that you're cool with know that you got a CD that you're trying to trade. This is how I added new CDs to my collection. Inmates are constantly getting burnt out on a CD, it won't be hard at all finding an inmate to do a CD trade with.

Big O.G. Homie

In prison there's going to be a lot of your Big O.G. Homies locked up behind bars. And as a youngster you're going to be looking for better guidance from your Big O.G. Homie. When choosing the right Big O.G. to soak up game from try your best to use your common sense to see if all the stuff he is telling you is making any sense. I mentioned earlier, you do have them arrested development inmates and those crazy in the mind inmates who you might think is the perfect guy to get positive knowledge from, but actually he's only lacing you up with negative words, advice, and knowledge. All of which will eventually bring you right back to prison.

So if you're a youngster inmate reading this and is soaking up game from an O.G., know that positive knowledge is knowledge that's going to keep you out of trouble. They are words that's going to get you on the right track in life and keep you there. If the O.G. you chose to soak up game from is not on that page, then I'll advise you to find another O.G. Homie to soak up game from. You'll eventually find that O.G. inmate because in prison there will always be those O.G. inmates that can't wait to take a youngster under his wing so he can begin schooling him on the right way to be living as a real man in society.

The sad thing about this is you got some youngsters that go to prison and don't fully know how to be a real man and he will choose one of his Big O.G. Homie from his hood as the one to soak up game and advice from and not even realizing that his Big O.G. Homie is one of them arrested development type, or the real crazy mentally disturbed type, simply because he's too young to recognize the signs. All the youngster knows is that this is his Big O.G. Homie from his hood with all the stripes and who he looks up to and wants to be just like. His Big O.G. Homie will have a life sentence and is still on the negative path and the youngster will be getting out in like 3 or 4 years but since he got soaked up by his Big O.G. Homie with nothing but negative advice and knowledge from - the youngster ends up returning right back to prison for committing a bad crime.

Growing up my real dad was never in my life and my step dad was always working. When he did come home, my step dad would walk straight to his room and close the door. My step dad barely said a word to me. I lacked positive fatherly words and advice growing up as a youngster. I chose to learn how to be a man by soaking up fatherly words and advice from these two ballers in my hood that I looked up to, not realizing that they both were negative people. I wanted to be so much like them. They had nice cars, nice jewelry, and lots of money. When I would hang with either one of them I would mimic their ways and behavior. I took what they said as the way a man was supposed to be. Not even realizing I was soaking up negative fatherly words and advice. I was being molded into a drug dealer, robber, and killer.

Unfortunately, it took for me to have to go to prison to find that right father figure to help get me back on the right track. I found this person one day when I had decided to go to church at the prison chapel at Soledad State Prison. I ended up choosing him to be the one to soak up positive fatherly words after hearing him preach to all of us inmates during a Sunday church service. At the time he was 62 years old and some of the stuff he was preaching damn near had me in tears. His preaching was so deep and the stuff he was saying was heavy. After a while of hanging with this guy he started calling me son and one day he told me that he looks at me like a son. With all the positive fatherly words, advice, and knowledge that he gave me, I can honestly say that he helped change me to become a way better man.

Doing Bad

If you're doing bad in prison with no financial support from your friends or family members, there are several things you could do to stay above water while you do your prison time.

The first thing is to walk around in your dayroom and ask only those inmates that you trust, do they want to use your name for a package? If one says yeah, he will give you $20 or $25 to do so. He will tell you what company catalog he's going to go through then he will tell you to make yourself out a $20 to $25 list of all the stuff you want out of the package. This allows you to get the important stuff you need, like toothpaste, deodorant, etc. You will be able to get four packages a year, but only one package every quarter. This hustle will get you $80 to $100 of free stuff a year to get the important cosmetics that you need.

The reason why I said ask only those inmates that you trust a little bit to get a package in your name is because you do have those inmates that be working with deception. They will use a bad credit card to order that package in your name leaving you in debt with that catalog company. You will be cut off from that company catalog and will no longer be able to order from them again. You won't know it was a bad credit card until weeks after you've gotten the package. Then you'll get a notice in the mail from the catalog company letting you know. That's why I say only ask those inmates that you trust to avoid putting yourself in a situation like this. The best thing to do is watch and see who is always going to the store or is always using the phone, this will let you know that he has money which lessens the chances of him trying to pull a fast one on you by using a bad credit card.

The second thing you could do that will keep you above water is try to get a job working in the kitchen. Getting a job working in the kitchen isn't hard because there's always a job opening. There's two ways to get that kitchen job, one way is by filling out an inmate request form and sending it to inmate work assignment. The other way is by writing down your name and CDC number on a piece of paper and when you go to breakfast or dinner chow, ask anyone of the kitchen workers if they are hiring. He will point you to that CO that is doing all the kitchen hiring. Go over there and speak to him, tell him that you want a kitchen job and that you're a very hard worker. Hand him your hook up name and CDC number that you wrote down on that piece of paper.

When you hand the CO your hook up, make sure you got an inmate standing right there with you because some inmates might think that you just dropped a kite on somebody. But your witness can verify your story. You could also ask one of those kitchen workers if they could give your hook up to the kitchen CO that be doing all the hiring. Once you finally get your kitchen job, you'll be able to eat more plus, you have a pay number so you will be getting money on your books. All the extra food that you bring back to your building from the kitchen, such as burgers, hot dogs, etc, you'll be able to sell it to the inmates in your building. That will be extra money you'll be making to stay above water in prison.

The third thing you could do that will keep you above water is if you don't owe any restitution, you can let an inmate put money on your books and go to the store for him. The going rate in prison is you get $20 for every $100 that he puts on your books. Being you're able to go to the store with $240 dollars a month, you'll be getting $40 a month. But if he puts the whole $240 on your books, then you get $50 a month. With this hustle, you'll be making $440 - $600 dollars a year. You'll be able to get everything you need and then some. But this hustle can be kind of dangerous and frustrating. Let's say an inmate did put money on your books to go to the store for him, but for some odd reason, you weren't able to make it to the store. This might have him thinking that you're playing with his money and he's likely to be getting at you aggressively.

Another reason how this hustle could be dangerous and frustrating is by an inmate telling you that his family just told him that they sent the money to your books but you never received the JPay receipt. Now you're telling him you never got the money but he is telling you that the money is on your books because his family sent it.

If you do decide to do this hustle just be very careful with who you mess with.

Store

If you have money on your books, you will be able to go to the store once a month. They run the store by draws they go off the last two digits of your CDC number. On the day that store is to be run, that morning at breakfast you will need to walk over to the canteen area and drop your canteen slip list in the canteen list slip box. This should be located by the canteen window. As soon as the yard opens up, the store will be open. The canteen staff will randomly call our inmates last names to come to the window to get their store. Listen up for your last name to be called, there will be a big crowd of inmates all standing around so make sure you have your prison laundry bag handy. You can put your food in it because the canteen staff will not give you any trash bags. Also, make sure you have your prison ID.

Man Down

When you start hearing inmates yelling out, "Man down! Man down! Man down!" This means there is an inmate down on the ground and is in need of serious medical assistance. The yelling is intended to try to get the COs attention so he can quickly call for medical assistance.

Man Downs consists of an overdose, a seizure, falling down and can't get up, choking, feeling dizzy, or feel like their blood sugar is too low, etc.

If you're on the top bunk, be very careful getting down because a lot of Man Down's do get called this way due to the guy on the top bunk slipping while getting down off the top bunk and hitting his head on the toilet or floor knocking him unconcious.

Bulletin Board

Every prison dayroom has a bulletin board and it's important to pay attention to what's being posted. That way you can stay up on what is current and what's to come. You'll see things posted on the bulletin board such as, a new self help group that's about to start, or a basketball tournament, or chest tournament, baseball, football, Domino tournaments, college course, a new law that's going into effect soon that will benefit you.

You'll even see sticky notes posted up by inmates on the bulletin board where they're trying to sell something. Paying attention to the bulletin board is how I found out about the stimulus checks economic impact payment that all us inmates were now allowed to get due to the pandemic. Attached next to it was an example of a 1040 tax form showing inmates how to fill it out. Pay attention to the bulletin board, it's a part of being super observant.

Counselor

Every inmate will be given a counselor. A counselor will have an office that you can go to on open line and you will be able to ask him or her any question that you may have, or get something done, a counselor can help you get transferred to another prison that you want to go to. The counselor can also help you get enrolled into any class you want to get into, or work assignments. When you get to prison, find out who your counselor is so you will know who to go to when you have some questions or need something done.

Chow Food

Never just dig right into your prison food without first examining it for stuff that's not supposed to be in it. Before you eat your prison food, take your spoon and move your food around a bit to look for things that's not supposed to be in there. Here are some of the things you need to be looking for. These are the most common things I found in my prison food:

Stickers-the stickers that be taped on to fruit somehow will wind up in my food

Plastic-I would find a little corner piece of plastic like it had been torn off the bag they were opening up to add to the food

Hair-you will find more hair in your food than anything else. This is what you really need to be checking your food for.

There are inmates that are working in the kitchen that really don't want to be working in there anymore, they only go to work to avoid getting a write-up or disciplinary action. Not showing up to work will get you a write up. They are not taking their job seriously and putting very little energy and effort. When any man is being forced to do a job that they really don't want to do, their performance is poor. This is why the prison food will be undercooked or overcooked sometimes. Also, make sure before you take a big gulp of your breakfast milk, that you check the expiration date on the milk carton and always give your milk a sniff before you drink it to see if it has a sour smell. Even though the date on the milk is showing that it's not expired, it can still be spoiled from the milk handlers letting the milk sit out too long before putting it back in the freezer. Trust me I know. Unfortunately, I had to learn this the hard way from me taking a big gulp of my milk before checking it - learn from my experience. It's not cool eating your food then all of a sudden tasting hair in your food. It's not cool taking a big gulp of your milk only to find out that it's been spoiled. The aftertaste that the milk leaves in your mouth will almost make you want to throw up. So always examine your prison food and milk.

Also know that when you go to chow, this is when the COs like to run up in inmate cells or check bunk area's to try to find pruno or contraband. If you are making pruno or got contraband in your cell, know that the CO might find it when you go to chow.

Blood Work

If you have no money on your books, then it will be free to get your blood work done. If you do have money on your books, then it will cost you only $5 to get your blood work done. I strongly advise you to get your blood work done every year so you can see what's going on with your glucose level, LDL level cholesterol level, protein level, calcium level, white blood cell count, red blood cell count - I'm going to stop there but there's at least 35 things they check for in your blood including hepatitis a, b, and c and HIV AIDS. If something is off you can hurry up and start trying to get it back right.

And if it just so happens to be your cholesterol levels that are way too high, you can stop this silent killer from occurring. If you never get your blood work done, then how will you ever know you will pretty much be getting added to the statistic list of people dying from having too much plaque buildup in their arteries, where it cuts off your blood circulation and causes a heart attack or stroke? Did you know many car engines blow up prematurely all because of the owner of the car failing to see what's going on with the engine oil? He will go on his hundred mile road trip, not even realizing that his engine oil is way too low until it's too late and his engine blows up. Be smart and frequently check your oil (blood), that way your engine (heart/brain), don't blow up prematurely (heart attack or stroke).

If you're up there in age, getting your colon and prostate checked for cancer is not a bad idea either. If you catch the cancer early enough before it starts to spread, you may be able to fight it. If you haven't already been doing all this, I would advise you to start doing it so you can live longer.

Any type of surgery you get in prison is free, whether it be a knee surgery, gallbladder, hernia surgery, etc. Back in 1996 I ended up getting an inguinal hernia surgery done. So take advantage of these free surgeries. You can begin to feel better and move better.

Teeth Cleaned

If you have no money on your books, then it will be free to get your teeth cleaned, cavities filled, or get that rotten tooth pulled out that's causing your breath to smell like hell. But if you got money on your books then it will only cost you $5 dollars. Till this day I still don't understand why so many inmates choose to walk around smiling with that yellow hard plaque buildup in between and on their teeth, or blackish stains inbetween their teeth when all they had to do was fill out a medical slip to request to see the dentist to get their teeth cleaned.

You only get one pair of adult teeths. Start taking good care of them by getting your yearly teeth cleaning and flossing. When you get out of prison, don't let your teeth be why it's hard to get a woman. You'll approach her and she thinks you're cute but as soon as you start smiling, she's like, "Oh hell nah, I got to go."

Another reason why you would want to start taking care of your teeth is that way when you get older you won't have to be wearing dentures permanently.

Angel Tree

Every year around June or July a Christian organization called Angel Tree starts sending out their Angel Tree applications along with their Angel Tree Catalog to all prisons in California. Once the prison gets their Angel Tree applications, they start dropping off stacks of applications to every building. If all the Angel Tree applications are gone by the time you get one of them in your building, you can always go to the prison chaplain and pick one up.

The Angel Tree organization provides assistance to inmates so that they can send a free Christmas gift home to their kids that are between the ages of 1 to 18 years old. Once you've chosen the gift that you want to send, fill out the application and drop it off to the prison chaplain.

The type of gifts the Angel Tree Catalog have are books, bibles, girly plastic jewelry, color crowns, and markers. There are basketballs, footballs, plastic cars, dolls, action figures, building sets, and arts and craft supplies. If you're unable to send money home to your kid for Christmas, take advantage of this free Christian Angel Tree gift and send your kid a Christmas gift for Christmas.

Title 15/Dom

In California, every inmate is issued a Title 15. Inmates are not issued a Dom book. If you want to read the Dom book, then you have to go to the law library to check it out. These two books show you all the prison systems rules, regulations, and procedures. When you get ready to file a 602 grievance form for some type of wrong you felt was done to you by the prison system or staff member, it will be a good idea to look inside the Title 15 first and find the section where it points out that you were in fact done wrong. Take that section and write it down on your 602 grievance form to show the prison system that even the Title 15/Dom shows that you were done wrong and now they must correct their mistake. Whatever the wrong was, you can use Title 15 or Dom to quickly find the section that pertains to you.

For example, your wrong was mail do to the mailroom confiscating something in your mail. Go to the index section in the Title 15/ Dom and find the mail section. Read the whole mail section till you find what you're looking for. Whatever you need to find out, go to the index section and read up on it. That way, you can find out if you were done wrong, or if you just want to learn more about the prison systems rules and regulations.

The Yard

On the prison yard there will be areas that you can't walk through because that area belongs to a different race. You will see different races chilling on different benches on the yard. This will be an easy way for you to tell what race is holding down that area on a Level 4 or 3 yard, it can easily get cracking (a race riot) if you walk through another race's area.

On Level 2 or Level 1 yards, you might get a pass for trying to walk through another race's area only because inmates are more focused on trying to go home. It's rare you'll get a second pass if you try to walk in their area again when you have already been warned. Quickly learn what areas are not cool to walk through. That goes for the different races, basketball court, and workout area too.

There is a toilet on the yard but inmates never take a crap on it, they only take pisses. The toilet is filthy plus, there's never any toilet paper. When you take a piss on the yard, have someone in your car standing a few feet away with his back toward you. If you're by yourself and don't have no one to keep guard for you, you can easily find somebody by just asking anybody that's the same race as you can they post up for you while you take a piss and he will do it.

Haircut

Only one inmate from each race will be assigned as the barber to cut his race's hair. You can easily spot who's the barber for your race because he will be walking around with a red metal tool box that will have all his hair cutting supplies in it. The barber goes building to building on a certain day and cut only their race's hair. If you decide that you want to get a haircut from these types of barbers, I would advise you that once you ask him to cut your hair, offer to give him one or two dollars to do it. Even though it is his job title to cut hair for free, he's only getting paid by the prison .11 cents an hour. When these barbers cut your hair they normally will give you an .11 cent haircut, and believe me, them .11 cent haircuts ain't cool looking. That's why whenever you ask these barbers to cut your hair, always offer him $1 or $2.

I remember this one time I went to get my haircut by the prison barber. I got up and walked over to him to see if I could get a haircut. He told me yeah, but then told me that two other inmates are in front of me. I said cool and watched as an inmate handed the barber 4 soups, then sat down to start getting his haircut. When he was finally finished, the other inmate did the same thing. The barber was doing a great job on these inmates' hair. He carefully was taking his time to line the hair up to make sure all the edges were straight and sharp.

When it was finally my turn, I told the barber I wanted the same thing those other 2 inmates got which was to give me a taper fade. I told him I don't got no money right now because I was waiting for my package. I asked him if he'd cut my hair for free. He hesitated for a second and then told me, "All right man, come on here and sit down." When I sat down, he began putting this cape thing around my neck. He began lining my hair up but he didn't use any razor blades to carefully line my edges like he did the other two inmates. Instead, he was using his clippers. He was giving me a rush job. I asked him can he instead line me up with a razor blade like he did those other two inmates. He told me that if he's going to put in that kind of work, he's going to have to get paid for it.

When he was done, I looked in the mirror and saw one side of my hair line was pushed back further than the other side. When I grabbed another mirror, I could use both mirrors to look at the back of my head, one side went up more than the other side. My bunky walked over to me and started laughing. He asked me how much did I pay the barber for that cut? I said nothing. My celly said, "That checks out." I was about to confront the barber about giving me this messed up haircut but my bunky said something to me that made me change my mind. My bunky said, "You can't get mad at the barber for giving you a hair cut like that. You get what you pay for! Since you didn't pay him anything, you got to respect the game." I asked my bunky could he shave my head bald and he did.

Money motivates people to want to work. The more money you pay the person, the more they put into their work. Make sure you always pay the barber, even if he says, "Don't trip." Know that there are other good inmate barbers around who also are not assigned as the prison yard barber. These inmate barbers charge $3 to $4 dollars to cut hair. They are very good at what they do. There are also inmates that French braid hair and will even start you up some dreadlocks. If you want to locate these types of barbers just ask around in your building. They'll point you to him. There's always one in every building and when you do finally find him, for your own sake, don't try to talk him down on his hair price. I'm sure by now you understand why I say that.

Today I decided to forgive you.

Not because you apologized,

or because you acknowledged

the pain that you caused me,

but because my

soul deserves peace.

~ Najwa Zebian

11
The Hole

If you decide that you don't want to equip yourself with the dummy down tool, or the anger management tools that's in this book, then this next chapter will be a place that you will be visiting frequently and it's called the hole.

The hole is a place that the COs send inmates who get in trouble. Being in the hole is the lowest of the lowest in life. You can't get no lower than this. Here are some of the things you'll be sent to the hole for participating in; a race riot or fight, getting caught with drugs, over familiarity with the COs or free staff, getting caught with a knife, or sexual assault.

Two inmates that were caught can avoid going to the hole if they both agree to sign the Marriage Chrono. In doing so, you are saying that the issue between you is resolved and that no further incidents will occur. If you give the other inmate GBI stitches, knock him unconscious, fracture or break bones, then you won't be able to sign a Marriage Chrono and will be going to the hole. Depending on what prison you're at, it will be determined if you're allowed to take your TV to the hole with you. Some prisons allow it and some don't. Some prison holes will even provide you with a crank up radio. That's a radio that has a crank on it and you crank it to juice up the batteries once a week. The CO will come around with books for you to read and you will get yard but it's way different from what you're used to.

When it's your yard time the CO will come to your cell and handcuff you and escort you to the strip out cage. Once you're in the strip down cage the CO will remove your handcuffs, you will then be told to take all your clothes off, squat and cough. You will then be told to put all your clothes back and the CO will cuff you again. The hole yards are just cages about 10 x 15ft. The cages are lined up alongside each other and you will be put inside that cage with just you and your celly. They will remove the handcuffs once you're inside the cage, there's no dip bars or pull up bars, so you'll see inmates doing calisthenics, push-ups, and burpees. You'll see some inmates just walking around in circles in the cage or talking to the next inmate in the cage next to him. The yard is about an hour and a half long.

You'll get handcuffed going back to your cell and escorted. When it's shower time, the CO will handcuff you and escort you. Also, you will be given a face razor to shave but once your shower is over you must return the razor to the CO. The CO will also ask you if you want to use the nail clippers to clip your nails. They're the same nail clippers that all the inmates use in the hole.

You're going to be hearing some inmates communicating to one another by yelling through their cell doors, but the majority of the inmates in the hole communicate to one another by using sign language. Using sign language to communicate is better because it keeps the whole building out of your business. Inmates use the same sign language that deaf people use.

American Sign Language Alphabet

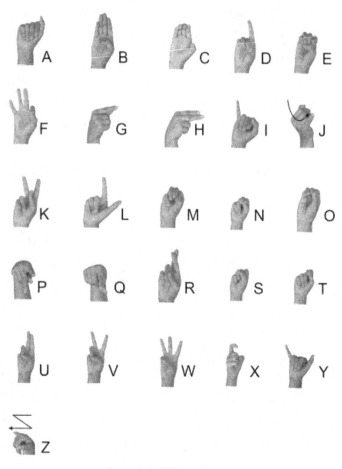

Copyright © 2008 StartASL.com

https://www.startasl.com

Inmates in the hole will spell a word out using the sign language alphabets and once we finish will swat the air one time like you would swat the air to get a mosquito or fly out your face. Then we move on to the next word. We will swat the air or pause between each word.

Being new to sign language you might have to tell him to go slow with his sign language so you can write each letter out until you got the word spelled out on paper so you can read what he's saying. You may just have to do it like that for a while until you get the hang of reading sign language. But if the inmate you're trying to communicate with isn't on the same tier as you then it will be impossible to communicate with him through sign language. The best way to get your message to him will be by fishing him a kite.

Fishing Him a Kite

The best way to communicate with inmates that's on the same tier as you is to fish him a kite. The way you do this is by first making yourself a fishing line.

Here's how, you need to cut several strips of shoestring size strips of material from your sheet and tie them all together creating yourself a very, very long string or rope. Take one of your state peanut butter packs and tie it nice and tight to the end of your fishing line. Write whatever you're trying to tell the inmate on a kite or piece of paper and fold it up and tie it to your fishing line below the state peanut butter pack.

Once you got your kite tied to your fishing line, start calling out the dude's name through your cell door. When he answers you, let him know that you got a kite for him and that it is on the way down. He'll now be standing by his cell door with his fishing line in hand ready to pull your line in. Depending on how far down the tier he is will determine how hard you need to slide the peanut butter pack under your cell door. If he's all the way down the tier then slide the peanut butter pack underneath your door with all your might. If he's just a few cells down from you, you don't need to use that much force.

Once he pulls your line in and reads your kite, he will quickly respond back to your kite and tie his kite to your line. He'll then yell to you to pull your line in. Not only can a kite be tied to your line, you can also tie food, books, papers, and things to your line and then you could pull it in. Once he gets all the stuff off your line that you sent to him. he would then tell you to pull your line in.

If you're on the top tier and you're trying to get something from the man that's on the bottom tier right underneath, there is a way for you to shoot your line down there. I know that sounds impossible but it can be done. With a little skill, you'll be able to hop your fishing line over the rail guarding to get your line to the inmate that's underneath you.

In the morning around 5:00 a.m. to 6:00 a.m. you will hear inmates doing a roll call. Normally this is done with the Southerners or Northes and white race inmates. They will yell out each one of their people's names one by one. This is done to make sure that they're up and programming. They must be up programming when their name is called or they will get in trouble with their people.

When I was in the hole from June 2015 to December 2017 I was going back and forth to court for fracturing an inmate's face. Unfortunately, the prison I was at didn't allow inmates to bring their TV to the hole. Instead, they provide inmates with a crank up radio. The only stations you're able to pick up at that prison was two Mexicans stations, one rock and roll station, and an alternative rock music station. I wasn't feeling none of these radio stations at first but being in the cell with nothing else to do but read a book, I gave the alternative rock music station a try. After a while, the music started to grow on me. To this day I still listen to alternative rock music sometimes.

Never have I heard so many people full of regret until my trip to the hole. When I would go to the yard I heard inmates saying things like, "Damn, how in the hell did I get myself into this?" or "If God gets me through this, I promise I'll start doing better." or "I can't believe I messed up like this." or "I can't believe I let that dude piss me off to the point I ended up socking him in the face like that." It was a lot of shoulda, coulda, woulda.

When I was in the hole the DA was picking up all cases that involved a DA referral. Once inmates court procedures were over and they finally got sentence to their time, I would ask them at yard time, "How much time did they give you?" This one inmate told me that he got seven years for having a knife in the cell. The crazy thing about this guy was the knife he had was just one of those puny fingernail clippers where he broke off the back piece and sharpen it down. It was nothing but a one and a half inch blade. Another inmate got 12 years for threatening a CO where he told the CO,

"I'll kill you." Another got 12 years for getting caught trying to sneak meth and heron in at visiting. He got caught red-handed.

I ended up taking a plea bargain deal for 4 years for my assault with GBI charge. I only got that deal because my victim was telling the courts that his face was already swollen before I hit him. He made a written statement saying that his face was already bruised so the GBI part of my charge went away along with the strike - which all could have gotten me a total of 16 extra years in prison.

I would advise you to try your best to stay out of the hole because your weeks are going to seem like months, and your months are going to seem like years. Your time is going to turn into hard time. Try your best to stay out of trouble while you're on the main line so your time could fly by as your programming.

*I release all things from the
past year that have echoed
any negative attachments
from my early life.
I prepare and welcome
new changes,
new lessons and
new adventures.*

~Ellen Seigel

12
Preparing for Your Parole Board Hearing

If you're not a lifer inmate and don't have to go to a parole board hearing then you might want to skip this chapter. If you just want to learn all that a lifer must learn in order for him to get found suitable for parole and get out of prison, then read on.

The only way a lifer inmate will get out of prison is by learning all that I'm going to share with you in this chapter. In California, a youth offender that got sentenced to over 20 years, but didn't get life in prison has a chance to get out of prison early due to the Youth Offender Board Hearing, Senate Bill 260. This allows youth offenders that committed their crime when they were 25 years old or younger, a chance to go to the parole board. They first must complete 15 years of their sentence. If a youth offender has a life sentence then you must complete 25 years in prison before you could go to the board.

The parole board commissioner is looking to see if you've matured any since the time you committed your crime and got incarcerated. The parole board commissioners understands that being you committed your crime when you were at the age of 25 years old or younger, scientifically, your brain was not fully developed yet. You're more capable of making mistakes - opposed to an inmate that is over the age of 25 years old. Commissioners are looking to see if you have changed your way of thinking and behavior. They are also looking to see if you know all your stuff. The stuff I'm talking about is called a Relapse Prevention Plan and your self help material.

Before I get into a Relapse Prevention Plan, let me first tell you the process leading up to your parole board hearing. You will first be given a consultation hearing which will be 4 to 5 months before your actual parole board hearing. You will go to a real parole board hearing room and sit down with a real parole board hearing commissioner. He or she is going to be looking at your prison file and will tell you what you need to hurry up and make happen to have a better shot at getting found suitable for parole. He might tell you what self help certificates you need to try to get. He might even tell you to get all your Laudatory Chorono. At your hearing, they can see how your prison supervisors judge you on your work performance and what your work ethics are. The parole board commissioner might tell you that you need to get your GED, or a vocational trade. If he or she tells you that you need to get your GED or a vocational trade, there won't be enough time for you to get it before your actual parole board hearing date. So things won't be looking good for you already.

Sample of a Laudatory Chorono

I will advise you if you know you have an upcoming parole board hearing a few years from now, start trying to get your GED or a vocational trade under your belt. That way, when you do go to the board it looks better for you.

When I went to my youth offender consultation hearing the only thing he told me that I needed to get was a domestic violence certificate. I was able to get it just in time before my parole board hearing. It's real good to have a vocational trade under your belt such as, plumbing, welding, carpentry, or painting when you go to your parole board hearing. It shows them that you got the skills to make a career for yourself once you're released from prison.

Soon after your consultation hearing you will be getting a letter in the mail from your state appointed attorney - the person that's going to be representing you at your parole board hearing. If you have money you can get your own good paid lawyer to represent you. Your lawyer will be coming up to the prison to visit you, helping you by giving you tips and knowledge to better prepare for you. Before your parole board hearing, a certified psychologist will be coming to visit you to give you a psych evaluation. The parole board commissioner would know if you pose a low risk, moderate risk, or a high risk to society once released.

If you score a **low risk** at your psych evaluation, that's letting them know that your chances of reoffending or of using violence is this low. Scoring a low risk at your psych evaluation is what you want to try to get.

Moderate risk is basically saying you're in the middle of being a low risk and high risk scoring. A moderate risk is still good. I know plenty of lifers that went to their parole board hearing with a moderate and still got found suitable.

High risk is saying that your chances of reoffending again and your chances of using violence again is high. Getting found suitable with a high score it's not likely. I don't know anybody that went to their parole board hearing with a high risk and got found suitable.

When I went to my youth offender parole board hearing psych evaluation for the first time, I scored a low risk assessment score, but I did not get found suitable. It's rare for any inmate to get his parole granted at first initial parole board hearing. It's always either the second or the third time they go that they will be found suitable. As long as you remember everything I am sharing with you right now, you will get found suitable for parole one day. How I know you will - is because everything I'm sharing with you is everything that some lifer inmates taught me before they left prison after they got found suitable for parole.

This is the phyc evaluation letter showing that I scored a low risk.

STATE OF CALIFORNIA — DEPARTMENT OF CORRECTIONS AND REHABILITATION   GAVIN NEWSOM, GOVERNOR

BOARD OF PAROLE HEARINGS
EXECUTIVE OFFICE
P.O. Box 4036
Sacramento, CA 95812-4036

supervised or sustained experiences from a positive role model in appropriately managing his impulses and behavior in his early adolescence. .

These antisocial behaviors have been evident throughout this term in prison including receiving sanctions for violence. However, these susceptibilities appear to have stabilized in 2015 and he has had no write-ups since then. He also reported he has not used substances the entirety of his incarceration. This suggests he has started to learn the ability to appropriately manage stressors and utilize coping skills on an ongoing basis in prison and which has also coincided with increased maturity and insight. However, he needs to maximize on these gains by continued self-help programming. He should be encouraged to continue his disciplinary free programming and expand his level of insight and awareness into the role of substances in his criminal history.

A risk rating of moderate was strongly considered since the changes noted have been recent and he has mostly had violence related RVRs with the last occurring about 4 years ago. Nevertheless, a low risk estimate was ultimately given due to his lack of substance use in prison (*which was impactful in the instant offense*), completing substance abuse treatment, avoiding negative peers in prison, gaining increased insight and empathy into his criminal history, obtaining certifications and having solid parole plans. The certifications should assist him in obtaining a job upon release. He should be encouraged to continue his disciplinary-free programming and expand his level of insight and awareness and continue taking more substance abuse courses.

Based upon an analysis of the presence and relevance of empirically supported risk factors, case formulation of risk, and consideration of the inmate's anticipated risk management needs if granted parole supervision (i.e., intervention, monitoring), <u>Mr. Bell represents a low risk for violence.</u> He presents with non-elevated risk relative to long-term inmates and other parolees. Low-risk examinees are expected to commit violence much less frequently than all other parolees.

Generally speaking, the current recidivism rates for long term offenders are lower than those of other prisoners released from shorter sentences. The board defines overall risk ratings relative to other life prisoners.

Charles Odipo, Ed. D., CCHP, CA License # PSY19345
Forensic Psychologist
Board of Parole Hearings / Forensic Assessment Division
California Department of Corrections and Rehabilitation

BELL, Emanuel   V60946   Page 14 of 15   BPH COMPREHENSIVE RISK ASSESSMENT

Some of the information I'm about to share with you is taken from actual self help parole board hearing material.

The first step in doing good at your psych evaluation and parole board hearing is remaining disciplinary free for at least 8 years the more years you stay disciplinary free the better.

Secondly, you must have some self help certificates and will need to be able to speak on all of your self help certificates, knowing the meat and potatoes of them. In other words, knowing all about it. The more self help certificates you get the better. You will need to write a book report for all your self help groups. This will show them that you know your stuff.

When I went to my psych evaluation, I handed over book reports on every self help group I took. It was a book report on Anger Management, Criminal Thinking, Substance Abuse Program, Domestic Violence, NA, AA, Victim Awareness/Impact, Family Relationship, and Emotional Management.

Going to the law library to check out self help books to do your book reports is also good. If you can't get a particular self help group that you need within the time of your parole board hearing, then go to the library and check out a book on it. It looks even better when you got the actual self help group certificate to show them.

And when you do a book report, try to get it all down to one page. The psychologist and parole board commissioners don't really have time to be reading a three or four page book report. If you hand over to them six book reports and each book report is three to four pages long, that would take a long time to read. Being your parole board hearing is only one and a half to two hours long, and time needs to be spent on answering their questions instead of on your book reports. Narrow your book report down to just one page for each self help group.

You must know all the 12 steps to an AA class or NA class by heart which are:

1. We admitted we were powerless over alcohol — that our lives had become unmanageable.

2. Came to believe that a Power greater than ourselves could restore us to sanity.

3. Made a decision to turn our will and our lives over to the care of God as we understood Him.

4. Made a searching and fearless moral inventory of ourselves.

5. Admitted to God, to ourselves, and to another human being the exact nature of our wrongs.

6. Were entirely ready to have God remove all these defects of character.

7. Humbly asked Him to remove our shortcomings.

8. Made a list of all persons we had harmed, and became willing to make amends to them all.

9. Made direct amends to such people wherever possible, except when to do so would injure them or others.

10. Continued to take personal inventory and when we were wrong promptly admitted it.

11. Sought through prayer and meditation to improve our conscious contact with God as we understood Him, praying only for knowledge of His will for us and the power to carry that out.

12. Having had a spiritual awakening as the result of these Steps, we tried to carry this message to alcoholics, and to practice these principles in all our affairs.

You must remember these 12 steps because you will be asked what's your favorite step, what step has been the most useful for you, and which step are you currently working on right now? If you're unable to tell them the answer to these questions then that will be a strike against you.

When I was asked what steps have been the most useful for me - was step 4. Taking a personal inventory of my insight, I was able to gain better insight of my past along with my triggers and causative factors.

And to answer the second question, which step am I currently working on right now? I said step 10 because. I'm constantly taking a personal inventory of myself and when I am wrong I promptly admit it.

The psychologists might ask you to recite the whole 12 steps. Don't get caught off guard. Turn off the TV and radio and start remembering the 12 steps - like you would if you had to remember lines for an audition you are about to attend for a star character role.

You must take a searching and fearless moral inventory of yourself. That will help you with gaining insight of yourself. Not taking a personal inventory of yourself is like going to take a college finals exam test without ever reading and studying the necessary college textbook. You will not do well.

To take your personal inventory, grab a piece of paper and pen and write down on the top of the paper the year you were born. Now skip four lines down and write down the year you were 1 years old then skip four more lines down and write down the year you were 2 years old. Repeat the same method of numbering the years and ages of your youth all the way up until the present age that you are now.

Now start writing down the tragic events that you witnessed or been through at that age. Such as when you were 7 years old all the way until your parents got a divorce. You used to always witness your dad beating your mom. This shaped your way of thinking and believing that a man is supposed to hit his girlfriend or wife to keep her in check.

Also find the year and age you joined a gang and write that down. If you are a gang member and not knowing what year or age you join a game is considered lack of insight. Having lack of insight can be grounds for denying your parole. Find the year and age you first started using drugs, that goes for any type of drug you took. Write that down next to the year in age. Remember, lack of insight can be grounds for denying your parole.

Find out what age you first:
    started drinking alcohol
    started carrying a gun
    first had sex with a woman
    first time you had a girlfriend
    worked at a job
    times you were arrested
    molested as a child if you were

If you were abandoned by either your mom or dad, write down that year. Being abandoned by your dad at a young age shows you lack the fatherly words, advice, and guidance. This could be a good reason to show why you grew up behaving like a menace to society.

If you're in prison for murdering or attempted to murder your girl friend wife, showing the parole board that you were abandoned at a young age by your mom will help make sense to the reason why you killed your girlfriend or wife when she tried to get a divorce or break up with you. Her trying to leave you, brought back your old heartbreaking feelings of being abandoned as a child. With those old abandonment feelings that you carried with you until this new relationship, when she tried to leave you - it brought back your abandonment feeling which drove you to the point where you lost control and snapped. Explaining that you understand how you got triggered (abandonment issues) and why your crime happened, shows you got insight and this is what they want to know that you know.

You're going to need to tell when you decided to turn your life around. It's a guarantee that the psychologist and the parole board commissioners will talk to you about your childhood, adolescence, and your adult days. If you fail to know what year and age something happened in your life then this is considered lack of insight which is grounds for a denial of your parole. Carefully study and remember your year and age chart. You need to be able to connect the dots leading up to your crime.

While doing your psych evaluation, the psychologist is typing on his computer your answers. You need to be careful what you tell him because his job is to send a copy of your psych evaluation to your parole board commissioners. They will be talking to you about it. You will also get a copy of your psych evaluation. Try your best to remember everything that you said, because what you say to your parole board commissioners when they ask you questions needs to match up with your psych evaluation report.

You must also know your core beliefs. A core belief is your view towards the world and life in general such as, all polices are corrupt, or trust no one. Normally poor core beliefs get instilled in us as a child by people like your parents, uncles, big brothers, someone in your gang or someone we look up to.

Here are a few examples of how core beliefs get instilled in us:
Your dad is always hitting your mom and one day your dad tells you that the best way to keep your woman in check is by hitting her. Believing what your dad told you, you're now quick to hit your girlfriend to try to keep her in check.
Your uncle tells you that you got to get it how you live and being you're out there in the streets running around, you now believe robbing people and breaking into homes is how you got to make money.

As a youngster, we take what they say to us and start acting accordingly and we end up carrying that negative core belief all the way up into our adulthood. This is how many prisoners end up in prison. Think back to your younger days and try to figure out who it was that instilled such negative core beliefs inside of you. The psychologist and parole board commissioners are going to want to know that you know who it was.

They're also going to want to know that you know your internal triggers and external triggers to your anger.

Internal triggers for anger - being rejected, betrayed, being pressured, being left out, abandoned, humiliated, or losing at something. Have specific triggers so they know you understand what they are.

External triggers for anger - seeing somebody getting bullied, seeing your girlfriend flirting with another man, having to wait in a long line, being put on hold for a long time on the phone, having a friend not pay you back the money that he owes you, being wrongfully accused, having rumors that are not true spread about you, or somebody stealing from you. Just think of the things that anger you.

Warning signs to your anger - my physical warning signs to my anger is my heart rate increasing, tightening in my throat, or my body begins to get hot. And my behavioral warning signs are when I begin pacing back and forth, throwing things, swearing, withdrawing from others.

My emotional warning signs are when I feel hurt or sad. **My cognitive warning signs** are when I start thinking about causing harm to that person that triggered my anger, or having hostile self-talk to myself saying, "I don't know who the hell he thinks I am, but I ain't the one to be messing around with I'll bust your head."

Coping skills for controlling anger - when they ask you what are your coping skills for your anger they want to know what things you do once your warning signs starts happening. They want to hear things like:

> **Thought stopping -** this is when I tell myself to stop thinking those negative thoughts because they're only going to get me in trouble.
>
> **Time out -** this is when I remove myself from the person that's getting me angry and go for a walk. While I'm walking I'm simultaneously taking in deep breaths and counting to 10 over and over while I think of the best way possible to handle

the situation peacefully and respectfully. Once I'm finally calm down and come up with the solution to handle the situation peacefully and respectfully, return back speaking assertively and calm in a respectful manner

Positive visionary - this is when I go to a peaceful or beautiful place in my head. Other words, a happy place in my head. Visualizing me either surfing on the beach or riding in my car with the top down as the wind blows in my face. Whatever your happy places, let them know what calms you down. Visualizing these things always seem to work with controlling my anger, because it shows me that if I ever want this picture in my head to come true, I need to stay focused and not let my anger get the best of me.

Positive self talk - this is when I tell myself that I'm doing good in life right now I'm finally on the right track and I can't allow this person that's triggering my anger to derail me and throw me off the right track.

Weigh the consequences - this is when you tell them that I weigh the consequences in my head, seeing the negative outcome of my actions if I allow my anger to get the best of me and using violence will only cause me a setback. Saying that the negative outcome will either land me in prison or cost me a lot of money, or even losing a friendship relationship, it shows me that to use violence is just not worth it.

Exercise - I go exercise to blow off some steam and this always seems to do the trick.

I vent - I call up a trusted friend or whoever you trust to vent all my problems.

Meditate - I find a quiet place and meditate.

I pray to God - whenever I pray to God connecting myself to him. It puts me in a humble peaceful state of mind which always do the trick with lowering my anger.

Listen to music - when I listen to soothing music, it helps bring my anger down. These are all good coping skills but if you got something else that works better for you, add that too.

Internal triggers for drug use and alcohol - feeling bored, depressed, lonely, mad, grieving for a loved ones, wanting to fit in, wanting to feel pleasure, or just wanting to escape.

External triggers for drug use and alcohol use - know that external triggers for drugs and alcohol use are people, places, and things. When they ask you what are your external triggers for drugs and alcohol use, they want to hear things like bars, clubs, or parties. The reason why those places are considered external triggers is because at those places people are using drugs and alcohol, seeing someone using drugs or alcohol will cause you to develop a craving and if you're not strong enough, you will give in.

Warning signs - not eating regularly, not sleeping regularly, stop going to your NA and AA meetings, you getting the I don't care anymore attitude, stuck in self pity, constantly thinking about using drugs or alcohol, or stop calling your sponsor those are all good warning signs you can tell your psychologist.

Coping skills to help prevent a relapse - I call my spiritual advisor or sponsor, I read my Bible or a book to take my mind off the use of drugs and alcohol, or the way the negative consequences of using drugs and see the outcome is not good, or I will avoid even going to bars clubs or parties. If somebody was to ask me to use drugs or alcohol, I would say no and walk away.

Support group - the psychologist and the parole board commissioner will ask you do you have a support group meeting people that's going to help you get on your feet once your parole?

Causative factors - the parole board commissioner and the psychologist will want to know that you know why you committed this crime? Some examples of causative factors can be lack of anger control, childhood abuse, or abandonment issues, etc.

C-file - you will get a chance to get on the computer with your counselor before you go to your parole board hearing to take a look at your c-file. When you get that chance, make sure everything is correct and updated in there because that same c-file of yours is what the parole board commissioners will be looking at. If you see an error in your c-file tell your counselor so he/she can fix it.

Remorse - not showing remorse can be ground for denying someone's parole. Never use the word victim when talking about your victim to the psychologist or parole board commissioner, you must say your victim's name. And no, not only do you need to show remorse for your primary victim, you must also show remorse to your secondary victims that were effected by your crime. This is called the ripple effect and it includes the first responder, the police officers, the witnesses, and the victim's family.

Also know that there's three types of ways to show amends to your victim:

The first way is called **direct amends-**this is when you write your victim an apology letter showing remorse.

The second way is called **indirect amands-**this is when you're helping, our assisting people that are close to your victim, such as, volunteering your time to help out with something or giving money to a charity that you know he or she is a part of. Being you know your victim love dogs, you can make a charity donation to the animal shelter.

The third way is called **living amends-**this is when you completely turn your life around and start doing things to better yourself and become a better person, such as, involving yourself in self help groups or going to church.

WHAT DOES IT MEAN TO HAVE "INSIGHT" (Culpability, Causative Factors, and Remorse)

☆ Insight ──▶ Culpability
──▶ Causative Factors (What led up to the crime) ── understand of self
──▶ Remorse

* These three components are essential to be found suitable for parole.

CULPABILITY

* Def. deserving blame; meriting condemnation or blame esp. as wrong or harmful. Blameworthy.

* By having culpability, you're taking FULL RESPONSIBILITY!!!!

* My def. Even though I could've prevented, avoided, and alleviated the life crime, I deliberately chose not to; and I am the only one who is responsible for this horrible crime.

* Just by saying "I take full responsibility . . . " doesn't mean you're taking full responsibility.

* To be culpable, you first have to know what happened in your life crime. It means you know the facts of the crime.

* To find out what happened, you should study your probation report, court transcript, Board Packet, Appelate Decision, or police report.

* One of the first statements you'll hear in the hearing is "Nothing that happens here today is going to change the findings of the court. We're not here to retry your case. We're going to accept as true the findings of the court."

* When your description of the life crime shows difference to the records that the CDCR has, the commissioners WILL say that you are not taking full responsibility.

* Often, when there's a discrepancy between your version and the records, the commissioners will say that you're 1)minimizing, 2)justifying (rationalizing), or 3)blaming.

* Understanding your conviction
  - First degree murder and attempted murder have premeditation.
  - Second degree murder conviction requires malice.

* Common statements of not taking FULL RESPONSIBILITY:
  - "it was an accident"
  - "I didn't meant to . . ."
  - "He started the fight; I was defending"
  - "I didn't participate in the murder; I was just . . ."
  - "I didn't know he would die"
  - "I only wanted to rob him"
  - "I didn't know my codefendant would kill him"
  - "I didn't pull the trigger"

* Mindset that leads to Minimization, Justification, and Blaming

- Good guy stance: When you adopt this thinking, you consider yourself to be a good person, no matter what. You may not only consider yourself a good person, you may think you're better than others! You probably don't think you're a criminal thinker at all.

- Victim stance: You view yourself as a victim first. It doesn't matter what you have done to victimize others. The victim stance is a common way to defend yourself when you are held accountable for your behavior. The victim stance allows you to blame others for the situations you usually have created for yourself.

- (obtained from Criminal & Addictive Thinking)

* Taking culpability (Full Responsibility)

- Accept your conviction and know your conviction.
- If you minimized, justified, or blamed in the previous hearing(s), tell commissioners about the denial or shame you may have had.
- Tell commissioners about the intricate parts of the crime by revealing the details about the crime that you only know.

e.g. "Before I went in to the store, I told myself that if anyone resisted, I would shoot him."
"I wasn't taking 'no' for answer."
"My gang mentality at the time wasn't going to let this person disrespect me."

* Often the commissioner will give you a lead way of explaining your version of the crime on your initial to set the record. It's VERY IMPORTANT that you describe your version of the crime without any discrepancy from the record that CDCR has!!!!

* If you're innocent of your crime, you will need to discuss this issue with your attorney.

Credibility - you are being judged on your credibility. No matter how honest, a mistake you make about your childhood insight, or your record, will lessen your credibility. That's why you need to go with what your court records and probation report says about how your crime happened. The psychologist and parole board commissioners are going to believe your court records over what you're saying. If you try to change up the story, they will say you're either downplaying the situation, minimizing, or not taking full responsibility. Yeah, I know some of the facts in the court records and probation report are probably not 100% accurate, but you still need to agree to it and just go with it. I know this is pretty unfair but to avoid them even thinking you are not being credible, you need to just go with what your court records and probation report says.

Take full responsibility-you must take full responsibility for your actions involving your crime. You must also take full responsibility for all the write-ups you've got while in prison because they are going to bring up - every one of them.

You got to avoid saying things like;
    it was an accident
    I didn't mean to do it
    he started the fight
    I was just defending myself
    I didn't know that my co-defendant was going to shoot him
    Etc, etc...
Using statements like those show you are not taking full responsibility for your actions.

Don't minimize - avoid using words like just, only, or never. You will get denied parole if they see that you're minimizing. Here are some examples of minimizing, blaming, and justifying sounds like this;
    He came after me so I shot him. If you say something like that, you are blaming. Instead, you will want to say something like, my gang mentality at the time wasn't going to let anybody come after me so I shot him.

    I saw my girlfriend in bed with him. I shot them both. If you say something like that you are justifying. Instead say, I felt betrayed by my girlfriend when I seen her in the bed with another man. I immediately got mad. I felt abandoned all over again. I felt they both needed to be punished, so I shot them both dead.

    I only shot him one time. If you say something like that you are minimizing. Instead, you should say, when I pointed the gun at him and shot him my intentions was to kill him.

Know that what you say in your parole board hearing will not be retried again. You will not be taken back to court. Just agree with everything that's in your court records and probation report.

Contributing factors - substance use or carrying a gun or weapon or being dependent on others or not being employed or hard time maintaining a job or partying or hanging out with negative people

Underlying issues - experiencing traumatic events at a young age is usually strong emotions that is within you often without your awareness examples of underlying issues are:
> Being abused physically or emotionally by parent
> Witnessing a death
> Lack of anger control
> Low self-esteem
> Being ridiculed and picked on at school

You must be able to articulate where your causative factors, contributing factors, and underlying issues all came from. Failing to identify the life experience will just be buzz words to them, meaning you know the words causative factors, contributing factors, and underlying issues but you really don't know what they mean or how to put the words into use.

Causative factors - in other words, why did you commit this crime? Here are some examples of causative factors:
> Childhood abuse
> Abandonment issues

Here's a look at how roots grow before a tree grows a trunk, branches, or leaves and that is all similar to how the causative factors, underlying factors and contributing factors all work.

UNDERLYING ISSUE(S)

* Underlying issue (also known as underlying causative factor(s)) is the issue (problem) that initiated all your deviancy (straying away from the norm of society).

* Think of your underlying issue(s) as the root of a tree.

* As a root grows before a tree grows a trunk, branches, or leaves; your causative and contributing factors grow out of your underlying issue(s).

*

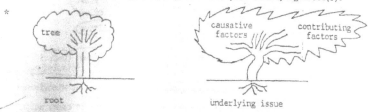

tree

root

causative factors

contributing factors

underlying issue

* Underlying issue(s) is (are) usually developed at a young age through experiencing traumautic event or period in life.

* It or (they) is(are) usually strong emotion that is within you, often without your awareness.

* Common experiences that create underlying issue(s):

- being abused or neglected (physically or emotionally) by a care-giver (parent(s))

- witnessing perpetual violence growing up. Circle of violences

- witnessing violent death.

- being ridiculed or ashamed by peers.

- being raised in a household that normalizes violence and/or criminality.

* Common underlying issues

- Hurt (pain)    - Resentment   - Abandonment

* Understanding where your causative, contributing factors, and underlying issues come from.

- unless you can identify the life experience where they were created, what you tell the psych or commissioner will just be "BUZZ WORDS."

* Examples:

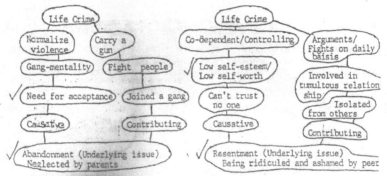

* Being able to articulate without Blaming or Justifying or Minimizing!

- When you merely speak of the life experience, often it comes out as you're blaming or justifying.

- To explain what factors led up to the life crime, you should identify your causative factor(s) first then state what happened.

"He came after me so I shot him." (Blaming)
"My gang mentality at the time wasn't going to let anyone come after me, so I shot him."

"When I saw her in bed with him, I shot them both." (Can sound like a justificat
"I felt betrayed and instantly I became angry. I felt abandoned all over again. My mindset at the time wasn't going to let this go and I shot both of them to punish them."

"My co-defendant shot the worker, and we ran out." (May sound like shifting blam
"Before we went in to the store, my greed for money wasn't going to tolerate any resistance. My co-defendant and I made up our minds that we'll shoot anyone who may come across our way."

Your causative factors and contributing factors grows out of your underlying issues.

You must be able to articulate where your causative factors, contributing factors, and underlying issues all came from. Failing to identify the life experience, where they were created, will show the parole or commissioner and psych evaluation you don't know your lifestyle history, in other words - connecting the dots, leading up to the crime and that will be grounds to deny your parole.

So with your fearless and searching moral inventory chart that you made out for yourself began connecting the dots and tie your core beliefs that will be the only way you'll ever get found suitable for parole and out of prison.

There's different formats on what a relapse prevention plan looks like. This is how my relapse prevention plan looked. This is the one I took with me when I went to see the psychologist for my psych evaluation and when I went to my parole board hearing. They both said it was a good, relapse prevention plan.

My Relapse Prevention Plan

EMANUEL BELL-V69940
C16-102 low

Relapse Prevention Plan

I realize staying drug free will heighten my chances of becoming and staying successful. I will also enroll myself in anger management class and if the anger management class is already filled up I will enroll in an alternative to violence class .in order to ensure Im successful on parole I'll avoid high risk situations by avoiding bars,clubs,and other places where drugs and alcohol are used..Not if but when temptation to use drugs or alcohol arises I'll seek help from my sponsor or spiritual advisor. Other techniques that I can use should I be tempted are reading sobriety literature, praying or urge surfing. I will think of the negative consequences when tempted. I have learned what my triggers are and I will avoid them whenever possible. I have accepted that my sobriety is my responsibility and that relapse is a process (trigger, thought, craving, then use). By knowing this I can interrupt the process before it accelerates.

EMANUEL BELL-V69940

C16-102 low

THEN AND NOW

2003 age 24	------	2019 age 40

I didn't realize how many people were victims in my crime.

I now understand the ripple effect of my crime.

I was an alcohalic and a narcotic abuser I was insane and my life was unmanageable.

I'm no longer an alcoholic or narcotic abuser. I got 16 years clean. I'm now restored back to sanity and my life is now manageable.

I was impulsive in my thinking and actions

I now take at least a minute to think things through and ask myself about the consequences.

Had no religion and did not know who Jesus or God were.

I am now a Christian and read my Bible daily to and go to church.

I thought police were the enemy.

I now realize the police are not my enemies, we need police to keep the world safe. They are here to protect me from criminals.

I did not know who to control my anger.

I now have great tools to manage my anger.

I did not respect a woman's free will to leave me in a relationship.	I now respect a woman's right to do as she pleases. I now respect a woman's free will to do as she pleases.
Didn't really know how to treat my girlfriend.	I now treat my girlfriend like I would want someone to treat my mom, niece, or daughters.
I was belligerent, hateful, and emotionally immature.	With God in my life now, I'm now more at peace with the help of my self-help classes and with growth. I'm no longer emotionally immature.
Did not take self help groups.	I will keep my AA, NA, and anger management groups in my life even after I get out of prison. I now see the importance of them. While incarcerated. I achieved over 13 self-help group certificates and I will continue to take self help groups even after I get out of prison. I now see the importance of them.

EMANUEL BELL-V69940

C16-102 low

I now realize it's very important to be surrounded by only positive people. Because having negative friends around me. I will eventually get in trouble. When I get out of prison I will continue to use all the tools that I learned in my self help groups. To avoid a drug relapse. Plus I'll use all the tools that I have learned in my anger management and emotional management class to control my anger.

Special Events - I will avoid bars, clubs, and house parties where alcohol is being used. Alcohol will be a trigger for me.

Environments - I will avoid known drug areas where drugs are being sold. I must avoid known drug areas not only because of the drugs around but also because drug areas are filled with negative people.

MANAGING MY ANGER -COPING SKILLS

Not if but when I get mad or angry I will quickly use my anger management tools to stop the climb on my anger meter scale. I understand that anger is an emotion that is within me for the rest of my life and if I didn't take the necessary time-out to work on myself to gather anger management tools to handle anger, I would have remained a threat to society and myself. Some of the tools I now have to control my anger are:

Decisional Balancing - that's when I weigh the pros and cons of a situation so I can see all the negativity that will follow my actions.

Thought Stopping - That's when I tell myself through a self-command to stop thinking of thoughts that are making me angry, such as," I need to stop thinking these thoughts I will only get myself in trouble if I continue thinking this way," or, "I will tell myself it's not worth it I will not allow him or her to derail me from goals."

Time-Out - Remove myself from the situation by telling him or her that we'll talk about this later. As I'm walking away, I'll be taking deep breaths, counting them as I breathe. Plus, I will think about the consequences of the situation and thinking about the best way to handle the situation peacefully. Once I figure it out I will return talkin assertively to resolve the situation.

Positive Self-Talk - Remove myself from the situation and go take a walk, taking deep breaths and telling myself positive self-talk, such as, "I'm doing good in life right now plus I got my freedom and I can't allow him or her to throw me off track."

Positive Imagery - Remove myself from the situation, take deep breaths and count each deep breath. At the same time, I'm flashing beautiful peaceful images in my head, such as me walking on the beach on a hot summer day, or me on a cruise ship relaxing by the pool.

MY INTERNAL WARNING SIGNS TO MY ANGER

I now know my body very well and know when I'm getting angry because my body gives off warning signs.

EMANUEL BELL-V69940
C16-102 low

Internal Triggers to My Anger
Rejection
Betrayal
Being Humiliated
Abandonment

Solutions
Read my Bible, pray, exercise, read a book, talk to sponsor, call
spiritual advisor, attend my anger management group, and deep
breathing.

My Internal Warning Signs to My Anger

My Physical Cues
Heart rate increases, tightness in my throat, feeling hot, or body
tensing up.

My Behavioral Cues
Pacing back and forth
Raising my voice
Stare angrily at a person
Handshaking unsteadily
Clenched jaw

Emotional Cues
Hurt, sad, disrespected, fear

Cognitive Cues
Hostile self-talk

Images of me hitting the person
Thoughts of revenge

Solutions
Not to take everything personally, relax my body and take deep breaths in and out.
I can even have positive imagery.
Thought stopping.
Count to 10
Positive self-talk
Tell him or her we'll talk about this later and walk away

MY SUPPORT GROUP

Mary and John Doe- They will be here for me giving me words of encouragement. They will help me by giving me positive advice and they will push me to continue in my recovery and assist me in living a positive lifestyle. They are my Spiritual Advisors.

My uncle John Doe- He will give me the push to achieve all my goals just like a big brother would.

My Parole Agent - I will add him to my support group on the day I parole he will assist me in a lot of ways, encouragement, bus passes, words of advice, and much more.

Sponsor - Upon enrolling in my NA group I will get a sponsor.

EMANUEL BELL-V69940

C16-102 low

GOALS

My Most Immediate Goals

Get my ID card - 1 week

Get to my accepted transitional housing and utilize all services there - 1 day

Get my Social Security card - 1 week

Get medical card for healthcare and dental - 3 weeks

Get clothing for job interview - 2 days

Get cell phone and set up email account so employers can either call me or email me - 3 days

Get bus passes - 1 week

Find out which trucking school offers the best opportunity for me so once I graduate from there I can drive a truck for the company - 4 days

Get copy of birth certificate - 2 weeks

Get list of parole resources from my parole agent - 2 days

Look on the internet to find the closest NA group by my residence - 5 days

Enroll in that group - 1 week

Look on the internet to find the closest anger management class by my residence - 5 days

Enroll in that group - 1 week

My Short Term Goal

Find a good Baptist Church to attend - 1 month

Find a gym and get membership to maintain my physical fitness and good health - 2 weeks

Get a small apartment for rent - 6 months

Get my Trucking license by enrolling in trucking school - 10 months

Open a savings account for my two daughters - 6 months

Get my Class C driver's license so I can start driving back and forth to work - 1 month

Begin getting a quite reacquainted with my positive family members only - 3 months

My Long-Term Goals

Begin paying mortgage on a home - 2 years

By my own big rig truck - 3 years

Donate money to Shriners Kids - 3 years

Send my two daughters to college and make a better life for them - 2 years

---

PAROLE PLANS

I will be paroling to a transitional housing on day one of my release. I will begin working on getting my ID card with the help of my transitional home. I will gain full-time employment and work hard. In the months to follow I will save as much money as possible. I am confident I'll be able to support myself Upon finishing up my stay at the transitional home which will be in 6 months, but if they allow me to stay a little longer I will do that so I can save up even more money. I know I have a hard road ahead of me. I know everything takes time it don't happen overnight. But with the help of my support system and with God on my side I am confident I will reach all my goals and become a positive tax paying citizen upon paroling.

Contact parole agent -1 day
Go to my transitional home - 1 day
Add to my parole agent to my support group -1 day
New ID card - 1 week
Get birth certificate - 3 weeks
Get list of parole resources from my parole agent - 2 days
Employment will get help from my transitional home to find job - 1 week
Get bus passes - 1 week
Get my Social Security card - 1 week
Enroll in NA management. I will get on the internet to find the closest groups by my residence.
Get clothing for job interview

There's still a lot more to be learned about your psych evaluation and going to your parole board hearing. There have been over 80 to 90 books that have been written on this subject but I narrowed it down a bit. What I shared with you is pretty much the basics. Incorporate those words into your vocabulary and know what they mean. I would still advise you to attend a prison self-help group on preparing an inmate for his psych evaluation and parole board hearing. One of the best groups I know about in prison is called Bridge to Freedom. Try to enroll yourself in this group because it is a good group to help prepare you for your up and coming parole board hearing.

Remember, if you don't know this stuff (relaspe prevention plan material) and don't have a relaspe prevention plan written out for yourself, you will not get found suitable for parole.

My Story
How I Started Using Drugs

In 1991 I was 12 years old. I was like most kids my age that had parents who smoked crack cocaine. Being they smoked crack cocaine in those years, they paid very little attention to their kids, failing to give us that parental guidance that a kid really needs in order to stay on the right track, away from drugs, and out of trouble. I was able to do whatever I wanted to without having to worry about getting in trouble with my parents. I was born in Salinas, California in 1978 on November 19th. I was raised in a city called Seaside in California about 30 minutes away from Salinas.

From the age one through 14 years old, my life was pain-free. I had no hurt inside of me. In 1993, when I was in the 8th grade going to Martin Luther King Middle School at the age of 14 was when my hurt and pain began. That was also the age I started using drugs, weed, and alcohol to try to numb the pain I felt inside of me.

It happened like this - my mom had gave me $100 to buy this moped. I kept asking her to buy for me. About 3 weeks later, my younger cousin Fred Wyer Jr. who was 13 years old, saw me riding my moped and now he wanted one. So he asked his dad Fred Wyer SR. to buy him one and his dad bought it for him. Two days later, me and my cousin Fred met up on mopeds at my grandma's house. I told my cousin Fred, "Let's play follow the leader on our mopeds." He agreed. So we rode off on our mopeds on that April 3, 1993 day in Seaside with Fred following me. I was the leader then later on, we switched up and I began following him on the moped. At the top of

Broadway Street, which has now been changed to Obama Way, we switched back to where I was now the leader and Fred was to follow me. I pulled the moped throttle all the way back and began heading down Broadway Street. I looked back and saw Fred was about two bus lengths behind me. My moped was a little faster than his (my cousin) moped. I made a left turn into a apartment complex right on the corner of San Lucas Street. I stopped to wait for my cousin Fred to catch up. As I'm stopped, looked back, waiting for my cousin. As I watched him began to make his left turn into the apartment complex - that's when a truck speeding up Broadway hit Fred from the side. I watched as Fred flew about 6ft in the air with his helmet flying off his head. I watched as Fred came landing down hard on the street hitting his head on the concrete. I quickly got off my moped and ran over to Fred and what I saw is still vivid in my mind today. I watched as blood oozed out of his mouth and him twisted all up like a pretzel with his arms and legs all twisted up in every direction. Paramedics eventually came and later that night the word came back that Fred had died.

R.I.P.
Fred Wyer Jr.

Not too long after my cousin's death I began using drugs. I would go over to one of my partner's house who used to go in his dad's stash spot for weed. At the age of 15 years old, I began driving a car. My first car was a 1973 comet Mercury with a 302 engine. This also was the age I started drinking liquor. I would pick my partners up in my car and head on over to Safeway where we would steal some liquor. By the time I was 16 years old I started selling crack cocaine and because the money was coming in so fast, I smoked weed everyday.

After school I would drive over to one of my partners house that we labeled the station. Members of my crew would all pile up in my car and another car sometimes, and we would drive back to back to get weed and liquor and head down to the beach to HotBox. Sometimes we would just park right in front of my partner's house - the station - and we would all get our smoke and drink on.

Around this time I was known in the city for tearing the streets up by burning long ass rubber up and down the street and doing donuts. Mostly everytime me and my partners finished getting high and drunk, I would drive around Seaside burning long ass rubber in my 302 Comet Mercury with the 302 engine in it.

My life took another turn for the worst when I was in the 10th grade at school. Me and 2 of my homies from my crew decided to ditch last period of class and go to my car that I always parked on campus and smoke a blunt. As me and my 2 homies passed the blunt around in my car, a PE class was being let out and they began walking past the car parking lot heading to the baseball field. My partner was in the back of the seat and seeing somebody that he knew he rolled the window down and started to call his name. The student that he called out to, started walking towards us. That's when my other partner that was in the front seat rolled down his window and yelled to the student that was walking towards my car to not come over here. But the student kept coming towards us smiling the whole way as he approached us.

When he finally got to my car he said, "Damn that weed smells hella good. Let me get a hit." As soon as he said that, the school security guard came out of nowhere and began shouting to the PE student that was standing by my car. "Hey, what you doing over there? Get away from there!" The school security guard started walking fast towards my car. My homie in the back seat said, "I'm out of here!" He opened his door and ran like he was in a track race. Thats when me and my other partner got out and started running too. We all went our separate ways. I ran straight to my last period class and when I sat down the student next to me said, "Damn you smell like weed."

After class as I'm heading to my car, I was stopped by the school principal who had a police officer with him. The principal said that he needed to talk to me inside his office so we began walking there. As I walked into the building heading to the principal's office, I saw both of my partners sitting on the bench with a police officer standing next to them. Once I finally made it to the principal's office I was told that I was being expelled from high school. The principal continued talking to me and I learned the reason for me being expelled was cuz when my car got searched after we ran, they found a weed pipe, a pocket knife, and a $20 bag of weed. Later that day I went to my crews hangout spot and found out that my other two potnas that was in the car smoking with me also got expelled.

So I ended up going to a continuation school at Monterey Adult School and got my high school diploma. I was now 18 years old. Shortly after that, I ended up being homeless and this is how that happened - I was chilling in my room in Seaside, California when I began to hear my dad yelling my mom's name over and over again. When I opened up my door, I ran to where my step dad was yelling from which led me to the garage. When I opened up the door, a cloud of smoke hit me in the face I began breathing in the crack smoke. I watched my stepdad vigorously shake my mom by her shoulders as she lay on the ground, yelling out her name, "Cathy, Cathy, Cathy," over and over again. Two of my parents' friends just stood by in shock as my mom just layed there on the floor motionless. My dad looked over to me and yelled out to me, "Call an ambulance!" I sprinted to the phone that was in the living room and dialed 911. My mom was taken to the hospital and we later found out she had a brain aneurysm caused by years of smoking lots and lots of crack cocaine. I guess it's true what they say that last hit could be your last hit. Even though my mom pulled through the brain aneurysm, she was no longer the same person. That brain aneurysm did major damage to her brain to where now she needed a caretaker. Because Mom was no longer able to help Dad out with the rent, we lost our housing and me and my parents became homeless.

At the time I had a yellow 1972 Malibu Chevy and that's what I slept in for about 3 weeks until I decided to ask my brother that lived in Salinas with the mother of his child, "Can I stay with you for a while?" and he allowed me to. My mom eventually found her a place to stay which was with one of her friends, but my stepdad couldn't find him anywhere to live, so he just continued to sleep in his 1984 BMW. He lived in his car for about 2 months until he decided to just move back to his home land in Florida.

Not too far from my brother's house in Salinas was a well-known drug area called Chinatown. In Chinatown, I was able to start making some money to feed myself by selling crack cocaine. I eventually made enough money to be able to get my own apartment upstairs in my brothers apartment complex. But I lost that apartment one day when I went to jail at the age of 19 for a DUI. When I got out of jail, I began living with my brother again and I began back selling crack cocaine down in Chinatown.

I eventually meet a woman named - I'll just call her Smookums. Smookums had her own place and she ended up letting me move in with her. One night I was driving in Salinas around 11:00 p.m. heading to 7-Eleven to check to see if my mega lottery ticket was a winner. I never made it to 7-Eleven because to my surprise I had a backlight out on my car and when I got pulled over by the police, he told me that he smelled alcohol on my breath. He then asked me have I been drinking I lied and said no. The officer then asked for my driver's license, insurance, and registration. As I dug into my pockets looking for my driver's license I couldn't find it. I began frantically looking in the glove compartment for my driver's license but I couldn't find it there either. I told the police officer that I can't find my driver's license, that was when the police officer told me to step out of the car. He did a sobriety test on me telling me to blow in this machine and it showed that I was over the 00.8 limit. I was then booked into the county jail and my car got towed. I was told to strip naked then squat and cough, that was when my bag of rocks fell from my butt cheeks. The police officer told me to step back and when I did, he quickly picked up my dope sack. Later I was charged with possession of crack cocaine for sale being my 22 baggies of 20 dollar rocks were all individually wrapped up.

My girlfriend Smookums ended up bailing me out of jail that night and as I'm out of jail going, back and forth to court, me and Smookums were getting into lots of arguments. Before I got sentenced to the 4 months with 5 years joint suspended, me and Smookums ended up breaking up.

This is my Possession of Cocaine Charge

SINGLE, CONCURRENT, OR FULL-TERM CONSECUTIVE COUNT FORM
[Not to be used for multiple count convictions or for 1/3 consecutive sentences]

SUPERIOR COURT OF CALIFORNIA, COUNTY OF: MONTEREY

FILED
JAN - 5 2004

PEOPLE OF THE STATE OF CALIFORNIA vs.
DEFENDANT: EMANUEL BELL
AKA: EMANUEL DEON BELL

DOB: 11-19-78
CASE NUMBER: SS012332A

SHERRI L. PEDERSEN
CLERK OF THE SUPERIOR COURT
DEPUTY

ABSTRACT OF JUDGMENT – PRISON COMMITMENT – DETERMINATE
SINGLE, CONCURRENT, OR FULL-TERM CONSECUTIVE COUNT FORM

For those of y'all that don't know what a 5-year joint suspension is that means once you get out of jail you will be on probation for 5 years and if you mess up on probation within those 5 years, you will have to go serve those 5 years in prison.

My Story
How I Ended Up in Prison

To make a very long story short, I ended up getting two woman present at the same time. I don't want to say their real names so I'll just call one of my baby mom's Smookums and the other Johnson.

I decided to go to Johnson's house on the day of Oct. 19, 2003 to try to work things out between us, but we ended up getting into an argument while I was loaded on P.C.P. (sherm) and I lost my cool and freedom for 18 years for stabbing her.

ABSTRACT OF JUDGMENT – PRISON COMMITMENT - DETERMINATE
[NOT VALID WITHOUT COMPLETED PAGE TWO OF CR-290 ATTACHED]

CR-290

SUPERIOR COURT OF CALIFORNIA, COUNTY OF: MONTEREY, SALINAS DIVISION

PEOPLE OF THE STATE OF CALIFORNIA vs.
DEFENDANT: EMANUEL BELL
AKA:
CII# A11540134
BOOKING #: N/A
COMMITMENT TO STATE PRISON
ABSTRACT OF JUDGMENT

DOB 11-19-78

SS033129-A   -A
-B
☐ NOT PRESENT   -C
☐ AMENDED
ABSTRACT   -D

FILED

MAY 1 3 2005

LISA M. GALDOS
CLERK OF THE SUPERIOR C
J. NICHOLSON

DATE OF HEARING: 02-03-05
DEPT. NO: 10
JUDGE: LYDIA VILLAREAL

CLERK: DEANNA DERUOSI
REPORTER: TINA GORRELL
PROBATION NO. OR PROBATION OFFICER: DAVID VARGAS

COUNSEL FOR PEOPLE: ELAINE MCCLEAF, DDA
COUNSEL FOR DEFENDANT: LORRAINE FAHERTY, DPD   ☒ APPTD

1. Defendant was convicted of the commission of the following felonies:
☐ Additional counts are listed on attachment ___ (number of pages attached)

CNT	CODE	SECTION NO	CRIME	YEAR CRIME COMMITTED	DATE OF CONVICTION (MO/DATE/YEAR)	JURY	COURT	PLEA	TERM (L,M,U)	CONCURRENT	CONSECUTIVE 1/3 VIOLENT	CONSECUTIVE 1/3 NON-VIOLENT	CONSECUTIVE FULL TERM	INCOMPLETE SENTENCE	NEW STAY	PRINCIPAL OR CONSECUTIVE TIME IMPOSED YRS	MOS
1	PC	664/187(a)	ATTEMPTED MURDER	2003	12-09-04		X		U							9	0
2	PC	273.5(a)	INFLICT CORP INJ ON SPOUSE	2003	12-09-04		X					X				1	0
3	PC	273a(a)	GBI CHILD	2003	12-09-03		X					X				1	4
4	PC	243(b)	BATTERY ON PEACE OFFICER	2003	12-09-03		X					X				0	8

2. ENHANCEMENTS charged and found to be true TIED TO SPECIFIC COUNTS (mainly in the PC 12022 series). List each count enhancement horizontally. Enter time imposed for each or "S" for stayed. DO NOT LIST ANY STRICKEN ENHANCEMENT(S).

CNT	ENHANCEMENT	Y/S	ENHANCEMENT	Y/S	ENHANCEMENT	Y/S	ENHANCEMENT	Y/S	TOTAL
1	PC12022(b)	1	PC 12022.7(e)	5					6	0

3. ENHANCEMENTS charged and found to be true FOR PRIOR CONVICTIONS OR PRISON TERMS (mainly in the PC 667 series). List all enhancements horizontally. Enter time imposed for each or "S" for stayed. DO NOT LIST ANY STRICKEN ENHANCEMENT(S).

ENHANCEMENT	Y/S	ENHANCEMENT	Y/S	ENHANCEMENT	Y/S	ENHANCEMENT	Y/S	TOTAL

4. ☐ Defendant was sentenced pursuant to PC 667 (b)-(i) or PC 1170.12 (two-strikes).

5. INCOMPLETED SENTENCE(S) CONSECUTIVE

COUNTY	CASE NUMBER

6. TOTAL TIME ON ATTACHED PAGES.

7. ☐ Additional Indeterminate term (see CR-292).

8. TOTAL TIME EXCLUDING COUNTY JAIL TERM: 18 | 0

This form is prescribed under PC 1213.5 to satisfy the requirements of PC 1213 for determinate sentences. Attachments may be used but must be referred to in this document.

Page 1 of

Form Adopted for Mandatory Use
Judicial Council of California
CR-290 (Rev. January 1, 2003)

ABSTRACT OF JUDGMENT – PRISON COMMITMENT – DETERMINATE
[NOT VALID WITHOUT COMPLETED PAGE TWO OF CR-290 ATTACHED]

Penal Code
§§ 1213, 1213.

I am not lucky.

I am blessed.

13
Preparing for Release

Anxiety

Once you are finally within one month of release, anxiety will begin to build up inside of you. The closer you get to your release date, the more anxiety you'll experience. This is normal and all inmates experience this kind of anxiety as they get closer and closer to our release date.

Anxiety means anticipating a negative outcome and having self-doubt about once capacity to cope with it.

That's why it is very important that you continue to remind yourself that you will do okay upon parole from prison, that you will easily find a job, get back on your feet, stay above water, and become successful in life. Even if you got nobody in your corner, or no family members house to parole to, you will still do good upon parole from prison.

Tell the parole plan person that will come to see you 90 days from your release date that you want to parole to a transitional house. They will find you one in your community. Normally you have to parole back to the county that you got arrested in, but if you have safety concerns paroling back to your own county then tell the parole plan person and he or she will find you a transitional home in a different county. By law you cannot parole within 35 miles from the victim's home.

Transitional homes will have resources to help you find work. You'll be able to leave the transitional home and find a job. Employers know that convicts allow them to receive a $9,000 credit towards W.O.T.C. You will be able to save up thousands of dollars from your job, once your stay is finally over at the transitional home, which is normally 6 months - but you can get an extension if you ask, it will not be hard for you to get yourself a nice size one bedroom apartment.

And if you are a religious person know that the devil will be trying to destroy your blessing. He will be sending some of his inmate demon possessed troops at you to try to mess your out of prison release date up. Around this time you're really going to need to be using all the tools and knowledge that is in this book. Don't give the devil the satisfaction at laughing at you because he was able to mess up your release date.

When I was at Solano Prison on the Level 2 side from 2019-2020. I was enrolled in a NA group. Every Friday my NA group was held from 5:30 p.m. to 8:00 p.m. A total of 60 inmates were in my group. There was this one inmate that all us other inmates called the life of the NA group because he would always be quick to raise his hand to read when nobody else wanted to. He made us laugh with his jokes and when there was a silent moment in the class, he was quick to come up with something to talk about. I'll just call him Boobie. One day Boobie had happily told all of us how he only had 4 months left until he gets out of prison and how he can't wait to get back to his kids.

Two weeks after Boobie made that statement, he was sent to the hole for murder. A stabbing took place on the yard and the inmate that got stabbed died on the scene. The CO believed Boobie was the one that did the murder cuz the blood that was all on Boobie allegedly came from the dead victim and anyone that was at Solona Prison on the Level 2 side in 2021 knows exactly what I'm talking about. So when you get close to the house, know that the devil is laying traps out for you to hold you back from getting out of prison.

On Your Stuff

Without a doubt some of the inmates that know you are to be getting out of prison soon will be hitting you up, trying to get locked in on some of your property. They'll be like, "Let me get all your CDs when you leave." Or "Let me get your Hot pot, CD player, TV, etc."

They're going to be trying to strip you for everything that you own all the way down to the shirt off your back. This can become pretty annoying because once you do finally tell them they can have a particular item, they will be constantly reminding you until the day you leave making sure you haven't forgotten about him.

When I was in dual vocational institution AKA Tracy State Prison general population during the pandemic from April 1st 20 until the day I paroled on 6/8/2021, one of the biggest mistakes I made was letting inmates know when I was to be released. The first thing that came out their mouth was, "What you going to do with your TV?" Or "What you going to do with your hot pot?" Once I told them, "Nothing. I'm not doing nothing with it," they'd quickly say, "Let me get it when you leave."

I had a total of 8 inmates that were all locked in on my stuff and on the morning I was paroleing, I made sure they all got what they had asked of me. But before I paroled, they all annoyed me a bit with all the constant reminders. At least every 3 to 4 days, one of them came to my cell and asked me if I am still locked in. On the yard when I'd be walking, they saw me and be like, "Don't forget about me! You ain't forgot about me have you?" The only time I caught a break from the constant reminders was whenever my building would go on a 14-day quarantine lockdown due to somebody testing positive for the covid-19. As soon as the 14-day quarantine lockdown was over, the constant reminders will start back up.

So know you will be getting constant reminders too once you let inmates know the day you are to parole.

Dressouts

If you look inside any of the catalogs that you're allowed to order a quarterly package, turn towards the back of the catalog and you will see a section called Parole Items. This section allows inmates an opportunity to buy themselves some real street clothes to walk out of prison. Within 2 months of your paroleing, order your dress out like Levi pants and shoes. Once it gets to the prison, the prison R&R department will hold your clothes for you until the morning that you are to parole. If you're unable to afford some brand new dress out clothes from the catalog then you will be able to parole in your gray or white sweatpants that you've been wearing in prison with your sneakers. If you have no prison clothes to parole in, your prison R&R will provide you with some free clothes and shoes. They'll give you some free sweatpants and t-shirt and black prison shoes.

When I was paroled my dress out clothes was a pair of new 550 Levi fitted jeans, a white T-shirt, and some new Nike Cortez shoes. I will admit it felt good leaving prison in some real street clothes. I like the way I was able to blend right in with society without anyone even knowing from my clothes that I had just recently walked out of prison.

$200 Gate Money

On the day that you parole you will get $200. This money is called gate money. All inmates paroling from prison gets this money. It's supposed to be used for your transportation fee so you can catch the bus home, but a lot of inmates use it for other things.

I remember 4 different inmates that told me how that after receiving that $200 gate money the last time they got out of prison, they went to spend some of it on drugs. One of them said he bought some heroin. The other 3 inmates said they went and bought some meth. Hearing these inmates tell me about their trip to the dope man's house with some of their gate money, made it obvious for me to see how they all ended up right back in prison. Their main focus after getting out of prison was to get loaded on drugs instead of trying to keep a clear mind. A mind that will help them better with making better decisions and better judgment. Staying clear minded fresh out of prison will make it a lot easier for a person to get back on their feet.

They'll be able to read the required handbook for the job, retain all the information better, and be able to pass the required knowledge test for the job. A lot easier due to their brain not being in a fog on drugs. I would advise you to at least give yourself a fighting chance at becoming successful in life and getting back on your feet by not going out like them. These dudes chose to instantly get high with some of their gate money. Be smart! You only get one life to live and know that using them heavy drugs is like pushing the fast forward button on your life.

Hard Work

When you're out looking for a job don't be one of them foolish guys that will see a job for hire but see that the job duties is hard work and start telling yourself that this job is too much for you. You mustn't be foolish like that. You can't afford to let good opportunities pass you by. Being fresh out of prison, you got to rise to the occasion and work your hardest no matter what the job is. You're starting from scratch, trying to get on your feet and the only thing that's going to get the ball rolling so you can become successful in life, is a job and hard work. Believe me when I tell you that the work you're looking at eventually gets easier. The same way doing prison time was hard for you at first but as the weeks and months went by, prison time got a lot easier for you to do well. As your body constantly do the hard work, your body will eventually get used to it. Just like when you are starting out working out a muscle that you haven't worked out in years. At first, the workout will be difficult and strenuous but as you keep at it and start building, the workout becomes a lot easier to do. Same is true with that hard job.

In the meantime, on them days when you like throwing in the towel and quitting your job, I want you to start thinking back to those days when you were locked up in prison, how you were forced to shower with all those naked men, how you were forced to live in a bathroom size cell, how sad your kids sounded on the phone when they told you that they miss you and can't wait for you to come home, to get back in their lives. How you had to go all them years without a woman's touch. Think back to all the mess you had to go through in prison and let that be used as motivation to give you the push you need so you can keep pushing on to do the hard work at your job that's required. Also, think forward, picturing yourself one day finally reaching that goal that you set for yourself in life and how that a job and hard work will be the only way to make that happen.

Also, when you're homey approaches you, talking about how he knows how you just got out of prison and if you ever need a front or some ounces of meth or cocaine to just let him know and he'll front you the drugs - again, think back to all the mess you had to go through in prison and ask yourself, "Do I want to go through all that mess again?" Because, if you accept his offer, then 9 times out of 10, that's where you'll be headed because selling drugs won't last forever and you'll eventually get caught.

Be the turtle, making that slow money from working a job and let your homie continue being the rabbit making that fast money from selling drugs. I promise you will one day eventually pass your homie, the rabbit, up. One day when he gets caught selling drugs - and I'm not trying to sound like no hater but selling drugs don't last forever. He will eventually get caught one day - it will stop his flow of money and while you're still working your job. That's when you'll pass that rabbit up financially. Your money will still be flowing in. It may take a year or two or more, but you will eventually pass him up as he sits in prison.

There are resources available to help you find a good job. Check in your local resource center.

But know that hard work alone won't make you successful in life. You also going to need to have faith. Without faith, you're likely to start believing that becoming successful in life is not possible. Not having faith in anything you do can discourage you and start making you lose self-confidence, feel discouraged, and lack self-confidence. These can make you lose your motivation and willpower to keep fighting on to becoming successful in life.

When hard times hit you or when you have a set back it's your faith that gets you through it. Believe that you will come out of it okay and that everything will work itself out. If you have faith in yourself and are a hard worker - you will truly one day reach all your goals in life.

Building a Safety Net

Being fresh out of prison, a smart thing to start doing right now is to start building yourself a safety net of at least $10,000 saved up in the bank. You may have to make a temporary adjustment on your spending habits and lifestyle, but the sacrifice will be well worth it. Instead of going out to eat at restaurants everyday, get yourself some rice and beans to eat. Basically, go out and buy some of that cheap food you been eating up in prison. Instead of trying to look flossy with that new whip with the nice rims that you got to pay a high car note on, go to marketplace on Facebook or Craigslist and find a cheap car for yourself. They have plenty of cars in there for under $2,000 that runs good. This sacrifice that you're making on your lifestyle won't be long and once you finally have that $10,000 safety net saved up in the bank for yourself, you will be glad you made the sacrifice that you did for the peace of mind you will now be experiencing. If for some odd reason you end up losing your job, or get evicted, you will know that you still be able to stay above water with your safety net funds. Until you find yourself a new apartment or job, you won't have to go into panic mode, frantically moving around like you're on a ship that is sinking. That safety net is also good to have for any type of emergency that life may throw at you such as, your transmission went out and now you quickly need a new one. That safety net will also bring more joy and laughter into your life simply from getting that uplifted spirit that money somehow brings upon a person that have thousands saved up in the bank.

Remain Fit and Healthy Like You Were in Prison

You've been working out all those years in prison so now you're fit, in good shape, and healthy. Don't end up losing focus on keeping your body in good shape and healthy by working out and eating right. Don't make excuses for not working out like when you get off work you're too tired to do anything, or have other important things to do instead.

If you look at a lot of COs in your building, you'll see that a lot of them are out of shape with Homer Simpson bellies. That's cuz they're putting in so much overtime at work that they just can't find the time to work out. This is one of the reasons why so many COs have died at work due to a heart attack or stroke. They failed to work out to keep their bodies healthy and in shape. Try to find time for yourself to work out, not only will it keep you fit healthy and in good shape, but it will also expand your life expectations and give you extra stamina so you can perform your job duties at work more easily going that extra mile. If you find yourself like most tax paying citizens that are too tired after work to work out, then I would advise you to get up an hour early then what you normally do and use that time to work out. Remember, there's no point in slaving yourself working all those long hours to make that money if you're not even going to be able to even live long enough to spend it.

Home

You finally made it out of prison but the war isn't over yet. Getting out of prison was only half the battle. You still got to fight the other half by becoming successful in life and becoming a homeowner. Daily, you're getting older and that time will come where you're going to be too old to work. While your body is still functional and able to work, the smartest thing to be doing right now is working towards becoming a homeowner. When the time comes when you're too old to work, you will have peace of mind knowing that you have enough money saved up to take care of yourself and that you have a house that you paid for. You won't have to worry about being old and homeless. Not only will becoming a homeowner be good for yourself, but it will also be good for your kids and your grandkids - for in time of need, you could be there to catch any of them. When they're falling, you could be their safety net, providing any one of them a temporary place to stay until he or she gets back on his or her feet. You will be helping to keep your bloodline living on. Your home can also be a place where family gatherings are held such as Thanksgiving dinners, birthday parties, etc. How wonderful would it be to be throwing your grandkids a birthday party at your house. An event they will always remember, or just having your grandkids sleep over at Grandad's house.

This battle of becoming successful in life and becoming a homeowner can be won, but you're going to need to equip yourself with a lot of the tools provided to you in this book such as, the anger management tool, the dumbing down tool, the weighing the consequences tool, etc. That way you don't easily slip on a banana peel and lose all your coins and have to start all over again - collecting coins like in one of those video games.

I ran into a lot of inmates that told me they were in the process of buying a house, paying off their mortgage, until one day they let somebody piss them off to the point where they lost their cool and either shot the person, killed him, or beat him to the point he suffered GBI. Because they let somebody piss them off to the point they lost their cool, they ended up losing their house. Don't get added to the statistics list. Your haters are hating you because they can't stand seeing you doing better than them in life. They're trying to get you to stumble so that you fall back down financially to their mediocre broke level. Envy and jealousy are emotions that eat people up inside. To get rid of this unwanted feeling inside of them, they began doing hating things to bring you back down to their level financially. It's kind of like how when there's a lot of crabs in a bucket and one crab is about to make it out of the bucket - there is that crab that will grab a hold of that crab that's about to make it out of the bucket and drag him back down. Be smart!

Stop the Cycle

If you're one of those guys who's had a granddad that's been to prison and also had your dad go to prison and now you're up in prison with a young son living with his mom, or a family member, know that it could be you as to the one that puts a stop this cycle and end this curse on your generation. It could be you who gets up out of prison and changes the negative core beliefs and knowledge that's been trickling down from generation to generation. Those same negative core beliefs and knowledge that played a big role in your granddad, your dad, and now you, once you get out of prison, you can hurry up and find your son, set him down and start rooting out all those negative core beliefs and knowledge that you instilled in him before you went to prison. Then you can start planting positive core beliefs and knowledge inside of him to put a stop to this going to prison cycle with your generation curse. But you just can't talk the talk with your son, you got to walk the walk and lead by example. By doing so, you will be creating a future generation of successful people in your family bloodline, perhaps doctors, lawyers, big-rig truck drivers, ect. Your son will now pass on those same positive core beliefs and knowledge that you've instilled in him to his son, and his son would then pass it on down to his son or daughter, and on and on. You've seen how bad prison is. You shouldn't want none of your kids to go through something like that. Pick up your phone when you get out of prison and tell your son you need to have a serious talk with him.

Old Hangout Spots

If you're trying to lessen your chances of going back to prison then you're going to have to make some adjustments in your life, such as, avoiding your old hangout spots. Being all your drug dealing, robbing, burglary, murderous, homeboys all chill around there - it was them that played a major role and part in shaping your negative criminal behavior and ways which resulted in you going to prison In the first place. This is a hard pill to swallow. You can hang with your negative homies who you grew up with, but since they're still all involved in criminal behavior, it will be just a matter of time until you're back involved in your criminal behavior and heavy drug usage simply because you're going to be trying to fit in with the crowd and not seem like a square.

What I learned from talking to hundreds of inmates while I was in prison is that the best way to stay out of prison is to become a family man and just work a 9 to 5 job. When you're a family man, you become a different person. You're now trying to keep all that negative criminal behavior away from your wife and kids. Being you're the protector of your family, you're now trying your best to keep your family out of harm's way. You'll be trying your best to stay out of trouble and prison so you can be there for them.

When a man has a family to look after, he's more hesitant to engage in criminal activities from fear of losing his family by going to prison. All the inmates that I knew that were getting family visits every 3 months, or regular visits every weekend from their girlfriend or wife, was that those particular inmates were really focus on trying to stay out of trouble so that the following weekend they could see their girlfriend again or get to spend time with their wife/ girlfriend at a conjugal visits.

I remember when I was at Solano State Prison, there was this one inmate who I will just call AJ. AJ always got visits every weekend from his wife. Every 3 months, he got family visits, also known as sex visits or conjugal visits with his wife, where he'd be left alone for 3 days in a trailer that's on the side of the prison. I remember one day on the yard, this one inmate had a problem with AJ, even challenged AJ to a fight by calling him a sucker. All AJ did was stare at the dude for a quick 2 seconds and said, "Whatever man." Then AJ walked away. What this showed me was that AJ was more focused on rolling around in the sheets with his wife at his up and coming conjugal visit, instead of rolling around on the ground wrestling and fighting that inmate who disrespected him.

If you don't already have a woman in your life, try to find yourself one because when you find the right one, she will also make sure you stay on the right track and out of trouble. She be arguing with you when you go to talking about engaging in any type of negative criminal behavior that will possibly land you right back in prison.

While you're out mingling with different women trying to find the right one for you, try not to get caught up in the game some of them women's play. The game I'm talking about is called the "whipping it on you game". See, she knows the power of her pussy and she knows from past experience that a man can get addicted to her pussy. Once she finally starts to see that she got you pussy whipped, she will start playing her little game with you a game that she done mastered.

She sees that you're addicted to her vagina and she sees that she's the only woman that can give you the fix that you're craving for. Once she sees this, she will then start looking at you like a slave - her being the slave owner. She will start asking you can you do this or that for her, such as pay her light bill, go to the store for her, pay her car note, etc. If you try to refuse her, she will refuse you your drug that she knows that you so desperately need. You will then start acting like a dope fien and begin feening for a hit, her pussy, and eventually you'll give in to her wishes so you can get your fix.

These type of women will continue to play her game with you until you're broke and then she will leave you broken-hearted. She'll be moving on to her next victim to get p**** whipped so she could suck him dry financially. That's what she does. Be careful of these type of women when you're out there looking for the right woman for you. Be smart and think more with your big head instead of your little head. Alway remember a woman's bloodline comes from Eve and Jezebel and just look at how many man's lives they have ruined.

Positive Wisdom

If you were like me and committed you're crime when you were considered a youth offender, you must not beat yourself up about losing all those precious years of your life in prison. Understand that scientists have proved that when you committed your crime as a youth offender, under 25 years of age, that your brain wasn't even fully developed yet. When a brain is not fully developed, it's more likely to make mistakes in life. We all made mistakes when we were younger, even the judge that sentenced you made mistakes when he/ she was younger. All them other people that's now looking at you as though you're such a bad person, they all made mistakes in their life too. It's just that your mistake was a little more serious then theirs. We must learn from our mistakes never to make that mistake again and to move on with life. You must now stay focused so you can give your CDCR number back to the prison system by getting off parole. You can fully get that weight of being held down by the prison system totally off your back. You can gain full control of your freedom and go anywhere in the world you want to.

Put a smile on all those people's faces that invested in you while you were in prison by sending you packages and putting money on your books. Show them all that they all made the right decision by investing in you and believing that you will get out of prison and do the right thing. Be determined never to return to prison again.

One of the saddest things I've seen while I was in prison was seeing all them frail old men in their 70s and '80s either limping around with a cane or getting pushed around in their wheelchair by an inmate. I would talk to these old inmates and I would always find out that they all had a life sentence. After talking to them even more, I would find out that they all had a bucket list of all the things they wanted to do before they died. What made this so sad to me was the fact that they all had a life sentence and any day now, they may die from old age. They will never be able to check one thing off their bucket list. Once you get out of prison and your back in society try your best not to get added to the statistic list of being a very old man in prison with a life sentence who is only dreaming of one day getting out of prison so you can check things off your bucket list. This is not a very good way to spend the last precious days of your life as an old crippled man.

Instead, remain free, having total control of your life, doing whatever you want - whenever you want; including sleeping on a nice soft marshmallow bed with your wife right by your side every night, spending time with your kids and grandkids, not missing them growing up, traveling around the world, vacationing to beautiful places, going to all family reunions and family get togethers, going camping, riding on a boat at the lake with family, checking off things to do on your bucket list before you die.

You only get one life to live and there's no coming back. Enjoy your life to the fullest while you're here on earth! The only way to do that is by keeping your freedom.

Welcome back home!

About the Author

Emanuel Deon Bell was born in the Central Coast of California in a city called Salinas on November 19th 1978. He was raised in a city 35 minutes away from Salinas called Seaside California.

While doing his 17 and a half years in prison, he did his time at these general population prisons; Salinas Valley, Ironwood State Prison, Soledad Tracy Prison, AKA Deuel Vocational Institution, Calipatria State Prison, Delano State Prison, and Solano State Prison. When the California prison system was sending inmates out of state due to prison overcrowding Emmanuel also did prison time at a Mississippi Prison, Oklahoma Prison, and Arizona Prison.

He is currently a cement truck driver and when he has extra time on his hand he enjoys making rap music. You will be able to hear some of his music on YouTube soon!

This was my 1973 Malibu Chevy
two months before I got locked up

This is me
2 months
before being
arrested

This is me first arriving to prison

This is my CA Prison ID

This is me in Oklahoma Prison due to the California prison system sending inmates out of state due to overcrowding.

This is me in Arizona Prison due to the California prison system sending inmates out of state due to overcrowding.

This is me in Mississippi Prison due to the California prison system sending inmates out of state due to overcrowding.

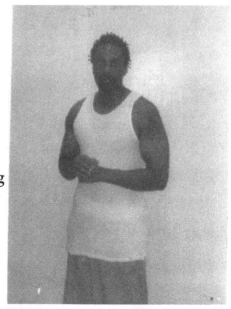

This is me at Soledad Prison CA.

This is me at Ironwood State Prison CA.

Meeting my 2 daughters for the first time
after serving 171/2 years in prison.

Glossary -

Battery pack - this is when you put some batteries in a sock or something hard in the sock and use it to swing and hit somebody it's called a battery pack.
"Did you see that Curtis just battery packed John?"

Booty bandit - these are the inmates that rape other inmates.
Purple passion was known to be a booty bandit in prison.

Car - numerous inmates that are from the same city or gang that got each other's back.
"When you're in the same car as an inmate he has your back and you're supposed to have his back."

Dayroom - when you come out your cell you will see the TV area with benches and tables that you can sit at all that is called the dayroom area.

Fe-Fe - a rolled up towel with a glove in the middle of it that haves vaseline and lotion inside the glove which some inmates use to create an artificial vagina and have sex with it.
"That inmate is nasty! I heard he be having sex with a fe-fe."

Fishing line - is a string size torn piece of sheet with a peanut butter pack or a flattened down milk carton with soap inside of it that's tied to the end of the string size sheet to create weight on the end which is used to slide it under your door to get, or shoot a kite or some food or books etc to another cell; normally fishing lines are used in the hole or segregated housing unit area.

Floor time - an inmate does certain things on the cell floor at a certain time and when he's on the floor don't interrupt his floor time cuz this is the time he does normally does things on the floor due to his program.

"I must have my floor time so I can do my workout."

Goon squad - these particular COs investigate who selling drugs and who's bringing it in. They also try to figure out who's in them high-powered criminal gangs such as black guerilla family, the cartel etc. The goon squad is known for running up in a cell between the hours of 2:00am to 5:00am looking for drugs. The goon squad wears a all black jumpsuit and wears a black CO patch on their uniform.

"Did you hear the goon squad last night? They ran up in cell 108 at 3:00 in the morning. And they must have found something inside the cell, because they took both of the inmates to the hole."

Hitting - when someone is going to visiting and his visitor is bringing him drugs.

That Carlos be hitting every time he go to visiting.

Hoop/keister - this is when you roll some drugs inside some plastic and stick it up your butt to hide it from the CO some people will even hoop their paperwork when they're being sent to a new prison that way soon as they get there and the shot callars are asking to see his paperwork he could quickly present it instead of having to tell them that I'm waiting for my paperwork to be transferred here from the prison I just left which would then put suspicious on you.

I'm fin to go to visiting and hoop some drugs.

Hot one - a murder charge.

Chris just caught a hot one for stabbing o-boy up on the yard.

Incense - rolled up toilet paper the size of a q-tip with Muslim oil rubbed on it. When lit, it gives off a good smelling aroma like real incense.

"Hey celly! Your farts stinks! Can you please light up an incense?"

Inmate Twitter - it's what everybody's talking about in the building and on the yard. One inmate will start something and it just gets spread like wildfire. But it's a 50/50 chance that it's even true.

"One time, on Twitter, I heard that the woman prison was going to have a dance party with the man prison.. You can't always believe what inmate Twitter is talking about."

Kite - a brief message on a little piece of torn off paper.

"Hey Porter! Can you do me a favor and go run this kite to cell 107 for me?"

Lock it up - rolled it up...is when you roll your stuff up to go to PC (protective custody).

Sam owed Curtis $100 and couldn't pay it, so he locked it up.

Mac Rep - in prison One inmate is assigned the speaker for his whole race so whenever there's an issue with the races the Mac reps will come together to resolve the issue such as if there was a riot on the yard with two different races and after the riot once we go on lockdown the Mac reps will come out and talk to the other Mac rep race to try to resolve the issue so we could get off lockdown when there's ever a race riot and they go on lockdown inmates will not get lifted off a lockdown until the Mac reps have a discussion to resolve the issue.

You must have good communication skills when being a mac rep because you got to try to resolve situations with other races.

On the line - when an inmate has something for sale, he puts it on the line by going out to the dayroom or yard and start telling inmates that he has whatever he has for sale; or he will put a note up inside the dayroom bullentin board stipulating what he has for sale.

"I'm trying to sell these shoes so I'm going to put it on the line."

Paperwork-your paperwork is all your charges and all your past charges and people look at your paperwork to determine if you're a Chester molester or a rapist because if those are on your paperwork and you're on general population you will get stabbed up quick

"Did you hear about Johnny his paperwork came back bad and they removed him off the yard yesterday?"

Pod Porter - the inmate building janitor that cleans the dayroom, showers, tables and every other thing that needs cleaning inside the building.

"The porter mop sweeps and wipe down tables in the dayroom."

Pruno - contraband alcohol made by inmates from rotten fruit and added sugar.

Removal - this is when somebody is going to get somebody off the yard mainly a removal is done because somebody's paperwork is no good and there then considered no good.

"Did you see that removal in the yard yesterday they stabbed him like 18 times."

Rice bowl - summer sausage or any type of meat or seafood mixed in a bowl with rice.
"I'm about to make me a rice bowl!"

Shank - a prison made knife.
Hey celly! You hear that metal scraping on the ground? It sounds like our cell neighbor is sharpening up a shank."

Shoot caller - one who holds the keys to his car and control his car and can make the people in his car do whatever he chooses such as do a hit.
"The shot callar to that car got all his boys ready to start a riot."

Short timer - somebody that is close to getting out of prison.
"He only got 2 months left so he's a short timer."

Smell good spray bottle - a nozzle spray bottle full of water with five to six drops of Muslim oil in it shake the bottle before you spray. When sprayed it acts like an air freshener.
"Hey celly! Your farts stink! Can you please spray the smell good spray bottle?"

Spread - a meal that inmates make using summer sausages or any type of meat or seafood mixed in a bowl of top ramen noodles.
"I'm about to make me a spread to eat!"

Stick - a Pinner joint.
"I got $5 let me buy a stick"

Turn ins - an old pair of shoes or anything that's used and old, which is used to turn in. You're only allowed one of these things each on your property card; a pair of shoes, a TV, CD player, hot pot, fan, etc. You must turn in the old to get the new appliances or shoes that you just ordered, you must turn in your old appliance or shoe. And you're only allowed 10 CDs, so when you go order another CD, you will have to turn in a CD to get your new CD... being you already got 10 CDs on your books.

"The CO said I can't get my new pair of shoes unless I got a turn-in."
to turn in."

White lightning - clear, pure liquor that's way stronger than pruno.

Zoom zooms and yam yams - snacks.

"I'm about to go to the store and get me some zoom zooms and yam yams."

CPSIA information can be obtained
at www.ICGtesting.com
Printed in the USA
BVHW081250120822
644456BV00002B/88